AF669395

*Netaji: Collected Works*

*Volume 7*

# *Letters to Emilie Schenkl 1934–1942*

Badgastein, March 1936.

*Netaji Collected Works Volume 7*

# LETTERS TO EMILIE SCHENKL 1934–1942

Subhas Chandra Bose

*edited by*

Sisir Kumar Bose and Sugata Bose

Orient BlackSwan

All rights reserved. No part of this book may be (i) modified, reproduced or utilised in any form, or by any means, electronic or mechanical, including photocopying, recording or by any information storage and retrieval system, in any form of binding or cover other than in which it is published, without permission in writing from the publisher; or (ii) used or reproduced in any manner for the purpose of training, development or operation of artificial intelligence (AI) technologies and systems, including generative AI technologies, without permission in writing from the copyright holder.

**SUBHAS CHANDRA BOSE: LETTERS TO EMILIE SCHENKL 1934–1942**

---

**ORIENT BLACKSWAN PRIVATE LIMITED**

*Registered Office*
3-6-752 Himayatnagar, Hyderabad 500 029, Telangana, India
e-mail: centraloffice@orientblackswan.com

*Other Offices*
Bengaluru, Chennai, Guwahati, Hyderabad,
Kolkata, Mumbai, New Delhi, Noida, Patna

© Netaji Research Bureau 2023
First published by the Netaji Research Bureau in 1994
First paperback printing 2004
Second impression 2016
This edition published by Orient Blackswan Private Limited 2023
Reprinted 2026

042043

ISBN 978-93-5442-379-6

*Printed in India at*
Yash Printographics, Noida 201 301

*Published by*
Orient Blackswan Private Limited
3-6-752, Himayatnagar, Hyderabad 500 029, Telangana, India
e-mail: info@orientblackswan.com

# Contents

# *Preface* *to the 2023 Edition*

'The bundle of letters,' my mother Krishna Bose writes in her book *Emilie and Subhas*, 'carefully tied with a ribbon and treasured by her more than her life could now be shared with the world'.[1] My grandaunt Emilie had just announced solemnly towards the end of a family dinner at Augsburg in June 1993 that she was giving permission to my father Sisir Kumar Bose to publish the letters that Netaji Subhas Chandra Bose had written to her. She had been concerned about my father's health and wished that these private letters should be brought before the public eye by him. My father and I set to work on what was to be a very special Volume 7 of Netaji's *Collected Works*. In June 1994 on the 60th anniversary of the first meeting between Subhas and Emilie, we were able to present to her the published volume.

'When she held the book in her hands,' Krishna records, 'her face lit up with a radiant happiness.' We had a celebratory roast turkey dinner, adorned Emilie with a beautiful scarf, and presented her a card with a picture of a tigress (Subhas affectionately called her 'Baghini') and inscribed in it 'Keep roaring'. She had a surprise in store for us, which is best narrated in Krishna's words:

> The next morning Auntie gave me a piece of folded paper and said, 'This is for you, Krishna, something from me.' Surprised, I looked at the rather worn-looking piece of paper and asked, 'What is it?' Auntie replied, 'It is a love letter.' It was, indeed, a beautiful love letter. I was deeply moved as I read it. It was undated but the envelope was postmarked 5$^{th}$ March 1936.[2]

True to form, my grandaunt Emilie had held back the most precious three-page handwritten letter written to her by Subhas from Badgastein to Vienna as he prepared to leave for India after three years of European exile. As editors, my father and I had missed the opportunity of printing

[1] Krishna Bose, *Emilie and Subhas: A True Love Story* (New Delhi: Niyogi Books, 2016), p. 9.

[2] Ibid.: 37–39.

it in *Letters to Emilie Schenkl* (1994), Volume 7 of Netaji's *Collected Works*. We included it in *The Essential Writings of Netaji Subhas Chandra Bose*, a one-volume distillation of the 12 volumes in the series, when it appeared on Netaji's centenary in 1997 (and more recently again on the occasion of the 75th anniversary of India's independence in 2022[3]). By that time Emilie had departed this world to be finally reunited with her lost beloved. 'If fate should thus separate us in this life,' Subhas had written to Emilie, '—I shall long for you in my next life.' We are appending this letter of March 1936 in the new edition of this book as it truly belongs here.

Emilie handed another letter to Krishna—this one of great historical significance. It was written at dawn on 9 February 1943, just before Netaji set off on his epic submarine voyage from Europe to Asia and was hand delivered by A. C. N. Nambiar to her. We have included this letter too in this new edition of Volume 7. The day before in Berlin on 8 February 1943, he had left with her a Bengali letter addressed to his *Mejdada*, Saṛat Chandra Bose, asking him to give his wife and daughter the same love that his elder brother had showered on him.

'You have an unselfish heart,' Subhas had written to Emilie in the now famous love letter of March 1936. My parents Sisir Kumar Bose and Krishna Bose had felt it was their duty to ensure that the people of India honoured the spirit of selflessness of the woman who enabled Netaji Subhas Chandra Bose to dedicate himself to a life of suffering, service, and sacrifice for his country, his 'first love'.

2 February 2023 SUGATA BOSE

[3] Sisir K. Bose and Sugata Bose (eds), *Netaji Collected Works: The Essential Writings of Netaji Subhas Chandra Bose* (Kolkata: Netaji Research Bureau and Hyderabad: Orient BlackSwan, 2022).

# *Preface*

For help in the preparation of this special volume of Netaji Subhas Chandra Bose's *Collected Works* we are deeply grateful to Emilie Schenkl, Anita Pfaff, Krishna Bose, Leonard Gordon, Sarmila Bose and Sumantra Bose. Naga Sundaram in the NRB archives and Kartic Chakraborty in the NRB secretariat gave unstinted practical support. We would also like to thank Oxford University Press for handling the publication process with care, efficiency and speed.

S.K.B & S.B.

# *Editors' Introduction*

'Just one thing more before I close this long letter. For your life, never pray for any selfish object or aim. Always pray for what is good for humanity—for what is good for all time—for what is good in the eyes of God. Pray in a *nishkama* way.'

Subhas Chandra Bose to Emilie Schenkl,
30 March 1936.

'Then suddenly I had the foolish idea of "Bleigiessen". It is done in this way. You melt on a spoon some metal (lead) and when it is melted, you pour it into cold water. At once it becomes hard and gets shaped. According to the shape, you foretell the future of the one who has poured his spoonful of metal. I had a very funny thing, looking like the map of India.'

Emilie Schenkl to Subhas Chandra Bose,
1 January 1937.

The ritual of 'Bleigiessen' performed in Vienna on New Year's Eve of 1936 had foretold with uncanny accuracy the future of a young Austrian woman whose destiny seemed inextricably linked with the fate of a country she would never see. 'India is my first love and my only love, that is what he told me,' Emilie Schenkl reminisced to Krishna Bose in the course of a conversation in her Vienna home in 1971. Subhas Chandra Bose, according to his close friend and political associate A.C.N. Nambiar, was 'a one-idea man . . . singly for the independence of India'. But he went on to add, 'I think the only departure, if one might use the word departure, was his love for Miss Schenkl, otherwise he was completely absorbed . . . He was deeply in love with her, you see. In fact, it was an enormous, intense love for her that he had.'[1]

Subhas Chandra Bose and Emilie Schenkl met for the first time in Vienna in June 1934. In the preface dated 29 November 1934 to his book *The Indian Struggle* she was the only person he mentioned by name. 'In conclusion,' he wrote, 'I have to express my thanks to Fraulein E. Schenkl who assisted me in writing this book and to all those friends who have been of help to me in many ways.'[2] That was also when their correspondence began as Subhas Chandra Bose, then exiled in Europe, travelled to India on being informed of the critical illness of his father. In his first letter from Rome on 30 November 1934 Bose wrote, 'I am always a bad correspondent—but not a bad man I hope.' This 'bad correspondent' nevertheless managed to write with unerring frequency to Emilie Schenkl whether he was in prison or hospital, home interned or in the midst of whirlwind political tours. One hundred and sixty-two of his letters written between 1934 and 1942 are being published for the first time in this volume. It is clear that Emilie Schenkl wrote with diligent regularity too, but only eighteen of her letters appear to have survived. They turned up in an old cigar box in 1980, carefully preserved along with the 1921 correspondence between the brothers Sarat and Subhas Chandra Bose concerning the latter's decision to resign from the Indian Civil Service. Subhas Chandra Bose was not 'bad' when it came to writing letters; he was only 'bad' about losing most of the ones he received.

The first fourteen letters in this collection were written between 30 November 1934 and 26 January 1935 during Bose's air journey to India via Italy, Greece, Egypt and Iraq, his home internment for the period of mourning following his father's death and his brief stop in Italy on his return voyage. He mentions in his letter of 25 January 1935 an interview with Mussolini scheduled for that eve-

[1] Krishna Bose, 'Important Women in Netaji's Life' in *The Illustrated Weekly of India*, 1973. See also Krishna Bose, *Itihaser Sandhane* (*In Search of History*) (Calcutta: Ananda Publishers, 1974), pp. 77–8.

[2] Netaji Subhas Chandra Bose, *The Indian Struggle, Collected Works Vol. 2* (Calcutta: Netaji Research Bureau, 1984).

ning. We also learn that he is pleased with the production of his book *The Indian Struggle.* He has not forgotten Emilie Schenkl's telephone number but had forgotten his own birthday on the 23rd. They had already become close friends in 1934. Emilie Schenkl had not only worked with Bose in Vienna, but had also accompanied him on trips to Badgastein and Karlovy Vary.

During much of 1935 they had the opportunity to see each other in Vienna and nearby health resorts. Consequently there were few occasions to write. Bose had a serious gall-bladder operation in Vienna in April 1935, which prevented him from being India's unofficial roving ambassador in the way that he had been in 1933 and 1934. The letters resume in early 1936 as Bose felt well enough to go on another European tour. Of particular interest are the letters he wrote from Ireland, where he had several meetings with Eamonn De Valera. In March 1936 Bose decided to return to India in defiance of British warnings that he would not be permitted to remain at liberty if he did so. Emilie Schenkl joined him briefly at Badgastein prior to his departure.

On 29 March 1936 Bose wrote from the ship Conte Verde, 'There are many things I want to write to you about—but I shall write in a disconnected way—so please read this letter carefully.' He wrote three letters in three consecutive days at the end of March 1936 which marked the beginning of nearly twenty months of geographical separation. All of the letters between 8 April 1936 and 15 March 1937 had to pass through police censors. Of these the first two were written from Arthur Road Prison in Bombay and Yeravda Central Prison in Poona, eleven from his internment in Kurseong and five as a prisoner in Medical College Hospital in Calcutta. Eight letters written by Emilie Schenkl during this period have also survived. One of Emilie Schenkl's letters (which has not been found) caused a break in his 'monstrous life' and took his 'thoughts away to Vienna for a while. The letters of this phase touch on a variety of topics, including Austrian politics, books, music, Bose's fascination with Budapest and Prague, jokes in Viennese cafes, spirituality and concern with each other's fragile health.

Bose promptly informed Emilie Schenkl of his release on 18 March 1937. 'My freedom means,' he wrote, 'that I can move about freely and that my correspondence will not be *officially* censored—though, of course, it will always be secretly censored.' In his letter of 25 March 1937 he promised to 'try to write a few lines every week', a promise he kept during the next few months as he corresponded regularly from Calcutta, Lahore, Dalhousie and Kurseong. He expressed his emotions in a couple of undated letters in block characters that he sent in the spring or early summer of 1937. In the first of these he wrote, 'I HAVE BEEN LONGING TO WRITE TO YOU FOR SOME TIME PAST—BUT YOU CAN EASILY UNDERSTAND HOW DIFFICULT IT WAS TO WRITE TO YOU ABOUT MY FEELINGS. I JUST WANT TO LET YOU KNOW NOW THAT I AM EXACTLY WHAT I WAS BEFORE, WHEN YOU KNEW ME. NOT A SINGLE DAY PASSES THAT I DO NOT THINK OF YOU. YOU ARE WITH ME ALL THE TIME. I CANNOT POSSIBLY THINK OF ANYONE ELSE IN THIS WORLD . . . I CANNOT TELL YOU HOW LONELY I HAVE BEEN FEELING ALL THESE MONTHS AND HOW SORROWFUL. ONLY ONE THING COULD MAKE ME HAPPY—BUT I DO NOT KNOW IF THAT IS POSSIBLE. HOWEVER, I AM THINKING OF IT DAY AND NIGHT AND PRAYING TO GOD TO SHOW ME THE RIGHT PATH.'

In another letter (in German) of 4 November 1937 again written in block characters Bose informed Emilie Schenkl of his forthcoming trip to Europe and asked her to make arrangements for them to stay in Kurhaus Hochland in Badgastein. Bose knew by now that he would be President of the Indian National Congress in 1938. On 26 December 1937 Subhas Chandra Bose secretly married Emilie Schenkl. We asked her why, despite the obvious anguish, they chose to keep their relationship and marriage a closely guarded secret. Emilie Schenkl explains that to Bose his 'country came first' and any public announcement would have caused unnecessary 'upheaval'. It is known, of course, that Bose wrote his unfinished autobiography in Badgastein in December 1937. Bose' biographer Leonard Gordon has underscored the significance of the treatment of the theme of love in a chapter entitled 'My Faith (Philosophical)' in this book. Gordon also points to a footnote in one of the early chapters in which Bose says: 'As I have gradually turned from a purely spiritual ideal to a life of social service, my views on sex have undergone transformation.'[3] Popular misconceptions of Subhas Chandra Bose's asceticism stem from an overemphasis on values and attitudes he may have held very early in his youth. In any event, Badgastein was more important in Bose's life than simply the place where he wrote his autobiography.

Bose's many letters written during 1938 provide glimpses into his hectic travel and work as Congress President. Several of the letters were written on trains as he criss-crossed the subcontinent. The reader will see that the more personal comments and endearments tend to be in German. In a letter dated 17 October 1938, he writes, 'I feel completely lonely all the time, even though I work hard day and night.' He repeats in a series of letters that he thinks of Emilie day and night. He sounds very detached about the prospects of his re-election as President. On 4 January 1939, he writes: 'Though there is a very general desire for my re-election as President —I do not think I shall be again President . . . In a way, it will be good not to be president again. I shall then be more free and have more time to myself.' After winning re-election he writes on 11 February 1939: 'I have been re-elected as President for another year. Mahatma Gandhi and his lieutenants opposed me and Pandit Nehru was indifferent. The result of the election is a great victory for me. The whole country is full of excitement over the election, but a terrible responsibility has come on my shoulders.'

Following his illness at the time of the controversial Tripuri Congress, Bose writes on 19 April 1939: 'I wish I could go to Badgastein . . . But I do not know if I can spare the time and the money.' He seemed to be quite content with his decision to resign as Congress President. 'India is a strange land,' he wrote on 15 June 1939, 'where people are loved not because they have power, but because they give up power. For instance, at Lahore I had a warmer welcome this time than when I went last year as Congress President.' He asked Emilie Schenkl on 21 June 1939 to 'please wait till

[3] Leonard A. Gordon, *Brothers against the Raj: A Biography of Indian Nationalists Sarat and Subhas Chandra Bose* (New York: Columbia University Press), p. 344. The full text of *The Indian Pilgrim* is available in Sisir K. Bose (ed.), Netaji Subhas Chandra Bose, *Collected Works Vol. 1* (Calcutta: Netaji Research Bureau, 1982).

August—probably I will come then to Gastein.' And then again on the train from Jubbulpore to Bombay on 6 July 1939: 'I must take a month's holiday at least—but I do not know if the holiday will begin in the middle of August or the beginning of September.'

The outbreak of war in September 1939 put paid to all these plans and also interrupted Bose's correspondence with Emilie Schenkl. The next letter is dated 3 April 1941, the day after his arrival in Berlin following his dramatic escape from India. It is well known that Bose went to Europe primarily in order to gain access to Indian soldiers in the British Indian Army. He had long believed that the subversion of the loyalty of Indian soldiers to the Raj had to be a crucial part of the anti-imperialist movement. What is less well known is that Bose at this time had also a strong personal reason to want to go to Europe. He would, of course, continue to make personal sacrifices to serve the cause of his country.

Emilie Schenkl joined Subhas Chandra Bose in Berlin in the spring of 1941. For the rest of the year and the first eight months of 1942 they lived together at their home on Sophienstrasse in Berlin. Their daughter Anita was born in Vienna on 29 November 1942. Although Bose wrote a few letters from Rome and Berlin in the latter half of 1942, he generally talked to Emilie Schenkl on the phone. Bose came to Vienna to see his daughter in December 1942. Emilie joined him in Berlin in January 1943, prior to his departure for East Asia by submarine on 8 February 1943. Subhas continued to send her radio letters from Asia, but these were taken away by officers of the British Army during their occupation of Vienna at the end of World War II.

Before starting on his perilous submarine journey Subhas wrote out a letter dated 8 February 1943 in Bengali to his elder brother Sarat: 'I am again embarking on the path of danger, but this time towards home. I do not know whether I shall see the end of this road . . . I have married here and have a daughter. In my absence please show them the love you have given me all my life.' After this letter reached Sarat Chandra Bose's hands, he visited Vienna in 1948 with his wife Bivabati and three of his children—Sisir, Roma and Chitra—and warmly welcomed Emilie and Anita into the Bose family. Four and a half decades later in June 1993 at another family gathering the intensely private Emilie finally gave permission for her letters from and to Subhas Chandra Bose to be brought before the public eye. After dinner at her daughter's home in Augsburg she declared to Sisir Kumar Bose, Krishna Bose, Anita Pfaff, Martin Pfaff, Sugata Bose and Maya Pfaff that she had an announcement to make. She had been deeply concerned about Sisir's health and wanted to see this volume published while he was active and well.

This special volume in the *Collected Works* illuminates the human and emotional aspects of the many-splendoured personality of Netaji Subhas Chandra Bose. Through its publication we wish to honour a woman of enormous courage, fierce independence and utmost dignity who added a new and deeply rewarding dimension to the life of India's leader.

S.K.B. & S.B.

# *Letters to Emilie Schenkl 1934–1942*

*Rome*
*30.11.34*

Dear Miss Schenkl,

The kind letter you gave me I read with great pleasure.

I had a nice journey to Rome. At times (near the Tyrol) we flew over the clouds and were bathed in sunshine, while the land below was misty and foggy. The 'dolomites' were white with snow.

In 2½ hours we reached Venice. From Venice to Rome it took 2 hours.

If ever I ask you to send me back any of my books or boxes you must destroy every bit of paper—every article and every letter. You should send me only the printed books. Please continue the French lessons.

If you can, buy a typewriter with the 210 sh: I gave you in an envelope.

I hope you have sent all the galleys, preface, etc. with care and have not made any mistakes.

I may not be able to write to you till I reach India. Do not worry. I am always a bad correspondent—but not a bad man I hope.

I am sending this by airmail. *Do not tell anyone* that I have written to you by airmail, because I am not writing to anyone else by airmail—and they may feel sorry.

Last night I had to work till 6.30 am to finish the book and could not sleep at all. Tomorrow morning I fly at 7.30 am. I have seen the plane in which I am going to fly from Rome to Calcutta. It has already arrived here from Amsterdam.

Write to me a short formal letter by airmail to 1 Woodburn Park, Calcutta informing me about the safe despatch of the galleys to Wishart. Please type the letter.

Best regards to your parents and warmest greetings from me.

Yours sincerely

Subhas C. Bose

*[undated, Nov. 1934]*

A present for buying a typewriter. Please write to me when the machine is bought and how it works.

*Venice*
*1.12.34*
*1.30 pm*

Just arrived here and am having a fast lunch; am flying again in a few minutes. Warmest greetings and regards to your parents.

S.C. Bose
30.XI.34

*Athens*
*[undated, 1.12.34]*

Recd. your telegram in Rome. I arrived here (Athens) about 3 pm. Journey was not bad. Feeling rather tired, otherwise am quite well. Regarding the memo of agreement, it is not necessary to sign because that is my own copy. The other copy which I have signed has already been sent to Wishart. When I ask you to send me any of my articles to India, please destroy all articles, letters, etc. only clothes and books should be sent. I do not think I shall be able to see anything of Athens. The time is short and I have many letters to write. After dark I cannot see anything. Hope you are all well.

S.C. Bose

10 pm. I was able to see something of Athens.

*Egypt*
*1.12.34*

Spent a very interesting time here in seeing the Pyramids, mosques, tomb, etc. which are 4000 years old. I am back again in the bosom of the East. While coming from Athens, we flew above the clouds in the early morning and saw a gorgeous sunrise, which we can see only in the East. In Europe, you rarely see a gorgeous sunrise. Am fairly well. Starting again tomorrow morning.

S.C. Bose

*Iraq*
*Sunday, 2.12.34*

Arrived here this afternoon from Cairo. Shall be in Karachi tomorrow evening and the day after (i.e. Tuesday) in Calcutta. It is so interesting to see these old places. The picture on the other side is a mosque with golden domes built 450 years ago. Hope you are well.

Yours sincerely

Subhas C. Bose

CENSORED AND PASSED

*38/2 Elgin Road or*
*1 Woodburn Park*
*Calcutta*
*7.12.34*

Dear Frl. Schenkl,

I arrived here on the 4th December without any trouble on the way. But I was too late. My father left this mortal world on the 2nd December—that is, about 40 hours before I reached Calcutta. My mother is utterly disconsolate, though we, brothers and sisters, are trying our best to console her. For a Westerner, it is difficult to understand our mentality. A Hindu wife's life is so bound up with that of her husband that life is unbearable to her in his absence. Nevertheless, we are hoping that she will be able to stand the bereavement. Recently, there have been many other bereavements in our family and all these have had a cumulative effect on my parents.

I do not know if I shall be able to write to you in future. But in case I cannot, please do not misunderstand me. At present I am living like a prisoner in our house. This order of 'home- internment' was served on me as soon as I landed in Calcutta. For the present, the Government have allowed me to stay with my mother for one week. During this week, I cannot communicate or associate with anybody outside the family, nor can I leave the house. When the week is over, I do not know what will happen to me. I may not be able to write to you in future. In any case, my future is quite uncertain.

My home address is 38/2 Elgin Road or 1 Woodburn Park, Calcutta. But as my mother is staying at the former address I have been 'interned' here.

The journey by air was interesting and if I did not have this mental anxiety, I would have enjoyed it. Every morning the sunrise was gorgeous. It was so enchanting to pass over so many countries in Europe and in Asia in 5 days' time.

Best regards for your parents and warmest greetings for yourself.

Yours sincerely

Subhas C. Bose

CENSORED AND PASSED

*38/2 Elgin Road or*
*1 Woodburn Park*
*20.12.34*

Dear Frl. Schenkl,

Your letter of the 2nd December by airmail reached me on 19th (yesterday). There was some delay in censoring. From the stamps, I find that it was posted on the 3rd, but actually dispatched from the Vienna Post Office on the 5th. It came by Dutch plane up to Karachi; from Karachi it came to Calcutta by train. It takes about 3 days from Karachi to Calcutta. The rest of the delay was due to censoring. As I have been 'interned' at home since my arrival here, all my correspondence has to be censored and passed by police officers. This entails some delay which is unavoidable.

You can write to me at *38/2 Elgin Road* or *1 Woodburn Park*, Calcutta. I generally live at the latter house (which is my brother's house)—but on this occasion I have been living at the former address, because my mother has been living here and this house belongs to my parents. The two houses are within a stone's throw of one another.

I wrote an airmail letter to you a few days after my arrival. I think it was dispatched from here on the 10th December. Therein I wrote about my father's death, about 40 hours before I reached home. My mother is still disconsolate. A separation after 50 years of happy married life is a shock which one cannot easily overcome. Moreover, the existence of a Hindu wife is so bound up with that of her husband that in his absence, life is meaningless to her. Nevertheless, we are hoping that since mother is of a deeply religious frame of mind, she will be able to stand the shock in the long run, if she can tide over a few months.

On my way to India, I found from the Captain of the aeroplane that the Dutch plane carries mail only upto Karachi. The Imperial Airways (British) carries mail right upto Calcutta. On the British plane you have to post at Vienna on Friday or Saturday, but for the Dutch line on Monday or Wednesday. Your letter of the 2nd December which was posted on the 3rd, did not catch the British plane—hence the delay. While posting for the Dutch plane, you should be careful to pay only the airmail charges upto Karachi.

Did you not receive the card I dropped to you from Venice?

I have not the patience to write to you at length about my journey, though you are so much interested. Well, the first evening I spent in Rome—the Eternal City. I got your telegram there, just before I left in the morning. The next night we spent at Athens. I had just enough time to look at the Acropolis and other ancient remains of Greece. The next evening we spent at Cairo. At Cairo, I had just enough time to have a look at the wonderful Tutakhamin Museum and pay a visit to the Pyramids. Owing to the insistence of the guide there, I had myself photographed there. I am enclosing herewith a copy of the photo. You will see in the background the pyramids and the Sphinx. [At] The Tutakhamin museum, I saw several mummies, besides many other wonderful things. The next night we spent at Baghdad, the Capital of Iraq. In Baghdad, I had time to see some of the old remains—especially the golden mosque which is 500 years old. We left Baghdad early in the morning on the 3rd inst. and reached Karachi the same evening. From Karachi we flew to Jodhpur and spent the night there. The next day we were in Calcutta at about 4 in the afternoon.

The journey was very interesting. What I enjoyed most was the glorious sunrise which we could see from a height of 2000 metres. Such glorious sunrises you can never see in Europe. I felt giddy in the head only when going up or coming down—but while flying at the same level, there was no discomfort at all. I could even write without difficulty while we were flying—there was so little jolting! The noise of the plane was of course uncomfortable but not unbearable.

Please remember me to Herr and Frau Lowy of Karlsbad. Please do not trouble about sending me the Karlsbad Album until I write to you for it.

I have already written to you from Athens (or Cairo) that you should not worry about the agreement with Wishart. That was a spare copy for my own use and hence my signature was not needed.

I am sorry to hear that it is so cold there now and that your cough is worse. Here it is cool—but not cold, if judged from your standpoint. Without any heating the temperature in the room at night is about 22°. We usually have the doors and windows open in this country.

You can keep Oxford History with you as long as you like and you can also borrow any books you want. Are you continuing your French lessons? If so I would like to know how you are progressing. About the book that you have inquired about, I shall write in my next letter. At the moment, I do not remember where it is published.

If you want to get any book that is published in England, I think it would be cheaper for you to buy it in England. You can do this in either of 2 ways. Ask your friend Ella to buy and send it to you—or write to a book-seller in England to send it to you. You can pay for it through the American Express Company or Wagonlits/Cook, both of whom have their offices in Kartnerring. If you deposit Viennese money with them, they will pay to your friend (or book-seller) in England in English money. I think you can also send small amounts through the post office, but I am not quite sure. My booksellers are Leighton Bell and Co. Ltd., 13 Trinity Street, Cambridge, England. If you like, you can order books of them. When ordering, you may mention that I have recommended them to you. I am afraid that if you order for an English book in Vienna, it will cost you more than if you buy in England.

You may keep my telegraphic address with you should any necessity arise in future. It is: ESCIBOS, Calcutta.

I hope you will be satisfied with this fairly long letter. Please convey my regards to your parents and accept my warmest greetings yourself.

Yours sincerely

Subhas C. Bose

*38/2 Elgin Road*
*or 1 Woodburn Park*
*Calcutta*
*31 Dec. 1934*

Dear Frl. Schenkl,

I was very glad to receive your airmail letters of the 10th December and 18th December. From the former letter I could see that your typewriter was working well.

I am sorrow [sic] to learn from your letter that your are having a bad winter and that you are ill. Let me hope that you will soon be able to shake off your illness and get out of bed.

I am glad to know that you are progressing well with your French. I envy all those who can pick up new languages. I have noted your enquiries about the books on India and Indian Philosophy and I shall try to give you the required information as soon as possible.

This is the last day of the year. I wish you with all my heart a happy new year and many many returns of the same. I am sending the same wishes for your parents—please convey them to your mother and father.

My health has not been at all satisfactory since coming here. During the last week there has been a serious aggravation of my old trouble—the internal pain. It has been the result partly at least of the special diet which I have to take during the mourning period. The period of mourning ends on January 3rd, 1935.

My home-coming would, in ordinary circumstances, have been a source of great delight and joy—but this time it is full of sorrow.

We are still living under the shadow of bereavement. Besides our domestic sorrow, I have to suffer from the restrictions imposed on me by the Government. As you have already seen in the papers, I am still 'interned' in my own home.

I am afraid I shall have to undergo an operation. There is no other way left open to me. But I do not want to go in for a major operation here. So I shall have to wait till I can come to Europe again.

I thank you very much for your kind wishes for the coming year.

I am glad to know that your gall-bladder trouble is better and that you may be able to avoid the knife. I wish you the best of luck in this aspect also.

Please convey my best respect to your parents and accept my warmest greetings.

You may be aware that the National Bibliothek, Vienna contains the complete works of Swami Vivekananda which I presented last year to them. Please make use of them if necessary. Swami Vivekananda's books contain one of the best expositions of Indian Philosophy.

Yours sincerely

Subhas C. Bose

CENSORED AND PASSED

*38/2 Elgin Road*
*Calcutta*
*8 January, 1935*

Dear Frl. Schenkl,

You will be surprised to learn that I am leaving for Europe today. I am leaving for Bombay today and am taking the boat (M.V. Victoria) from Bombay on the 10th inst. I shall reach Genoa (Genua) in Italy on the 21st January.

I thank you very much for the kind sympathy you have expressed for us in our bereavement. Please convey our thanks to your parents as well.

My trouble has aggravated since coming here. I shall therefore have to undergo an operation.

I thank you very much for the present you have sent me through Dr Sharma. I have also received your letter dated the 7th December accompanying the present.

I hope you have been able to shake off your cold by now. I am glad that you are otherwise better.

Please accept warmest greetings for the new year and convey same to your parents and your sister.

Yours sincerely

Subhas C. Bose

*Naples*
*20.1.35*

Dear Miss Schenkl,

Just a line to inform you that I have landed safely at Naples. We had wretched weather after Port Said and that was one of the reasons persuading me to get down here.

I shall spend about a week before coming to Vienna. The Italian Railways give a reduction of 50 per cent to foreign tourists if they stay for at least 6 days in Italy. Drop me a line to Hotel Excelsior, Rome to say how you are keeping.

I went to Pompeii this morning soon after landing. This afternoon I am going to see the Volcano Solfalara which is now active.

Best regards to your parents and warmest greetings.

Yours sincerely

Subhas C. Bose

PS  I shall leave tomorrow or the day after tomorrow for Rome. I am not writing airmail because today is Sunday. *Please reply by airmail* to Hotel Excelsior, Rome.

S.C.B.

*Naples*
*22.1.35*
*4 pm*

Dear Miss Schenkl,

I am writing this just before starting for the station to go to Rome and I shall post this letter in Rome.

Last three days I was busy sight seeing. Pompeii; the volcano Solfalara, 'the little Vesuvius' which is now active; the museums, etc. have all been visited. I bought tickets to go to Capri and to Vesuvius but had to give up the idea as it began to *snow* heavily here. You will be surprised to hear of snow in Naples. They have not had such snow for the last 30 years, they tell me. However, I returned the tickets for Capri and Vesuvius this morning and instead, I bought a through ticket for Vienna. I am going to break journey at Rome for 3 days and possibly for a day at Venice also. But most probably I shall go straight to Vienna from Rome. I am sure it has been snowing heavily in Vienna and the weather is very wet there. I hope you have already written to me from there by airmail. I shall be so glad to hear from you. Best regards for your parents and warmest greetings for your good self.

Yours sincerely

Subhas C. Bose

PS  I had to leave India in a hurry. Till the last, I was not certain about coming. However, I have brought the 'dhup' (incense) you wanted and also 'Thoughts on Vedanta' by Swami Vivekananda. Can you read my handwriting?

S.C.B.

*Hotel Palacer Ambassadeuro*
*Rome*
*25.1.35*

Dear Miss Schenkl,

Thank you so much for your kind letters—the envelope and the post card—sent by airmail from Vienna. They were to hand this morning. Hotel Excelsior is just opposite this hotel—so there is no difficulty in getting letters from there.

I am sorry I could not come to Vienna so soon from Naples. There is much work for me to do here—and it would not be right for me to neglect it. This evening I have an interview with Signor Mussolini, to whom I am going to present a copy of my book. (*Please treat this matter as strictly private.*)

The book has been published. The printing, etc. is quite good. The preface has been published, in which I have given you my thanks.

The weather here is glorious and my health is better than on the boat. On the boat I had severe pains and the Mediterranean Sea was very rough.

Please keep ready for my use a typed copy of the appendix—I mean, the last pages that I wrote on the day that I left Vienna for Rome.

Please do not come to the station to receive me. I shall telephone to you from the Hotel and there you may come to see me. I am thinking of leaving Rome on Sunday the 27th—but it is not quite sure. I may even stop at Venice for a day, if the weather there is good.

Do you think I have forgotten your telephone number?

Thanks very much for your kind message for my birthday. As a matter of fact, I had forgotten about it! I am so awful—am I not?

Please give my thanks to your parents also, and my regards. I am sorry for your old cough—mein kopf! mein kopf! My greetings to your sister and yourself. Auf wiedersehen!

Yours sincerely

Subhas C. Bose

PS I am sending this express so I hope you will get it on Sunday. I shall send a wire to Katyar about my arrival—you can telephone to him or to Hotel de France about my arrival.

S.C.B.

*Albergo Palazzo Ambasciatori*
*Roma*
*Saturday, 26.1.35*

Dear Miss Schenkl,

I have written to you yesterday. I find that I cannot start before Monday the 28th morning—reaching Vienna (Sudbahnhof) on Tuesday morning at about 8 am. I am also writing to Dr Katyar accordingly now. I think it is Sudbahnhof where we arrive at Vienna, but I am not sure. If I have to postpone my departure further, then I shall send a telegram to Dr Katyar in time. It is not necessary for you to come to the station. Hope you are better. Warmest greetings.

Yours sincerely

Subhas C. Bose

*Prague*
*13.1.36*

Dear Miss Schenkl,

Just a line to say that I arrived here safely this morning. After spending a busy day I shall be going to Berlin tonight. I met President B. Best regards to your parents.

Yours sincerely

Subhas C. Bose

*Berlin W 8 den*
*Unter den Linden 5–6*
*15.1.36*

Dear Miss Schenkl,

I arrived here from Prague yesterday morning and was kept very busy yesterday—so I could not write to you. The Congress has been postponed for a few days—so I think I can go by the Italian boat—but I am still not sure. I have received the redirected mail yesterday. Today also I hope to get some. Please send me 'Indian Struggle' *here*, if the parcel arrives. I shall probably stay here for 2 or 3 days more. Best regards to your parents—also to yourself.

Yours sincerely

Subhas C. Bose

*Hotel Bristol*
*Berlin W 8*
*17.1.36*

Dear Miss Schenkl,

Many thanks for two letters—one received yesterday and the other received today. I am with people most of the time and cannot therefore find time to write a long letter. Please excuse me for that.

I leave for Antwerp tomorrow and stay there for 3 days. From there I go to Paris.

My address in Antwerp: c/o Mon Nathalal D. Javeri, 24 Avenue van den Nest, Antwerp (Belgium). My address in Paris: c/o American Express Company, 11 Rue Scribe, Paris (FR)

Please redirect my mail accordingly. *And inform American Press and Pension Cosmopolite also.*

I have left 2 overcoats and 1 raincoat in the wardrobe in my room in Pension Cosmopolite. I should have brought the raincoat with me but forgot by mistake. Please ask Mrs Vecsei to look after these coats.

I am sending some stamps herewith.

Yours sincerely

Subhas C. Bose

*Koln*
*19.1.36*
*10 am*

Best greetings from Koln. Best regards to your parents. Leaving for Antwerp just now.

Subhas C. Bose

*Brussels*
*20.1.36*

Warmest greetings from Subhas C. Bose.

Please continue sending mail to the forwarding address until further instructions: c/o N.D. Jhaveri, 14 Avenue van den Nest, Antwerp.

*c/o N.D. Jhaveri*
*14 Avenue van den Nest*
*Antwerp (Belgien)*
*22.1.36*

Dear Miss Schenkl,

Thanks for your card of the 18th. I hope you got my card from Brussels. We drove to Brussels from here the other day. It is only one hour by car.

I shall stay on here longer than I had intended—so please write to me here. From here I go to Paris and then take the boat to Ireland on the 30th from Havre. I return from Ireland about the middle of February and then go to India by 'Victoria' on the 28th February from Italy.

My address in Paris: c/o American Express Company, 11 Rue Scribe, Paris (IXe)

I got 2 letters in Berlin and replied to them.

*Re. the papers*

I. Send Bengali papers *that you do not want*, to: c/o Dr K.L. Ganguli, Berlin-Wilmersdore, Zahinger Str. 38
II. KEEP ANY papers that you want.
III. Send me *only one paper*—Patrika or Forward.
IV. Send any papers that are left to the following address: c/o H. Ghoshal, ul. Lwowska 15. m. 14, Warszawa (Polen)

I hope these instructions are quite clear. Dr Katyar and Dr Selig should get their papers as usual.

I am sorry to hear of your cold. Please do the following:

(1) Ask Singh to take you for the light treatment one day—as you had once.
(2) Ask Dr Sen for a prescription for cold and cough.
(3) Try Solvents' Mixture. You may buy it yourself in an apotheke.

I may be able to send you a little money from Paris after one week.

Best regards to your parents and for yourself warm greetings from myself.

Yours sincerely

Subhas C. Bose

*Antwerp*
*24.1.36*

Dear Miss Schenkl,

As I stayed here longer, I wrote to Paris for my mail and they all came here this morning. I am leaving for Paris on Sunday the 26th inst. Please redirect my mail accordingly. I leave for Ireland by boat on the 30th from Havre. I shall ask the Paris office of American Express Co. to send my mail on to Ireland. I am going to Spa with friends today and shall see Waterloo and other historical places. We shall return tomorrow and I leave for Paris on Sunday. I have sent you a French paper of Antwerp containing an interview of mine. I have received this morning a card and a letter of yours. I am sorry to know of your health. Please take care, as I have suggested in my last letter. I hope you have sent the American magazine to Mrs Horup. When you have time, please go through all my papers. Have you arranged for getting the papers from some café at a reduced price. I think you should continue your French. I shall write more in my next. I have probably left a number of papers, letters, etc. with you. Please revise them so that you may know exactly what you have. Excuse haste. Best regards to your parents and to you.

Yours sincerely

Subhas C. Bose

*Waterloo*
*25.1.36*

Frl. E. Schenkl,

Warmest greetings from: Subhas C. Bose; [illegible]; K.D. Parikh; Chandulal Mohanlal; Nathalal Dayabhai Javeri.

*Hotel Ambassador*
*Boulevard Hausmann*
*Paris IXe*
*30.1.36*

Dear Miss Schenkl,

I am sorry I could not write to you from Paris. I was awfully busy. Now I am leaving for Dublin. My address there is: Shelbourne/ Hotel Dublin (Ireland).

But why don't you write to me?

I am enclosing herewith £ 2 which should give you about 50 shillings. Please continue French lessons and buy medicine for your cold and cough. I hope to hear soon that your cold and cough are better.

I have been officially informed that President De Valera will receive me as soon as I arrive in Dublin.

Kind regards

Yours sincerely

Subhas C. Bose

*United States Lines*
*on board*
*S.S. Washington*
*30.1.36*

Dear Frl. Schenkl,

I am now at Havre and am going to sail for Ireland soon. I reach there tomorrow evening. I shall probably be very busy and shall not be able to write. This morning I posted a registered letter to you from Paris. *When writing to Dublin, please remember that the post passes through England.* I shall leave Ireland on the 12th February. At Dublin I shall stay at Shelbourne Hotel, Dublin, Ireland. In Paris I shall stay at Hotel Ambassador, Boulevard Hausmann, Paris (IXe).

I am sorry to know of your ill-health. It pains me. Why don't you take more care of yourself?

Have I told you that it has been arranged that in Dublin my first visit will be to President De Valera.

I met many interesting people in Paris. On my return from Ireland, I shall spend a week in Paris, about a week in Switzerland and then 3 weeks in Gastein. The Congress has been postponed till the 7th April and I shall sail from Marseilles about the 20th March. I cannot now sail by Lloyd Triestino.

I have received all your letters. Many thanks.

Some of your words are wrongly written. Vienna is [Bengali script], Bande Mataram is [Bengali script]. I am sorry I have not yet read the article by Blan. As soon as I read it I shall write to you about it. Dr Selig can certainly take Pandit Nehru's book.

I am thinking of some journalist work for you. As soon as my idea is more clear, I shall write to you.

In one letter you have talked of my young life. But I am no longer young!

You must have already seen the new French Cabinet. Herriot is not there.

For the present you may buy at least one paper (old copy) and read it.

You need not send me the translation of 'Le Matin'. If there are any surplus non-Bengali papers, please send them to Mr Ghoshal at Warsaw. Have I not asked you to send some Bengali papers to Dr Ganguli in Berlin? His address is: Dr K.L. Ganguli, Zahringer Str. 38, Berlin-Wilmersdorf. To Dr Ganguli, please send only Bengali papers.

Shall I send you some French magazines or daily papers? By the way, why not ask the cafés for old copies of French papers as well?

The economic situation in Germany is really very bad. People are not afraid now of criticising the government for this. The 'Haus-frauen' especially are discontented.

I am glad that you have cut down your smoking.

Before I leave Paris, I shall try to find a correspondent for you. I have been already trying.

My health is fairly well though I am tired. I had plenty of Indian food at Antwerp and at Paris.

Asoke's address: c/o Grindlay and Co., 54 Parliament Street, London S.W.

Good-bye. Best regards for your parents. Greetings for your sister and yourself.

Yours sincerely

Subhas C. Bose

*Shelbourne Hotel*
*Dublin*
*7.2.36*

Dear Frl. Schenkl,

Thanks for your letter of the 3rd February. I am enclosing a letter for Dr Katyar which please repost to Rome from Vienna.

I am sending a cutting which please translate and send on to me.

I hope you have received the cuttings which I sent you from here. Please send them to Katyar in a closed cover for his perusal and ask him to return them to you.

I am so sorry that you are suffering from cold and cough.

I am leaving Dublin on the 11th and going to Paris—Hotel Ambassador, Boulevard Hausmann, Paris (9e).

You can always keep New Leader if you want it.

My health is fairly well considering how I am rushing from one place to another. But I am somewhat tired.

It was very good of you to send me the cutting from 'Das Echo'.

Kindest regards

Yours sincerely

Subhas C. Bose

I beg you to take more care of your health

S.C.

*Dublin*
*Tuesday, 11.2.36*

Dear Miss Schenkl,

Enclosed please find a letter from The Hindu which you should preserve carefully. It will show that they want 2 articles a month for which they will pay 30 shillings an article—making £ 3 or about 75 Austrian shillings a month. It is necessary that you should begin reading the papers regularly. For Viennese papers, Neue Freie Presse will do. But can you also get the Times (old copy) at a cheap price? If so, it would be good to get the Times regularly also. As long as I am in Europe, I shall be sending you cuttings from the Times—consequently reading the Times is not an urgent matter *just at present.* But you may only bear this in mind. There are really only 2 pages in the Times which give foreign news and other pages are not so necessary for you.

Next, you should read the Hindu regularly. I think the Hindu is coming for me now. If so, you could keep it for yourself. If you read the Hindu regularly, you will find out for yourself what its general policy is. It is one of the best papers in English—but it is moderately nationalist and I do not think that it is as strongly nationalistic as I would like it to be.

It is necessary for the Indian readers that you should in your first article about any country, give a general idea of the recent political history, so that the news that you may subsequently send may be intelligible to the Indian readers. You may begin with Yugoslavia and give a general account of its political history since the First War leading up to the present time. For this purpose you should get in touch with Yugoslavian journalists at once. Ask Mrs Fulop Miller to introduce you to Mr Maxim Kandt or some other intelligent journalist and get from them as much information as possible. My knowledge is not enough—but I can try to send you some notes which may be useful to you. These notes you can work up into an article.

If it is more convenient, you may begin with another country about which you may be able to collect information more quickly or more easily. The countries about which you can write are:

1) *Balkan States*—Yugoslavia, Bulgaria, Roumania, Greece and possibly Hungary also, though Hungary is not strictly speaking Balkan.
2) *Near East*—Turkey, Palestine, Syria, Egypt. You may even include Arabia.

*You will have to remember that Egypt now is very important.*

On second thought, I think you should read the Times regularly. I am therefore asking the Times Book Club to send my Times to you. You should read it and then send me the inside four pages of foreign news or a few cuttings only which are important.

You should print a visiting card as follows:

Fraulein E. Schenkl

(Special representative of 'The Hindu' of Madras,
India's most popular and influential daily paper)

Vien XVIII Tel. R60-2-67
Ferrogasse 24

*Of course the above must be in German.*

Then you must write to the Press Attache of all the countries of the Balkan and Near East that have a Legation in Vienna. Please write to them, enclosing your card, and ask them for an interview and also for information which they would like to see published about their countries in India. The address of the Press Attache or Press Chef will be c/o the Legation. Doing all this will require some money. I shall therefore try to send you two pounds (or about 50 shillings) from Paris.

I am leaving for Paris today and shall arrive there on the 14th (latest). Please write to me c/o Hotel Ambassador, Boulevard Hausmann, Paris IXe.

The first article may also be about the attitude of the Little Entente towards the Hapsburg restoration.

When you send your first article by airmail, please ask for a legitimation from the Editor of The Hindu.

Yours sincerely

Subhas C. Bose

*Hotel Ambassador*
*16 Boulevard Hausmann*
*Paris*
*18.2.36*

Dear Miss Schenkl,

I have not replied to 3 of your letters. Yours of the 15th was to hand *here* the other day. Many thanks. I am writing this in great hurry. So I shall write on one point only. *Do not send your first article to 'Hindu' this week.* Please take at least a week more to prepare the article and let me approve it first. *The first article must be a good one*—even if there is delay in sending it. I am anxious that you should not send an article in a hurry this week.

I shall order for a dictionary for you from London. I shall send you two pounds this week.

Little Entente means *Czechoslovakia, Roumania and Yugoslavia.*

I have got the address of two French ladies for your correspondence. Shall send them later.

I am always glad to be of any service to you.

More in my next letter. Once again I say—do not send your article to the 'Hindu' this week.

Yours sincerely

Subhas C. Bose

*Hotel Ambassador*
*Saturday, 22.2.36*

Dear Miss Schenkl,

Thanks for your letter which I received today. I am sending herewith 2 pounds. I am still too much in a hurry to write a long letter. My programme is as follows:

1) 25th Feb. Tuesday—leaving for Lausanne
2) 26th Lausanne—visiting Nehru
3) 27th Lausanne—visiting Rolland at Villeneuve
4) 27th or 28th—leaving for Badgastein (Kurhaus Hochland Badgastein).

Do not write any *important* matter when I leave Paris until I am settled down in Badgastein. The letter may miss me while I am moving. My address in Lausanne: c/o Messrs. Wagon-Lits/ Cook, Lausanne, Schweiz.

Yours sincerely

Subhas C. Bose

PS I have read all your letters.

S.C.B.

*Kurhaus Hochland*
*Badgastein*
*3.3.36*

Dear Frl. Schenkl,

I arrived here this morning. I was delayed at Lausanne because of the death of Mrs Nehru on the 28th February. I expected to find your letter and article here on my arrival. I am very tired and am glad to have some quiet rest now. How are you? It is beautiful here. I want to do some skiing here. Best regards for your parents.

Yours sincerely

Subhas C. Bose

*Badgastein*
*4.3.36*

Dear Miss Schenkl,

I am now sitting down to reply to your letters of the 22nd January; 8th, 12th, 15th, 19th, 20th and 25th February.

I am glad you are reading two Viennese papers regularly. Though they may not give full information about Austria, they will give useful information about the Balkans.

If you meet or talk to Dr Elvira, please give her my kindest regards. Please tell her that wherever I may happen to be in future, I shall never forget the sisterly care with which she nursed me in Rudolfiner Haus. I do not think I shall meet her again before I leave Europe, but she is such a good soul that I am sure that everything good will come to her in this life.

I received the enclosure with your letter of the 12th inst. Since the letter was opened, I am sure that the authorities in Bombay already have your name down in their list.

Is there no reference to Indians in 'Das Letzte Fort'? Is it only about Negroes and Kurds? Please let me have a small description of the film. Is the story much the same as that of Bosambo?

Owing to my negligence, I have not ordered for the English dictionary for you. I am doing so today. It will come in my name via Karlsbad and you must take delivery of it.

I am writing to the Times Book Club for a post-war European History. I am sorry I did not do so before. If I can get hold of the right book for you, I shall order one for you. I have among my books a masterly book on post-war international affairs—but I am afraid it will be too lengthy and learned for you. What you want is a more popular book.

Mr Steiner of Karlsbad may be able to give you useful information about the Jewish point of view. But you will require information more from the Arab point of view.

For Syria, I am enclosing a card for a Syrian exiled leader who lives in Geneva. You may enclose my card and ask for information for the Indian press. Please mention that he may write in French and send you information in French. If possible, please write in French as he knows only French. Failing French, write in English. I think he has a secretary who knows English.

Your visiting card is all right. Don't send this card to the Hindu along with your first article, but send your former card (personal). Ask for the legitimation (letter of appointment) from the Editor of Hindu. After you get it, you may send your new card. A visiting card in English is *not* necessary.

A presse-chef is *not* Seine Excellenz. The Austrian presse-chef has, however, got the rank of Minister. Therefore, he is entitled to be addressed as 'Herr-Minister'. You can also write to the Austrian presse-chef—but please wait till you get your legitimation. For writing to the other presse-chefs, you need not wait for the legitimation. You should also write to the Verkehrsburo, Wiener, Messe and other Viennese officials who are interested in foreign propaganda. The head of the Verkehrsburo is probably Strafella and Mr Faltis knows about him.

Regarding the legations: (1) Syria and Palestine being Colonial countries, have no legation (2) Egypt has a legation in Vienna (3) The Balkan countries, including Turkey, have each a legation (4) Arabia (Ibn Saud) has a legation in London—but not in Vienna (5) Iraq has a legation in London and some other capitals—but probably not in Vienna. It is *no* use writing to the British Legation for any information.

I am glad that you are continuing your French—it is very important. I am enclosing herewith two French addresses for your correspondence. You may write to them and introduce yourself by saying that Mrs and Miss Woods of 131 Morehampton Road, Dublin (Ireland) have kindly recommended them for correspondence. Write a very polite letter to begin with. The two addresses are quite different. But do not begin correspondence if you think that you will not have time to continue it.

I am glad that you are somewhat better now. Is it really so?

The 'Einschreiben' parcel from India redirected to Dublin was duly received by me.

The synopsis of your first article for Hindu is quite good. I now want to see the article itself.

You can cut out as much of the Times as you want. Don't worry about me.

I received two long letters from you when I was in Paris.

Palestine belongs to England (under British mandate). Syria is under French mandate. Arabia is independent—one part being ruled by Ibn Saud (including holy places like Mecca) and the lower part being ruled by the Imam of Yemen. Iraq is nominally independent but is under British influence. Egypt has a nominal King, but is a British protectorate.

You should approach the Turkish presse-chef if you have not done so already. It is no use writing to Nahas Pasha about Egypt.

You must be very careful before deciding to give lessons to Indians. Generally they want some lady who will flirt with them and also teach them dancing perhaps. There are such girls already and I am afraid that you may be taken as one among them. How is Dr Sen behaving towards you?

Who gave you the information about Udai Shankar? I hope he will not fall into the hands of Agnihotri.

I hope you have seen the Hungarian presse-chef by now. Please send me the article of Nariman about H.

I shall now end this letter by answering a few more questions of yours:

1) Locarno Treaty was signed by about 9 European powers at Locarno some years ago, promising that they would maintain the peace in Europe and also go to the help of any power that might be attacked by any other power in an unprovoked way. The exact year of the Treaty I forget—probably 1925.

2) Stresa Conference was held last year between England, France and Italy at Stresa in Italy. The object was to establish a close understanding among these three powers as against Germany.

3) Roman Pact is probably the understanding between Italy, Austria and Hungary for close co-operation—economic and political. This also took place last year.

4) Little Entente means Czechoslovakia, Yugoslavia and Roumania. Hungary is against it.

5) *Balkan Entente* means Turkey, Greece, Roumania and Yugoslavia. Bulgaria is outside it; also Albania.

Today or tomorrow I shall write another letter to you. Please call for it. It is beautiful here and quiet. Plenty of snow. How are you?

Yours sincerely

S.C. Bose

*Kurhaus Hochland*
*Badgastein*
*5.3.36*

Dear Miss Schenkl,

Your express letter of the 4th of March is just to hand. You seem to be very much excited over the telephone call. The best thing for you is to say that you are not quite sure if I had reached Badgastein and then give them my Badgastein address. Also say that you have got a letter from me from Lausanne saying that I shall soon be leaving for Badgastein.

Then please enquire from Pension Cosmopolite if they gave the British Consulate your telephone number.

I am just now writing a letter to the British Consul thanking him for his courtesy in the past. As a matter of fact, I have been thinking of writing to him for a long time. *I shall not of course mention that he was making enquiries in Vienna about my address.* When you get this letter, you can ring up the Consulate and give them the information contained in the first paragraph of this letter.

I am thinking of doing some skiing. I have already written to Singh for the boots. I want you to get ready the following things:

1) Long Indian breeches of rough grey cloth.
2) Coat (European style) of the same stuff.
3) Sweater (not the white but the coloured one).
4) Brown woollen shirt (tennis shirt pattern).

Please send them by parcel *when I write to you again.*

Do you know where are my looking glasses (binocular)? They are not with me.

I have received your letter of (not *from*) Monday.

Yours sincerely

Subhas C. Bose

*Kurhaus Hochland*
*Badgastein*
*7.3.36*

Dear Frl. Schenkl,

I think I have replied to all your letters except the last two ones which I received yesterday and today. Thanks for both of them.

(1) Did I send you from Paris a cutting from a French paper 'La Lumiere'? It contained an interview with me. If not, I shall send you one. I shall also send you a cutting from Petit Parisien containing an article about Pandit Nehru and myself.

(2) Do you remember where I have put the bundle of Patel

letters? If I can make time here, I would like to go through them. Please let me know where they are.

(3) I would have liked very much to come to Vienna but it is quite impossible. I must look after myself these few days because I have to leave Badgastein on the 18th. If I go to Vienna I shall have to miss the baths.

(4) Mathur wrote yesterday that he and Dr Sen may pay a visit to Badgastein. If any of them come, please don't forget to send me the clothes I want—viz. Indian breeches, Indian made coat of the same cloth, sweater and woollen shirt. Perhaps you could send me the binocular (looking glasses) as well. As they belong to my brother, I would like to return them. If anything else strikes you as necessary for me, you may also send them.

(5) I am thinking what I shall do with my boxes in Pension Cosmopolite. Shall I ask Mrs Vetter to keep them for me? In any case, I shall let you know soon.

(6) The address of Amir Chekib Arslan is as follows:

Mon. Arslan l'emir Chekib
Av. E. Hentseh 9
Geneve (Genf)

I hope he has not changed this address in the meantime. Please write 'absender' on the other side of the letter so that it may come back to you if it does not reach him. I have asked Mr Jenni to try and see him in this connection—and also another Syrian nationalist leader, Mon. El-Djabri.

(7) I am writing to Paris about information on Turkey. Meanwhile you can try to get at the Turkish presse-chef.

(8) I have subscribed to the Times upto the 16th March. It costs 8 shillings (English) per month. I wonder if you could get an old copy of the Times at a cheaper rate. There are at least a dozen cafés that keep the Times in Vienna. If you could arrange with one of them at a cheaper rate it would be good.

(9) It is no use writing to the Iraq and Arabian Legations in London.

(10) Yes, you must send me the light coat if any one is coming to Badgastein. What other things are with you?

(11) About the other points in your letters I shall write later. I must first go through your article. I shall try to post it tomorrow (Sunday), so that you may get it on Monday—type it at once and post it by Monday evening. I think that the Indian Air Mail leaves Vienna on Tuesdays and Saturdays (6 am) from the Hauptpost—so that you must post by Monday and Thursday evening in a Branch post office.

(12) I do not remember the length of the article which the Hindu wants from you. Your draft seems to be too small. You must count the number of words in one column of the Hindu and see that you do not send less that what the Editor wants.

(13) I have written by airmail to the Hindu saying that your first article will be despatched in the middle of the month. It will not matter, therefore, if you miss the Tuesday airmail. So long today.

Yours sincerely

Subhas C. Bose

*Kurhaus Hochland*
*Badgastein*
*Sunday,*
*8.3.36*

Dear Frl. Schenkl,

I am writing this card today to inform you that I shall not be able to send your article today. So you must wait for the next airmail (Friday, or Saturday) I hope to send you the article on Tuesday—so that you may get it on Wednesday.

Mr Nambiar has made two suggestions to yourself which are good and with which I agree.

(1) That you should send articles to Hindu re. *Women's movement and cinema news.* He says that the Hindu is greatly interested in these items. You must of course wait till your Balkan correspondence is finally fixed up. I am informing you at this stage so that

you may bear this in mind. If the Hindu is pleased with your Balkan correspondence—then you can suggest the other things (women and cinema).

(2) That you should get interesting photos from India and place them in the pictoral magazines like Wiener Bild, etc. Of course, I shall have to arrange so that you could get the pictures from India. Meanwhile you may write to Viennese and Swiss pictorial magazines asking if they will accept pictures from India and what they will pay for them. If we can get the pictures from India you will have to pay half of what you get to the Indian supplier.

More later.

Yours sincerely

Subhas C. Bose

*10.3.36*

Dear Frl. Schenkl,

Your article is unsatisfactory. Firstly, you have altogether forgotten that you are not a Vienna correspondent but a correspondent for the Balkans and Near East. Secondly, there are serious mistakes in it which an Austrian should be ashamed of. *The article is rejected.* (But I have corrected your article to show you your mistakes).

*I have written the first article for you.* Please type 3 copies and send one to me at once. I shall revise the typed copy and send it back to you. Then you will send it to Madras. If you post the typed copy on Wednesday, I shall get it on Thursday. I shall post it back at once and you will get it on Friday morning and you can mail it before evening.

Please return me your own article after you have seen my corrections. I shall make an article out of it for later use.

In my draft article I have said that the Austrian Archduke was murdered in June 1914. Please verify this from Mrs Vetter or somebody else—and if possible give the exact date, probably June 26 or June 29.

Please type the article as follows:

*The Balkans before the War*: (from our special correspondent) Vienna, 12.3.35

In 1453, the Ottoman Turks etc. etc. etc.

So long today.

Yours sincerely

Subhas C. Bose

*Remarks*

1) Bad English
2) The Social Democratic Party was never in charge of the Government (except for a few weeks). *It was in charge of Vienna City only.* In February 1934 it was driven out of the Vienna municipality (Gemeinde) only.
3) The Catholic Party in Austria was never called the Centre Party. It was called the Christian Social Party.
4) It is wrong to say that the Croats and Slovenes would like to come back to Austria. Who told you that?
5) You are wrong in saying that Italy is opposed to Hapsburg restoration. Only Germany is opposed—not Italy.

*Very bad! Very disappointing! English also is bad!*

In 1453, the Ottoman Turks crossed the Bosphorus and seized Constantinople. That was the dawn of the Ottoman or Turkish Empire in Europe. In 1918 the Allied Powers took possession of Constantinople and made the Sultan a virtual prisoner in his Palace. That was the end of Turkish domination in Europe. The wily Turks retired to the hills of Anatolia and fought bravely for their national existence. They saved Anatolia and recovered Constantinople and part of Thrace (THRACE) by 1922, but the Turkish Empire disappeared from the map of Europe once for all.

For nearly 500 years the history of the Balkans was the history of the Turkish Empire in Europe.

After Constantinople fell to the Turks in 1453, for two centuries Turkish rule began to spread to the west and north-west. Greece, Bulgaria, Yugoslavia, Hungary, Albania—all became Turkish provinces. Then one fine morning the Turkish cavalry appeared before the walls of Vienna. If Vienna had fallen, the Turks would have overrun Western Europe. But after two desperate assaults, the Turks were repulsed in 1683 and Christian Europe was saved. The Turks withdrew, but not before they had taught the Christians to drink coffee. After 1683, the decline of the Turkish Empire set in, but for nearly 250 years the Turks fought a losing game.

It was the French Revolution during the last years of the 18th century that sealed the doom of the Turkish Empire. Till then, people in Europe had thought and felt in terms of dynasties and tribes and clans. After the French Revolution and the Napoleonic wars—people began to think and feel in terms of their common nationality. The whole of the Balkan Peninsula was astir with a new national consciousness. Revolts against the Turkish rulers broke out among the Serbs, the Greeks and the Roumanians.

But the Turks were still very powerful and their army was excellent. Left to their own resources, the Balkan peoples would have taken ages to throw off the Turkish yoke. But external forces came to their aid. The fall of Napoleon in 1815 led to the rapid growth of two other Imperial powers in Europe—viz. Austria and Russia. Driven by their own imperialist urge and inspired also to some extent by sympathy for the Christian subjects of the Turkish despots—the overthrow of the Turkish Empire became one of the avowed objects of both Austria and Russia in the 19th century. The bond of sympathy was more marked in the case of Russia. Most of the Balkan peoples, like the Serbs and the Bulgars, being Slav in race, like the Russians themselves—began to look up to Russia as the Big Brother and as the Saviour of the enslaved Balkan peoples. Russia, on her part, sedulously nurtured this feeling and deliberately encouraged the Pan-Slav movement, hoping thereby to gain more and more influence in the Balkan peninsula.

It was the pressure of the Big European powers, more than the internal revolts within Turkey which forced the Ottoman rulers to make concessions to the nationalist aspirations of the Balkan peoples. The first stage came when countries like Serbia and Greece were granted autonomy, subject to the suzeranity of the Turkish Sultan. But it did not take long to break this slender thread which still bound them to Turkish overlordship. Between 1830 and 1880 most of the Balkan countries recovered some measure of independence and the Balkan peoples invariably profited from a war in which Turkey was involved.

It should be noted in this connection that as the Turks began to withdraw from the Balkans, step by step, the void was filled up not only by new and independent Balkan states but also in some cases, by the far-reaching tentacles of the Austrian Empire. For instance the major portion of present-day Yugoslavia excluding Serbia proper was shamelessly wrested by the Austrian Emperor from the hands of the Turkish Sultan. Russia intended to emulate Austria in grasping Turkish territory in the Balkans, but she could not do so, owing to the opposition of the Western powers—particularly of Great Britain. There were two sources of friction between Russia and Great Britain. Firstly, both Russia and Britain were rapidly expanding in Asia. Secondly, Great Britain was afraid that if the Turkish Empire was completely annihilated, the Bosphorus and the Dardanelles would pass into Russian hands—Russia would then become a Mediterranean power and would be a menace to the Suez Canal. The result of British and later on of German opposition to Russia was to prevent her (Russia) from grabbing Turkish territory in the Balkans.

. . . [illegible] that while during the 19th century, external forces like Austria and Russia were plotting the overthrow of the Turkish Empire, the Western European powers being highly suspicious of Russia, were endeavouring to prevent her from completely annihilating the Turkish Empire in Europe.

The ultimate fate of the Turkish Empire was, however, doomed and the question was as to who would step into the shoes of the retiring Turks. Would the Balkan Peninsula become a conglomeration of independent states or would another imperialist power extend its sway over that Peninsula? The question was solved by the fact that Austria had already grabbed a large portion of the Peninsula and had no intention of giving it up. In 1878, when

Bulgaria was freed from the Turks through the help of Russia, the latter (Russia) wanted to annex it—but owing to pressure from the other powers she could not do so. Bulgaria, thus, got her freedom, more or less, as a gift from Russia. This fact is gratefully remembered by the Bulgarians till today and in their capital, Sofia, they have a huge monument as a token of their gratitude to Russia.

The frustration of Russia's imperialist designs in the Balkan peninsula and the comparative success of Austria there created an acute tension between these two countries. With the dawn of the present century it became quite clear that these two powers would soon come to grips and solve once for all the question as to who would dominate the Balkan Peninsula. It was Anglo-German rivalry which converted a Balkan war into a World war. But even if the German Empire had not come into existence in 1870 and even if there had not been a world-war in 1914—the issue between Austria and Russia over the Balkan question would one day have been fought out on the field of battle.

An inquiry into the immediate causes of the Great War will convince any one that an explosion in that part of Europe had become unavoidable. The Austrian Archduke was assassinated at Sarajevo in Austrian territory in June 1914. But the assassin was a Serb and investigation revealed the fact that the conspirators were in league with the officers of the Serbian army and had been supplied arms etc. by them. A prima facie case was made out that the Serbian Government was behind the affair and a very stiff ultimatum was sent to Belgrade from Vienna. Though the ultimatum was too bitter a pill for any government to swallow, Serbia was too small a country to stand up against Austria. Left to herself, she would in all probability have made peace with Austria on any terms, but from the start, Russia was behind her and she (Serbia), therefore, refused to comply with the Austrian ultimatum. Austria, therefore, declared war on Serbia. Russia came to the aid of her protégé, Serbia, and the war-front began to expand until the outcome was a world-war. Looking back on these events there does not seem to be any doubt that Russia encouraged Serbia to create trouble in Austrian territory inhabited by Serbs and other kindred races. What both Russia and Serbia desired was emancipation of the Slav races in the Balkans from Austrian rule. The Serbs desired this on national grounds, while Russia desired this partly on Pan-Slavic grounds and partly out of hatred for Austria. The Great War has completely altered the situation in the Balkans. Till 1918, the Balkan Peninsula was a victim of imperialist aggression. But with the end of the War, three big Empires have disappeared from the Balkan zone—Turkey, Austria and Russia. One could very well assert today that the Balkan Peninsula has after all been rid of imperialist domination.

But does that mean that the Balkan problems have been finally solved. No. The Great War has cured old evils but has bred new ones. The Balkan countries today can be divided into the 'haves' and 'have-nots'. Among the 'haves' are Yugoslavia and Roumania. Among the 'have-nots' are Bulgaria and Hungary—if we may include that country within the Balkan zone. The 'have-nots' are clamouring for a revision of frontiers. In addition to this, there is internal trouble in Yugoslavia and there is the Macedonian question which is acute in Bulgaria but which exists also in Greece and Yugoslavia.

No, the Balkan problems are still far from a final solution. The Balkans are only superficially quiet. Beneath the surface the rumblings can always be heard. Though for the time being, Germany and Austria have drawn the world's attention—the Balkan Peninsula still remains the storm-centre in Europe.

*Kurhaus Hochland*
*Badgastein*
*11.3.36*

Dear Miss Schenkl,

(1) Enclosed please find some German stuff. Please translate it and send it to me with the original as early as possible.

(2) I have ordered for a European History for you. It will come direct from London in your name.

(3) The Oxford dictionary will come in my name via Karlsbad. Have you got it yet?

(4) Did you enquire about subscribing to the Times in some café?

(5) I got a postcard from you yesterday. You said that you were sending me my clothes and Patel letters. How? I hope you are not sending them by post. I don't want them now because the weather is not suitable for skiing and I don't want you to waste money by sending them by post. In my first letter I asked you to *keep them ready and to send them only when I write for them again.* In my last letter I said that if Mathur and Sen happened to come to Badgastein, then you could send these articles through them. *But I did not want them by post.* So do not send them by post now.

Hope you are well,

Yours sincerely

Subhas C. Bose

PS Did you inform the Consulate? What did they say?

S.C.B.

*Kurhaus Hochland, Bdg.*
*12.3.36*

Dear Miss Schenkl,

Herewith *your* article corrected. You may send it off at once. Please let me know in your next letter how many words there are in a full column of Hindu.

Yes, you must accept the offer of Major Basu. No doubt about it. This is a very good opportunity for you to go to England. I hope your parents will let you go.

I am writing this in haste as I want to catch the mail.

Let me know if you can get the Times from the café. Otherwise I must write to London at once. The Times will come from London till the 16th March only.

I am so so. Accept the offer of Major Basu.

Yours sincerely

Subhas C. Bose

*Kurhaus Hochland*
*Badgastein*
*Austria*
*12.3.36*

Dear Miss Schenkl,

I have just received the parcel you have sent and I cannot tell you how greatly annoyed I feel with you. I do not know under whose instructions you have sent them. They are quite useless—as there is no snow here. Moreover I cannot carry any more luggage than I have with me and I have to send them back to Vienna again.

I told you in a previous letter to keep the things ready, so that I could ask you to send them to me when necessary. In a recent letter I told you to send them with Mathur or Sen, if either of them came here. But who told you to send them by post:

*Please let me know how much money you have spent over this.*

I am sure you are always spending a lot of money in similar foolish ways.

I thought you had more intelligence but I find that you are very foolish. I am very very sorry.

Further, you could easily have made a parcel of the clothes. Why did you send a suitcase over and above the clothes. I wish you had used your brains less and followed instructions more.

Yours sincerely

Subhas C. Bose

PS Looking at the parcel I find that you have wasted some more money sending it *express.* What was the urgency—I wonder! So you have spent a good bit over this meaningless thing!

S.C.B.

*Kurhaus Hochland*
*Badgastein*
*15.3.36*

Dear Miss Schenkl,

I have received information *officially* from the Government of India (through the Consul at Vienna) that they will not allow me to remain at liberty when I reach India. This means that when I reach India I shall have to go straight to prison.

I am now thinking if I shall go, in spite of this official welcome. Most probably I shall. I shall, however, finally decide within 2 or 3 days.

In case I go by boat, I shall leave Badgastein on the 25th morning for an Italian port. In case I go by aeroplane, I shall leave Badgastein on the 31st March. Most probably I shall go by an Italian boat. If I have to go, there is some urgent work which I have to do—some articles to be written and the 2nd edition of my book to be prepared—which will require a about week's hard work. Can you please come here for one week? Please ask your parents if they will allow you to be away from home for one week or so.

I shall write to you again if it is necessary for you to come. Until you get my next letter, you need not do anything except revising the index of my book and doing other things in that connection.

If you come, you will have to bring my trench coat and looking glasses. You must bring few things with you so that you may not have too much luggage. I shall of course send you money for your railway expenses.

Please treat this whole matter as confidential and ask your parents also to keep it a secret. I have not informed anyone in Vienna about the official threat of the Govt. of India and you should therefore keep it a secret till I inform other friends.

In case I do not go home now, it will not be necessary for you to come here now. I am writing this now, so that you may be in readiness to come at short notice.

Best regards for your parents and greetings for yourself and your sister.

Yours sincerely

Subhas C. Bose

PS I hope you have sent off the first article to Hindu.

S.C.B.

*Kurhaus Hochland*
*Badgastein*
*Austria*
*Monday, 16.3.36*

Dear Miss Schenkl,

Yes, I must go home. I must therefore make all preparations at once. I am sending forty sh. herewith for your travelling expenses to this place. Please bring for me the following things:

1) Trench Coat
2) Mieder (corset)—this is packed in some box.

Please leave the light overcoat (grey colour) with the landlady at Cosmopolite—so that if I write to her she can send it by post or somebody could bring it. But do not trouble to bring it with you. *Only bring the trench coat.*

Just go through the 2 boxes of clothing. If you find anything which would be useful in India, bring it please. But you should not bring the Indian clothes (dhoties) of white cotton stuff. I have got one set with me and that is enough.

For your own use, please bring as little as possible, so that you are not bothered with too much luggage. You need bring clothes, etc. for only one week. It is possible that you may have to carry back some luggage with you.

If you can find a white cap (Gandhi cap) among my clothes, please bring it.

Today is Monday and you should get this letter in the evening.

Can you start tomorrow (Tuesday)? If you can, you may send me a wire—like this:

> Bose
> Kurhaus Hochland
> Badgastein
> arriving 10.15 (or 15.02 or 22.10)

This will be enough—you need not even give your name. If you cannot start tomorrow, you please write an express letter and it will be in time. But I hope that you will start latest on Wednesday.

You need not inform anybody in Vienna that you are coming here—or that they will take me to prison.

I got your letter of the 14th inst. yesterday. It is in a way lucky that your lessons are over—otherwise, I would have been sorry to disturb your work.

I am probably not sending you enough money now. Please manage somehow—I shall give you more when you come.

For your ticket, you need not go to any Reiseburo. Better not. Since Badgastein is in Austria, you can buy the ticket at the railway station. Third class will cost 33 sh. I think. I do not know exactly the train timing that you must find out for yourself by telephoning to the Oesterreicher Verkehrsburo. But I think there is no direct train now—you will have to change at Salzburg or at Schazach St Viel.

Keep the ticket with you when you arrive here. Aufwiedersehen. Best regards for your parents.

Yours sincerely

Subhas C. Bose

*Kurhaus Hochland*
*Badgastein*
*16.3.36*

Dear Miss Schenkl,

This morning I have written an express letter to you. I have forgotten three things:

1) You should bring 'Indian Struggle'—with any notes you might have made.
2) You must bring your typewriter. Also bring some typing paper (100 sheets) with carbon paper.
3) Please bring block post (50 sheets) with 50 covers and 25 thin covers for airmail letters.

In case you have no time do not bother about the stationery (papers, etc.)—but do not forget your typewriter, which is absolutely necessary.

Brief papier is very expensive here—therefore it is better to bring with you—if you have time.

I hope I am not bothering you too much. I am afraid you will be short of money—but please manage.

Yours

S.C. Bose

*Haus Hochland*
*Bg. 17.3.36 (Tuesday)*

Dear Miss Schenkl,

Perhaps you get this letter too late. If you do get it in time, please consider one thing. The lady here (Hausfrau) has a typewriter of Orgaprivat make (German) which she will gladly lend for my use. It is a table machine—not portable. If you think you can work with this machine, then you may not bring your own typewriter. The less luggage you bring the better.

If you have time, please bring my medical papers—a bundle of medical reports re. my health, etc. They are in some box in Cosmopolite.

The trains are as follows:

| | | |
|---|---|---|
| Vienna (West)—8.0 | 12.20 | 13.45 |
| Badgastein— 14.41 | 19.09 | 21.36 |

In all trains I think you have to change at Salzburg. In some trains you have also to change at Schwazach St Viel. Sorry to trouble you with another letter.

Yours sincerely

S.C. Bose

In case you don't bring your typewriter you may bring my grey overcoat in addition to the trench coat.

*Villach*
*Bahnhof Restaurant*
*26.3.36*

Dear Miss Schenkl,

I have just finished this article. Please scrap the other one I wrote in Gastein—and send this one on Monday by airmail. Along with this article, write a short note to the Editor asking for his opinion on the first two articles you have sent—and also for any suggestions for the future.

I shall send you a note regarding your future articles before I reach India. I hope you will arrive home safely. I am now waiting for my train.

Yours sincerely

Subhas C. Bose

PS I did not notice anyone following me. Maybe he is here, but I was too busy to notice.

*Vienna*
*30.3.36*

*The Balkans after the Great War*
(from our Balkan Correspondent)

The end of the Great War meant the break up of the Austro-Hungarian Empire and the virtual expulsion of the Turks from

Europe—leaving them but a tiny portion of Thrace and the city of Constantinople, as a remembrance of what was once the great Ottoman Empire extending from the Bosphorus to the vicinity of Vienna. There emerged from within the Balkan Peninsula the six states of Yugoslavia, Bulgaria, Albania, Roumania, Greece and 'Turkey in Europe'. Hungary, though not generally included among the Balkan states, is destined to play a role in the future of the Balkan Peninsula and may be regarded as coming within the Balkan zone. Of these six states, Albania and Turkey are comparatively small and both of them are Moslem by religion. The states that have enlarged territories considerably after the Great War are Yugoslavia and Roumania and they may therefore be ranked among the 'haves' (HAVES). Yugoslavia (meaning literally 'South Slav State') as its name will indicate is Slav by race. The component races in Yugoslavia are the Serbs, Croats and Slovenes. All these three races speak a Slav language which is not remote from the other Slav languages like Czech, Polish and Russian. The Roumanians are a distinct race, probably descended from the ancient Romans, and the Roumanian language is akin to Latin and Modern Italian. Greece also may be classed among the 'haves', because she had added to her territory after the Balkan Wars of 1912–1913 and the Great War—though her gains have not been probably as great as those of Yugoslavia and Roumania. Greece is now definitely interested in maintaining the status quo and the existing frontiers and has no territorial ambitions. Among the six Balkan states, Bulgaria today is the only country that can be definitely classed among the 'have-nots' (HAVE-NOTS). Turkey, of course, has lost her Empire both in Europe and in Asia—but she has resigned herself to her fate and has no 'revisionist' ideas. She is content with the territory which she now has and which is inhabited by Turks alone and she wants to live at peace within the Balkan zone that is definitely a 'have-not'.

I stated in my last article that the Balkan problems have not yet been solved, though Imperialism has been abolished from the Balkan Peninsula. The explosive forces in the Balkans are Bulgaria and Hungary—and Yugoslavia also, though for quite different reasons. I shall explain.

Bulgaria has long been dreaming of becoming a big Slav state but owing to her bad luck, she has been worsted by her Balkan neighbours. She expanded her territory at the cost of Turkey, but later on, portions of the territory to which she lay claim, were grabbed by Roumania on the north and by Greece on the South. This happened during the Balkan Wars of 1912–13. After the Great War, probably because of her crime in going against the Western Powers, Bulgaria lost some of her territory to Yugoslavia also. She has, thus, strong grievances against her neighbours—Roumania, Greece and Yugoslavia—and probably Turkey also. It is because of this that when the four important Balkan powers, Roumania, Greece, Yugoslavia and Turkey, launched the Balkan Entente recently, for the preservation of peace and of the 'status quo' in the Balkan Peninsula, Bulgaria refused to join in. Bulgaria, like Hungary, wants a revision of her frontiers.

The fate of Hungary is even more tragic than that of Bulgaria. Pre-war Hungary had a population of about eighteen millions. The Treaty of Trianon in 1919 almost halved that figure. It happened in this way. The Austro-Hungarian Empire was a dual-state under a common crown—the Austrian Kaiser or Emperor. One part of this Empire was directly ruled by the Austrians with the Headquarters in Vienna, while the other part was ruled by the Hungarians with the Headquarters in Budapest. The territories of Croatia and Slovenia were ruled from Vienna—while territories like Bohemia and Transylvania were ruled from Budapest. (The Austrians are German by race and have quite a different language) In the Great War, when the Western Powers became victorious, they decided to break up the Austro-Hungarian Empire. In order to do that, they had to set up new states in Central and South Eastern Europe. Thus Czechoslovakia came into existence as a new and independent state largely at the expense of Hungary. The small kingdom of Serbia with a population of about four million, became the enlarged 'Kingdom of the Serbs, Croats and Slovenes' largely at the expense of Austria. In this process of redivision, Hungary lost portions of her territory to Czechoslovakia, to Enlarged Serbia (now called Yugoslavia and to Roumania and her (Hungary's) territory and population shrunk almost by half. And while the pre-war Austro-Hungarian Empire had a population of about fifty million, present-day Austria has shrunk into a small state with a population of about 6½ million, with Vienna accounting for about 2 million. But Austria has resigned herself to her fate and there is now no movement in Austria for acquiring the former Austrian territories. On the contrary, a large section of the Austrian people are looking forward eagerly to a union with Germany, which has a population of about 65 millions. For good or for ill, Hungary has been unable to reconcile herself to her defeat and there is today in Hungary a strong movement for the 'revision' of the Treaty of Trianon, which is responsible for the present frontiers of Hungary.

The three states that have gained much out of the last war—the two Balkan states of Yugoslavia and Roumania and the Central European state of Czechoslovakia—have combined to protect their common interests and the 'status quo' in Europe. Out of this combination and alliances has emerged the Little Entente. Hungary regards the Little Entente as a menace to her aspirations.

As a supplement to the Little Entente, there has come into existence the Balkan Entente between the four states—Yugoslavia, Roumania, Greece and Turkey. Bulgaria regards the Balkan Entente as a menace to her revisionist aspirations. Albania, though a Balkan state, has not joined the Balkan Entente, because she is under Italian influence.

Both the Little Entente and the Balkan Entente are pro-French in their attitude towards bigger European problems. French diplomacy is very active in Central Europe and in the Balkans and French influence is very great. Individual states, like Yugoslavia, have however been showing of late an inclination towards an understanding with Germany.

To counteract excessive French influence in Central Europe and in the Balkans, and for extending her own influence therein, Italy has been active of late. Albania has for some time already been under her influence and now the Triple Pact between Italy, Austria and Hungary has brought Italy into the politics of Central Europe. Austria has turned to Italy because of her fear of German aggression and Hungary has turned to Italy because the latter encourages her revisionist aims.

Besides Bulgaria and Hungary—there are in the Balkan Peninsula two other sources of possible future trouble. Firstly, the internal situation in Yugoslavia is still acute. When the 'Kingdom of the Serbs, Croats and Slovenes' was founded after the war, the Croats and Slovenes expected to have local autonomy within a federal state. But in 1929, the late King Alexander set up a dictatorship and tried to unify the country, and accordingly suppressed provincialism in every form. He renamed the country Yugoslavia. Though all opposition was gagged for the time being, the feeling of revolt was intensified among the Croats and Slovenes. Today, the opposition parties are stronger than ever and every one feels that the internal problem of Yugoslavia is still far from a solution.

The other problem is that of Macedonia. The Macedonians are a people who are divided between Greece, Bulgaria and Yugoslavia— their greatest influence being in Bulgaria. Till quite recently, they had the benevolent mentality of the Bulgarian government in their campaign for Macedonian autonomy or independence. The Macedonians are all not quite clear about their objective. Some would welcome local autonomy within the existing states—while some of them dream of an independent Macedonian state, carved out of Bulgaria, Greece and Yugoslavia. Since the suppression of the Macedonian movement in Bulgaria about a year ago, one does not hear much about the Macedonian problem. But there is no doubt that the problem is still there and unsolved.

And allied to this, is the question of the relations between Yugoslavia and Bulgaria. During the last two years there has externally been considerable rapprochement between them—thanks to the efforts of the late King Alexander of Yugoslavia and King Boris of Bulgaria. But the crux of this problem is as to who will ultimately have the hegemony of the Southern Slavs. At one time, Bulgaria dreamed of it, now-a-days, she has been pushed aside and Yugoslavia has come into existence as the Southern Slav State. Now the Yugoslavs have gone so far as to talk openly of an union of Yugoslavia and Bulgaria, Yugoslavia being the big partner in the combine. The idea is a grand one—to unite all the South Slavs in one state. But what about the King of Bulgaria and his throne? With these problems we shall deal in greater detail in our next.

*Napoli*
*28.3.36*

Dear Miss Schenkl,

After a safe journey I arrived here this morning and shall soon be on the high seas. I send you my warmest greetings and also to your sister. Best regards to your parents. Please tell them that I got their letter while in Gastein. I posted an article on 'Balkans after the War' from Villach which you must have got by now.

Aufwiedersehen

Yours sincerely

Subhas C. Bose

*'Conte Verde'*
*29.3.36*

Dear Miss Schenkl,

There are many things that I want to write to you about—but I shall write in a disconnected way—so please read this letter carefully. We are now one day's journey from Naples. The sea is fairly calm—thank God! As I am now old, I cannot stand a rough sea, which I could do when I was a young man. It is beautiful and sunny—the blue sky above—the darker blue of the ocean all around us and in front of us—an unending expanse of water.

When I crossed the Italian frontier there was no trouble at all. They looked at me and did not even ask me to open my boxes. At Villach, I stopped at the Bahnhof Restaurant for three hours and then finished the article which I posted to you. I think there was somebody watching me there—but I did not care, as I was busy writing. If that letter did not reach you, then they must have stolen it, because I posted it myself in the station post-box. There is not much to report about, after I crossed the frontier. I posted the pencil for you and registered it. And I spoke to Dr K. about your cuttings. The journey to Naples was all right and we left Naples at 3 pm.

Life on a boat is comfortable, so far as animal comforts are concerned. Plenty of food to eat—in fact, too much. You can begin with bed-tea—then breakfast with plenty of courses—lunch at 1 pm with plenty of courses—then afternoon tea with cakes, etc. and last, but not least, evening dinner at 7.30 pm. In the first class, the food is even richer and between breakfast and lunch they also give you soup and sandwich. You have concert in the afternoon and a cinema-show at night. Last night we had a cinema show. Then you can have a daily bath of course and there is besides a swimming pool which you can visit when the weather is favourable. For killing time, you have deck sports. Today, there was a shooting competition and the Italian passengers showed remarkably good aim. They were shooting at a piece of wood thrown into the air automatically by a machine. In the first class there is also a gymnastic room.

My cabin-mates are an Indian and an Afghan. There are about six Indians on board. The boat is full of Italians but I think it will be empty at Massawa. We shall reach Port Said on the 30th or 31st March and I shall post this letter there.

I am glad that the sea is not rough. Generally the Mediterranean is rough in winter and the Arabian Sea is rough in summer. Only in spring (March, April, May) and in Autumn (October and November) one can find both the Mediterranean and the Arabian seas calm. The Red Sea is never rough—except when there is a storm—but it is awfully hot. I wonder how we shall find it now. They have started putting the electric fans in order, in anticipation of the Red Sea.

I hope you have done all the work that I had left for you, without bungling. There was really so much to do that I cannot blame you, if you did bungle. The two important things were—my statement to the press and the doctor's letters, all to be sent by airmail.

If I can manage, I shall send you (under another cover perhaps) notes for your further articles for the Hindu. If you could get additional information and rewrite the articles, it would be good. Try to remain in touch with the friend in Prague—he will be able to help you in journalism.

If you ever happen to travel to the East, choose Spring or

Autumn. And if you choose spring, you should have summer clothes to be used after Port Said. On the boat, European ladies wear even 'beach-pyjamas' when they move about on the deck.

This morning in the ship's wireless newspaper (a daily paper) there was a piece of wireless news about Vienna. One Dr Ochsner(?) belonging to the Phoenix Insurance Company was found dead on the banks of the Danube. There was also the news about De Valera's eye-operation in Zurich and a forecast of the German election which is to be held today.

I have with me some surplus lira which I *may* send you in this cover. I hear that in Port Said or in Bombay I shall get a very bad rate if I change. I may send you 100 or 150 lira in paper notes. If you get it, you may get it changed into Austrian money soon. The lira will probably be falling—so you should change it soon.

I think I shall write to the Times Book Club subscribing to the daily Times for about one month more—i.e. till the end of April. You may read the paper and send it to me once a week. Send only the inside four pages—but please don't make the cuttings. If there is anything important for your work, please make notes. You should collect notes and cuttings separately for each Balkan country—so that when you write an article, there will be no difficulty in picking out the information you want.

And then, take care of your health. At Gastein, the food was not very good. I hope that at home you are now feeling better. It is spring, so that you will not feel the cold any more and I hope the cough will disappear. I hope the gall-bladder trouble will disappear. I beg you to be careful about your diet. *If you are, then you may avoid an operation.* Otherwise they will cut you open one day.

Regarding my letters in English, you may perhaps consult the Prague friend *if necessary*. You know that I trust him in political matters. Keep the Patel letters carefully. Should you find in that bunch, any of my letters, please keep them separately. And if you find the release order at once mail it *registered* to my brother but do not put any 'absender.' (Re. Bengali letters, see note below).

I have spoken to Dr K. about taking some of my clothes to India and he has agreed. I think it would be best to divide my clothes into three boxes—two small boxes and one big box (leather).

Mathur and Katyar can probably take one box each without difficulty. The more useful and expensive clothes should be packed into the small boxes. If they can be put into one box—all the better. If Mathur agrees, it would be much better—because he will come straight to Calcutta. I shall of course pay for the expense from Bombay to Calcutta for the baggage and any incidental expenses in Europe. But you must use your common sense and see that the transport charges are not too much. If they are too much, then it is no use sending them to India. Dr K. told me that he could manage to bring them to the port from Vienna, without any extra charge. The extra charges, if any, for Europe or Bombay—should be paid by you—at least you should offer to pay on my behalf. If either Dr K or Mathur does not accept payment from me, that is a different matter—but I feel that I should offer, because they are students after all.

About my books, you must arrange with Dr V. or Mrs F.M. as you think best, please make a note of all books that are lent, and see that they are returned.

I have with the American Express the sum of £ 5. I shall ask them to pay this money in pounds to you. They will probably charge a commission. Please pay the commission yourself and take the money in pounds. You will have to pay out of this amount the sum of £ 1 to New Leader for my subscription. The balance of £ 4 you should keep. Perhaps you should better keep this in English money so that if you went to England, you could use it. If you change it, please ask Dr Sen if he could give you a better rate. Even if you do not go to England, English money would sometimes be useful.

I shall send with another letter to you, a letter to New Leader. Along with that letter, enclose £ 1 and send it to Nambiar by airmail. Ask Nambiar to register my letter and the £ 1 to the address I give. I am also writing to Nambiar now. The idea of sending it by airmail to Nambiar is on account of the fact that an airmail letter is more safe than an ordinary letter. The idea of sending it registered from Prague is because it will be delivered safely in London (As you know we cannot send money in a registered cover from Austria, but we can send it from Czechoslovakia).

Please read the New Leader and send it to India. Please send both the New Leader and the Times to my home address—1 Woodburn Park, Calcutta—by Book Post—Drucksache.

Re. Bengali letters let Dr Sen read them in your presence and translate them soon afterwards. Don't send them to Asoke. Destroy them after translation.

The big leather box is impossible to carry in a compartment in the train. It must be booked as 'gepack' and that means expense. You must wait for the time when some one will agree to bring it at his own expense, or if the transportation charge is not much empty the box as much as possible and offer him the box to carry his own clothes and things. I would only like to have the box—because it is useful and belongs to my brother. The white cotton things in the box you may give away. The typically Indian shirts which cannot be used in Europe—you may send with Katyar or Mathur *or destroy them, as they are of no value.* Pick out the useful and valuable things from the big box and put them into the other two boxes for Mathur or Katyar to bring with them. Please send the skating and skiing boots, as I want to keep them as a remembrance. Now I have written enough for one letter. Give my best regards to your parents and greetings to your sister. I wish you the best of luck and I hope and pray for the best. Please tell your parents that I request them to allow you to do journalism.

Yours sincerely

Subhas C. Bose

PS If there is anything else to write, I shall write another letter before reaching Port Said—but to another address.

S.C.B.

*'Conte Verde'*
*30.3.36*

Dear Miss Schenkl,

There are a few points which I forgot in my last letter— hence this supplementary note.

(1) If you get an opportunity, you may go to England. In case you go, don't forget to write to Mr Pulin Seal (17 Edith Grove, Chelsea London S.W. 10) and introduce yourself as my secretary mentioned in Indian Struggle. He may be of help to you. Better still, call him in London *instead of writing*. If Asoke is still there when you go, he may also help you. His address is 33 Connaught Mansions, Battersea Park, London S.W. 11. The letters of both are opened by police.

If you go to London, then you should visit Paris on your way. Paris is worth seeing. Perhaps Mrs Vetter could introduce you to some French ladies—or your teacher could.

(2) Write to the two French ladies to whom Mrs. and Miss Woods introduced you. Perhaps they have already informed the French ladies and if you do not write, they (French ladies) will be wondering about you.

(3) Do not write to Mukherji again if he does not write. Perhaps he does not like that you should write. He should have replied to your letter about the Bengali books. Perhaps he is suspicious as to why you want to learn Bengali.

(4) You should continue your French. And what about Spanish?

(5) You may take gymnastic lessons twice a week. Try without instruments. Failing anything better, you may try 'Jim'[?] where I used to go.

(6) I hope you will try to be as economical as possible. I want you to use this money as a reserve fund to depend upon in case of any serious trouble. Consequently do not waste it over unimportant things. (You may of course make a new dress or a new coat for summer)

(7) Please correspond with the pictorial journals and ask them if they will take Indian photos for reproduction on payment.

(8) When the 'Hindu' finally appoints you, please send them extra notes about *cinema news* and about *women's movement*. In forwarding them, please say that they may not publish if they don't like, but if they do publish, they will be so kind as to pay.

(9) You may get into touch with the Austrian Verkehrsburo through Dir. Faltis and ask them if they would like you to do some

propaganda for them in India. I am also writing to Dir. Faltis about this matter. I am enclosing a letter of introduction to the United Press of India asking them to publish what you send. If you could get something published, either for the Austrian or for the Hungarian Verkehrsburo, you could show that in Vienna and thereby prove your worth and importance. If they do not agree to pay you at the beginning, they will still begin to take interest in you when they see your publications in the Indian press. When you send any stuff for publication, please ask the United Press to send you cuttings from all the papers that publish your stuff.

As Mr Nambiar suggested, you should never fail to send to the Indian papers reports of such incidents as Vienna Fair, Budapest Fair. [The Hindu would have welcomed such reports as about Shankar and the lecture of Pichamuthu.] Reports of Vienna Fair should be sent to the United Press which would supply to all the papers—though without paying you anything. The Hindu, on the contrary, would pay you, but they would be interested only in women's movement, cinema and art news—besides Balkan reports. In short, write to the Hindu for payment—and to the United Press for showing people in Vienna that you have connection with all the Indian papers. As a first step, along with my letter of Introduction, send a short account of 'Der Letzte Fort' to the United Press. In that report, show that the plot (story) is similar to that of Bengali and Bosanto—only the background is different.

In case you do get an appointment from the United Press, please do not tell anyone that the United Press does not pay you—because they do not attach much importance in Europe to journalists who are not paid.

(10) I want you to realise how you bungle things where you do not obey my instructions faithfully. The last example is your telling Dr Sen about my postponing my departure for India. The difficulty with you is that you never think before acting. You must now cultivate the habit of always thinking before you do anything. *Think thrice before you act.* If you do this, you will seldom make any mistakes.

(11) I posted a short letter to you from Naples. Hope you got it.

(12) When writing to the United Press, please address the Editor formally and not Mr B. Sengupta by name.

(13) When writing to the Hindu and to the United Press—please see that you do not repeat the same matter. That would be disastrous. To avoid this, always keep typed copies of what you send out to India.

(14) Just one thing more before I close this long letter. For your life, never pray for any selfish object or aim. Always pray for what is good for humanity—for what is good for all time—for what is good in the eyes of God. Pray in a nishkama* [in Bengali script] way. Cordial greetings. Regards for your parents.

Yours sincerely

Subhas C. Bose

PS I am subscribing to the Times till the end of April when it will stop.

S.C.B.

* Nishkama (without expectation of gain) ed.

*'Conte Verde'*
*Suez Canal*
*31.3.36*

Dear Miss Schenkl,

Yesterday I posted two letters to your home address. I have written to American Express to pay you £ 5 in English money. Please pay the commission yourself and get this amount from them in full. I have not sent you the lira because I shall manage to spend the money on board I think.

I am writing again today because there is something interesting to report. We left Port Said at 9.30 in the morning and are now passing through the Suez Canal. We shall reach the end of the Canal (Suez) in the evening.

When we reached Port Said in the morning, police officers came on board in search of me. My passport was seized and a policeman was ordered to mount guard on me. The guard remained on duty as long as the boat remained at Port Said. When the boat sailed, the guard withdrew and the passport was left with the Purser of the boat. Evidently, the British did not want that I should get down from the boat or meet any one. (I had met Nahas Pasha before) You may give the widest publicity to this incident if you like. You may inform Dr Sen, Mme. F. Miller and others. You can judge from this what sort of official reception I shall have in Bombay.

Kindest regards

Yours sincerely

Subhas C. Bose

PS Best regards for your parents. I hope to post this letter at Suez this evening.

S.C.B.

PS The journalist in Palestine wrote to you about another canal to be constructed—probably from Akaba to Haifa. Akaba is on the northern end of the Red Sea (like Suez) and Haifa is on the Mediterranean Sea in Palestine. If you can get reliable information about this, please send a news-item to the 'Hindu'. *It will give you great credit as a correspondent if the news is correct.*

S.C.B.

*Arthur Road Prison*
*Bombay, India*
*8.4.36*

Dear Mlle. Schenkl,

I arrived here this morning and on opening my boxes I found that I had forgotten to bring my medical papers. They must be in the box which I have left behind at Mme. Vecsei's place. Will you be so good as to see her and arrange to send me my medical papers by ordinary registered post? It is possible that she has already discovered my mistake and forwarded those papers to my home address. In that case, you need not bother at all. Please convey my regards to Mme. Vetter and Mme. F. Miller to whom I cannot write seperately. The papers should be sent to me c/o the Superintendent, Arthur Road Prison, Bombay. As they are a big pile, it is not necessary to send them by airmail. Hoping to be excused for the trouble and with regards.

I am

Yours sincerely

Subhas C. Bose

Mr Jailor, I shall be obliged if you arranged to have this sent by airmail after it is censored and passed.

S.C.Bose

*Yeravda Central Prison*
*Poona (Bombay Presidency)*
*11.5.36*

Dear Frl. Schenkl,

I wonder if you got the letter I wrote to you from the Arthur Road Prison, Bombay, on the 8th April. In that letter I asked you to be so good as to arrange to send me my medical papers which I had left behind by mistake. I discovered my mistake just before I reached Bombay and I therefore took the earliest opportunity of writing to you after I landed and I did so by airmail. My medical papers must be in the box which I left behind with Mrs Vecsei and I shall be thankful if you could arrange to have them sent to me. Since I wrote to you last, I have been transferred to Poona. You may therefore address me c/o the Superintendent, Yeravda Central Prison , Poona. If you have already arranged to have the medical papers sent to Arthur Road Prison, Bombay, they will be forwarded to me here and I shall get them in due course.

It is possible that you are now out of Vienna and in the country. If so, please do not bother about sending medical papers just at present. You may do so when you return to town later on. In the meantime, if I need them urgently, I shall write to somebody else in Vienna—but I think I shall be able to wait till you return to Vienna.

Now that the 'dog days' of winter are over, I hope you have been enjoying your Continental spring and summer. Here we are now in the worst part of June. The heat here has been very oppressive, ever since I came here on the 13th April from Bombay. You cannot even imagine how hot it is here. I often think of the thick snow that was lying all round in Badgastein when I left Europe.

You will see from my letter that I am now in prison, having been arrested when I landed in Bombay on the 8th April. Consequently, there is little that I could write to you from here. I have not met my people (relatives) yet, except my younger brother and his wife who came to interview me two weeks ago. Perhaps it would interest you to know that I have been kept in the same prison and in the same yard where Mahatma Gandhi was confined some time ago.

I am sorry to give you this trouble (about sending my medical papers)—but I venture to do so, only because I know that you will not mind the trouble. I am glad that my mail is being duly forwarded from Vienna. I have already received some letters and journals, redirected to India from Vienna.

Please convey my warmest regards to your parents and accept same yourself. My cordial greetings to your sister. Please let me know how you all are keeping.

I have just been reading in the Illustrated Weekly of India about an Innsbruck girl 15 years old who has been painting wonderful pictures. She is regarded as an artistic prodigy and has created a sensation in Viennese art circles. Her name is Rosuritha Bitterlich. Have you also read about her?

Yours sincerely

Subhas C. Bose

To: Frl. E. Schenkl,
*Vienna*

CENSORED AND PASSED

*c/o The Superintendent of Police*
*Darjeeling (Bengal)*
*22.5.36*

Dear Frl. Schenkl,

I am grateful to you for taking the trouble of forwarding my medical papers, which I had left behind in Vienna by mistake. I got them about a week ago—as also your forwarding letter—when I was still at Poona. I would have written to you at once to thank you—but about that time, I received orders of transfer to this place which is near Darjeeling. I am sure you have never heard of this place—but you might have read of Darjeeling. At any rate, it is more likely that you will find Darjeeling on a map. It is to the extreme north of Bengal.

Owing to the delay in receiving the medical papers, I thought that you were in the country during the summer season. I, therefore, wrote to you again from Poona asking you not to bother about the papers till you got back to town. Soon after I sent this letter off—I got your letter and papers.

I am no longer in prison now. I have been 'interned' (I wonder if you know what that means!) in a bungalow (a small villa) belonging to one of my brothers which is situated near Kurseong on the way to Darjeeling. Darjeeling is about 7000 feet high—that is, approximately 2300 metres high—and this place is about 5000 feet high—that is, about 1600 metres high. Though I am not a free man yet—it is a welcome change from prison life in Poona where the heat was oppressive during the months of April and May. By contrast, it is delightfully cool here and the villa commands a nice view of the plains.

Please remember me to friends in Vienna and Prague. Should you care to write to me now and again—I shall of course be glad to hear from you. With kind regards to your parents and yourself and cordial greetings to your little sister,

I am yours sincerely

Subhas C. Bose

Giddapahar
Kurseong
Dt. Darjeeling
22.5.36

CENSORED AND PASSED

*c/o The Superintendent of Police*
*Darjeeling (Bengal)*
*The 11th June, 1936*

Dear Frl. Schenkl,

I am grateful for your long letter of the 26th May which reached me on the 9th inst. It caused a break in my monstrous life and took my thoughts away to Vienna for a while. Latterly, we have had plenty of Austrian news in our papers—especially about the fight going on between your chancellor (Kenzler?) and ex-vice-chancellor. These news are of course concerned with Austrian politics and I do not think you are much interested in politics. Even if you were, I cannot write to you about anything of a political nature.

It was kind of the nurses in 'Rudolfiner Haus' to think of me. If you happen to meet them again, please convey my cordial greetings. I am sorry to hear of Sister Elvira's illness. Please convey my warmest wishes for a speedy recovery. It always struck me when I was there, that she looked so tired from over-work. She did not look really well. I often wondered why she went in for nursing when she came from such a well-to-do and aristocratic family. Perhaps nursing was a hobby with her or perhaps she found happiness in serving. In any case, I shall always remain grateful to her for her nursing.

I was interested to read what you wrote about the unsympathetic nurse. Was she not the fat sister-in-charge (oberschwester?) in the ward where I was?

I now feel sorry that I missed the exhibition of the paintings of that girl-prodigy, Rosuritha Bitterlich. Was it the same exhibition which Sister Elvira spoke so highly of. Have you been to the exhibition yourself?

It is not surprising that you liked Budapest. There is hardly anyone who is not impressed by the beauty of that city. It is really the 'queen of the Danube'. Tourists from Great Britain are very fond of Budapest. Vienna is 'gemutlich' no doubt—but when compared to Budapest or even Prague—it gives the impression of a city that has been robbed of its past glory. But Budapest, and even Prague, still look prosperous and gay.

There is little I can write about myself. I am sorry I have made very little progress with my German. Occasionally, I turn over a few pages, but I feel too lazy to sit down at it every day. You see, I have still to master the German grammar and that is the most uninteresting part of the study. I do not know enough to be able to tackle a serious book, all by myself. I am thankful for your kind offer to send me literature in German—but at this stage, it will not be of much use to me. When one is alone, one likes to read something more interesting than German grammar.

I am glad to hear of your progress in French. So you will soon be knowing two languages besides your own! What about your Spanish?

I hope you will get this letter before you go out of town. In any case, I shall send this by airmail. Many people do not have their mail forwarded to them when they go out for their summer holidays. Do you follow this custom?

This place is about 1500 metres high and on the way to Darjeeling. It is on the Himalayan range. The climate is cool and pleasant and quite different from that of the plains below. The temperature indoors is about 20° C—without any heating of course. And one should be lucky to have such a low temperature in India at this time of the year. At Poona, it went up to 43° C in the shade.

In a way, the climate here is like that of Europe—except that it rains heavily for several months in the year. Besides rain, we have constant fog—and the weather is therefore changing every minute. Occasionally, we have a brief spell of sunshine— and then we can enjoy the sun all the more—as in Europe. In the plains, you have the burning sun all the day long—except during the rainy season. The result is that we are not so fond of the sun, as people in Europe are. You see, we have too much of it and would rather have a little more cold.

My elder brother has a small house here where I have been 'interned'. (I wonder if you know what that means). Though there are several restrictions, it is much better than being in a regular prison. The worst thing is being alone all the time, but somehow one gets accustomed to such circumstances. Recently, my elder brother was permitted by Government to spend a couple of days with me. That was a welcome change for me. I am not yet allowed to go out for walks, but the matter is being considered by Government.

I was interested to hear that you met Mrs Hargrove. Yes, she is a very cultured lady with a deeper understanding of men and things and with a great deal of spirituality. Did you meet her friend, Miss Greene, an American lady. She is also spiritually-minded.

So you are still collecting stamps! I have never seen such a universal craze in Europe—or at least, in Central Europe. Hotel porters, housemaids, postal clerks, hospital nurses, railway officials, aristocrats, students, old women—no one is free from this craze. Sometimes, utter strangers have come upto me and asked for Indian stamps. It is amusing to find how happy you can make them feel by giving them a few stamps. In Sanatorium Purkersdorf, there was an old Viennese lady—a patient, the first day she talked to me, she asked for some stamps—and her joy knew no bounds when I gave her some. Latterly, I became a stamp-collector myself in order to please other people. This craze has not yet spread in this country—but I daresay it will come with time. Autograph-hunting has already become a craze with younger people in India.

I am glad that you are feeling better now with the approach of summer. With us, it is different—we long for winter and are glad when summer is gone. Please give my best regards to your parents and greetings to your sister.

I cannot expect you to write a long letter every time, because you do not have as much time as I have at present. Nevertheless, when you have nothing better to do, you may pen me a few lines. I hope you will have time to read this long and trivial letter. With cordial remembrances to all friends and kind regards to yourself.

I am yours sincerely

Subhas C. Bose

PS I did not get the Times for about one week—from the 3rd to the 10th April. Perhaps it was not forwarded from my old address in Vienna. I received the subsequent copies all right.

If you want to read any French journal, please try 'Vendredi'. It has the same standing as the 'Spectator', 'New Statesman' in England.

S.C.B.

CENSORED AND PASSED

*c/o Superintendent of Police*
*Darjeeling, Bengal*
*India*
*22.6.36*

Dear Frl. Schenkl,

Your airmail letter of the 9th June reached me yesterday. You have asked me to write again. I gladly do so, because it is not trouble for me in my present circumstances. As a matter of fact, writing letters (within the limits allowed to me) sometimes helps me to while away my time—especially when time hangs heavy on me. Writing letters is certainly more interesting than studying an uninteresting book. But you need not at all bother about replying to my letters—unless you have time and inclination to do so. (I wonder if you can read my handwriting which is rather bad at times)

You have asked me if I have any interesting stamps. As my correspondence is more limited and my foreign correspondence is practically stopped, I rarely get any interesting stamps. However, I shall bear in my mind that you are interested in stamps. As for snaps, though the country is beautiful round about, I have not so far taken any snaps. I am thinking of taking some and if I am successful, I shall gladly send you some. But I am doubtful if I shall succeed. Apart from the fact that I am not a good photographer, the weather here is not at all suitable for photography. It is misty and foggy most of the time and rains are frequent. Occasionally we have snatches of sunshine. It is not possible to take snaps of mountain scenery unless the weather is clear. You know this quite well, since you are in the habit of taking snaps yourself.

I shall, of course, be glad to receive a few pictures (reproductions) of the girl-artist—if they are being sold in Vienna now. But I would request you not to go in for any expenditure on that account—in case they are expensive.

I am sorry to learn from your letter that one of my countrymen misbehaved himself in Bratislava. Did you come across his name in the press reports which you noticed?

I replied to your last airmail letter by airmail also. That was about a fortnight ago. I hope that letter will reach you in due course.

You have said in your letter that you are giving lessons now-a-days. I wonder if that will compel you to stay on in town instead of going out to Styria as you had originally planned. Should you be in town when this reaches you, will you please do me a favour? I have left behind some books at the place where I was last staying in Vienna—23 Alser Strasse. Could you please ask Mrs Vecsei if there is such a book as '*Planned Economy*' by Sir M. Visveswariya (or Visvesvaraya) among them? If there is such a book among them, she may be so kind as to send it to me by Book Post (Druck-Sache). I want this book now, but it is possible that I purchased one in Europe, in which case I would not like to buy it again. There is no hurry about sending this book if it is there. And in case you are out of Vienna please do not bother at all about it. I may write to Mrs Vecsei about it later on—if I feel like doing so.

Our papers here say that in all probability Prince Otto will be returning to Vienna. You will then have an Emperor again and the empty palaces of Vienna will once again be humming with life.

By the way, Kaffee in English is spelt as 'Café', what we drink is written as 'coffee' in English. I hope you will not mind my correcting you in this manner.

If you have seen the films 'Mandalay' or 'Das Letzte Fort' (the last fort)—please let me know how you liked them. The technique will probably be very good.

Government have allowed two nephews of mine (brother's sons) to spend about a fortnight here. They are at present here and so I am having some company. They will go down towards the end of this month. That is all the news I have to give about myself.

I hope this will find you all well. Please remember me to friends in Vienna and Prague, when you happen to meet any of them. Best regards for your parents and yourself and greetings for your sister.

Yours sincerely

Subhas C. Bose

CENSORED AND PASSED

*c/o Superintendent of Police,*
*Darjeeling, Bengal,*
*The 15th July, 1936*

Dear Frl. Schenkl,

Many thanks for your kind letter of the 27th June which was to hand on the 11th inst., together with the pictures of the girl-prodigy, Rosuritha Bitterlich. They reminded me of the children's paintings in Prof. Cizek's art-school in Vienna. I wonder if you have been to that school. It is worth visiting—if you have not visited it yet. Both Mrs Hargrove and Mrs Vetter are enthusiastic admirers of Prof. Cizek's art. They took me there and introduced me to the 70 year old Professor. This modest and humble old man has now acquired an international fame. Mrs Hargrove has lately sent me a book in English on Cizek's 'Child Art' which has come out.

I appears from your letter that you are getting more interested in spiritual things. Is that due to Mrs Hargrove's influence? In India when a young man becomes spiritually-minded, his people get alarmed, lest he should give up the world and become a Sanyasi—i.e. a monk.

So you are getting warm weather after all! I hope you will have a nice time in the country and will be able to recoup there. I am sorry to hear of your lung trouble. I hope you will not neglect it at this stage when it is so easy to cure medically. In most cases, lung-tuberculosis originates from an old pleurisy or neglected catar-rh. Pardon me for alarming you in this way, but I am saying what every medical man will confirm. I have been through it myself and I know something about it. Vienna is one of the best places for curing lung diseases and it would be a pity if you get ill in Vienna through neglect. You have a very famous man there for lung-disease —Prof. Neumann, under whose treatment I was for several months.

No, I have not heard from Mrs Vetter, though I wrote to her from Poona in April and as I did not get any reply, I wrote again about ten days ago. I was wondering why she did not write. I now understand from your letter that she did write about eight weeks ago—though I did not get her letter. I gather from your letter that Mrs Miller is still in Vienna. I thought that she had gone to London according to her previous intention. Will you please give her my best regards?

Vienna has become popular in India, I find—especially from the medical point of view. I think Viennese people should write articles about Vienna and Austria in our magazines—with beautiful pictures of the art museums and palaces of Vienna. A place like Badgastein, of which I have become very fond, would attract Indian tourists, if people here knew more about it. It was my intention to write about Badgastein and the bath treatment there in our papers, because I benefitted by my two visits to that place. Since Austria is very keen on attracting tourist- traffic as Switzerland is, she should not neglect India.

I am sorry I have not been able to take any good snaps of the scenery here. Now-a-days it is raining constantly here and when there is no rain, there is fog. The few snaps we took have not come out so well. There is a waterfall near this place called 'Pagla Jhora' or the 'Mad Waterfall', which I want to snap. Should I succeed in taking some good snaps, I shall send you some. The scenery here is, of course, nothing compared to what you see in Darjeeling. There you can see the entire snowy range with 'Kanchinjunga' peak in the middle shooting up into the sky. It is grand and sublime and before the huge mass of rock and snow, one feels so small and humble. I do not know if one could get Darjeeling pictures here. I shall enquire.

I am now alone again. Two of my nephews who had been permitted to visit me, have left. It is not bad being alone, but sometimes, one feels quite fed up. I have now got a gramophone to keep me company. I find that I can appreciate European music much more than I formerly could. Could you send me the name of some good records? I shall then order for them from Calcutta. It is impossible to choose from a distance, unless somebody who has heard the records can recommend.

I am now getting my usual papers and magazines from London and they help me to keep in touch with the world outside. In addition to them, I get the Indian magazines and newspapers. Without papers, I do not know what I would do.

May I correct a few sentinces in your letter which are typically Austrian. (1) You have said 'your letter *from* the 11th.' It should be 'of'. In German you use the same word 'von' for both 'of' and 'from' and that is how the mistake arises. (2) Again you have said 'she is looking forward with anxiety'. You meant 'pleasure' or 'eagerness' instead of 'anxiety'—because 'anxiety' is used when you anticipate something bad or unfavorable. (3) You have written '*an* neglected catarrh'—it should be '*a* neglected catarrh (?)'. If the next word begins with a vowel, it should be 'an'. But if it begins with a consonant, it should be 'a'. This is the general rule but there are exceptions. Since 'neglected' begins with a consonant, the article before it should be 'a' and not 'an'. I shall not criticise more, because you may consider it rude on my part to do so. Besides, you write fairly good English and I would be very glad if I knew as much German as you knew English.

You must be tired of this long letter—so I shall stop here. Kind regards to your parents and yourself and greetings to your sister. When do you return to town?

Yours sincerely

Subhas C. Bose

CENSORED AND PASSED

*c/o The Superintendent of Police,*
*Darjeeling,*
*The 30th July, 1936*

Dear Frl. Schenkl,

Thank you very much for the long and interesting letter of the 13th inst. from Pollau which reached me on the 24th inst. I cannot spot Pollau in my map of Austria, but I remember very well the place that you say you passed through—Monichkirchen—where I had once been on an excursion during winter. Snow was then lying thick and the skiiers were all busy with their skiis. Monichkirchen is a pretty place and judging from that, Pollau must be pretty too. I am glad to know that you are having a nice and warm summer there. You need it very much in a country where the winter is so severe.

What you have written about your Austrian affairs has come rather late, because thanks to Reuter, we had the fullest news here the next day. An important event like that is flashed over the wires at once—no matter in which part of the world it happens. It is only less important events that are not sent out to other countries.

Very wet weather is continuing here and it will be like this till the end of September—or middle of October. It is at times rather trying, but somehow one gets accustomed to it. I am now allowed to walk within a radius of one mile from the house—that is I can walk up to a distance of one mile from the house. But that is possible only when the weather is clear, which does not always happen in this season. People here say that from the point of view of health, this is the worst season. But in any case I am relieved from the heat of the plains of which I am not at all fond.

I am trying a few snaps and if they are not too bad, I shall send you some along with my next letter.

I find that the Times is coming direct from London. When I wrote to the Times Book Club renewing my subscription, I gave them my new address and they have made use of it.

Should you feel interested in any Indian magazines (published in English of course)—please let me know—I may ask some one to arrange to send them to you. Of the weekly illustrated papers, the best is the 'Times of India Illustrated Weekly' published from Bombay. Of the monthly papers, the best is the Modern Review published from Calcutta. I am fond of both and get them regularly.

Do you read any English newspapers or journals now for improving your English—or do you think you know enough already and should tackle French now?

The word 'Uhr' in German means watch (and time also) and is feminine gender. Why then do you say 'vor ein Uhr' instead of 'vor eine Uhr' (Before one o'clock). I came across this expression in my German grammar. Is it a misprint or do you really say in German 'vor ein uhr'.

Rom Landau is a very interesting and able writer—he generally writes biographies. I have read a book *of* his (not *from* him) on Pilandski. I am surprised that he is now writing on spiritual topics. In his biography of Pilandski I found that he was something of a mystic. You need not trouble about sending that book, because books on spiritual topics we have enough in this country.

I have been thinking of sending some Darjeeling Tea to Mrs Vetter, because she is very fond of Indian Tea and I think Darjeeling Tea is the best brand of Indian Tea. But I am afraid that the customs duty may be too much—in which case it will be an infliction to receive a parcel. I know that the Austrian Customs once charged me . . . [illegible] Austrian Schillings per pound (½ kilogram) as duty. Can you please find out, when possible, if any duty is charged on small parcels of tea sent as *sample post*—say ½ kilo or 1 kilo parcels? The proprietors of inns and cafes should be able to tell, because they are constantly buying tea and coffee. Please also enquire what is the ordinary duty on tea in Austria. What is the German expression for 'per sample post'—bei muster pst—or what? I am sorry I must trouble you for this because I cannot write to Mrs Vetter on this point when I want to send her some tea.

There is a drama in Sanskrit called 'Shakuntala' written by our greatest dramatist and poet—Kalidasa—who lived about 1000 years ago. The German poet Goethe was charmed when he read it and he wrote a poem in appreciation of it. I am sending a few lines from it (English translation) and shall be thankful if you could send me the original German with the full translation when you are back in Vienna.

> 'Wouldst thou the young years' blossoms and the fruits of its decline,
> And all whereby the soul is enraptured, feasted, fed;
> Wouldst thou the heaven and earth in one sole name combine,
> I name thee oh Shakuntala! and all at once is said.'

In case it is not Goethe, it must be some other German writer like Schopenhauer—but it must be Goethe.

I am well on the whole. There is a little trouble in the inside and some throat infection, I think. For the throat infection the doctor is preparing an auto-vaccine for me. Do you know what that means? I don't know the German for it. I hope you are all well. Best regards for your parents and yorself and greetings for you.

CENSORED AND PASSED

*Supdt. of Police*
*Darjeeling*
*3.8.36*

Dear Mr Bose,

Many thanks for your letter of the 15th July which was to hand on July 29.

I am glad to learn that you received the pictures of that girl prodigy Roswith Ritterlich. Yes, I have heard through Mrs Hargrove about Prof. Cizek's school. She also showed me the book which she sent to you. Unfortunately, I have not been to that school but I shall do so, when I come to Vienna and Mrs Hargrove is also back. Then I shall try to go and see the school.

You think that my interest in spiritual things is due to Mrs Hargrove's influence. No, not at all. I have been interested in these things already since I was 12 or 13 years. Not of course that I understood what I wanted and needed to get into the subject more deeply, but the interest was already there. The person who roused my consciousness in this direction was my first 'guru' (as Indians call it, I think), Hans Sterneder, the author whom I like most among German authors. I think, I spoke once about him to you. But all that does not mean that I am on the way to become saintly or so absorbed in spiritual things, in order to give up the world completely. First I think that it would not do good to give up the world, because in active life one can fulfill a mission, while as a monk or so, one does not fulfill a useful mission. The world as a whole is not yet ripe to penetrate into a more spiritual sphere.

Yes, the weather as a whole is very fine. Only for a few days the temperature fell again, but I did not mind so much. Regarding my health, I am feeling rather well now. Only a few days ago I used to get the pain in the gall-bladder regularly after mealtimes. But I counteracted it so far that I ate very little and did not take any meat at all. Alcohol I do generally not drink. Only yesterday I had to, because my father had his 60th birthday and our family with a whole party of young people and some priests even, went to an inn. I must say that the Roman-Catholic priests are a very worldly people, specially here. There is one, he sits night after night in the inns or in the cafés, dances with girls and drinks. The other does not dance openly, but he also is a very jolly chap. And the most funny thing is that the second one is very strict regarding the rules of his religion. I had a little talk with him once. We were talking about religion and I told him that I had not been to a church for years. He now tries to bring me back to the fold of his church. But he will never succeed in this direction. But nevertheless, I will have another talk with him once, in order to tell him how I think about all this.

No, you did not at all alarm me, because you spoke about my health. You see, I am always for frankness and I can appreciate the frank speech of a friend. Therefore, please do not be afraid you may alarm me or offend me.

I did not hear for a long time from Mrs Vetter. But I will write to her again and tell her that you have not got that letter of hers. Mrs Miller had been in London. I only saw her very little after she came back. But she was quite charmed by the town and the people there. She stayed there for about 6 weeks I think and told me, that she has considerably progressed in English. Her husband seems to have gone to America now. She told me that she would go for the summer somewhere to Italy, probably Abbazia. But I do not know anything about her actual plans, because as you know, I was never so very intimate with her.

So Vienna is becoming popular in India. All right, I shall be glad about it. You know, that I have not so much affection for Austria as I should have for the country where I spent my whole life. But you are right in what you say about the propaganda, Austria never understood to make use of her beauties. Only lately, Austria has become a little more popular. Specially in England.

I have taken some snaps of the surrounding but they are not yet developed. The others I have taken are of our family and I do not think that you have much interest in these. I will send you under separate cover by ordinary mail some snaps or picture post-cards of the place here. I think that scenery in Darjeeling must be gorgeous. Only a few days ago I had a funny dream that I was in the Himalayan mountains. But it was not Darjeeling. It was somewhere high up near the highest summits and I was so charmed by the beauty of this dream landscape that I was quite sorry when I woke up and the beautiful dream was gone. The scenery here has nothing grand and mighty, but it is lovely and beautifully calm like a sleeping maiden. The high mountains I always compare with a young man who wants to storm the summits of the heaven.

That is fine that you have got a gramophone. I shall certainly send you a list of records when I come to Vienna, because there I can get the exact number which is here impossible. But you must please tell me what sort of European music you would prefer. I am afraid that I personally am a bad judge regarding music As you may know, I hate heavy music, I cannot digest it. For instance one can drive me out with Wagner's operas. What I like is light music. Specially the Viennese songs. But I also like peasant songs, or even jazz-music. Anyway, I shall try to get you a fine list when back in Vienna.

Are you getting the 'Modern Review'? If so, please let me have the copy of *July* this year. I wrote a short article about Budapest and it has appeared. I got a copy but unfortunately they have sent me a bad one, because there are some pages double while others are missing. And just the pages with the article are missing. But it was certainly printed, because the title is given on the cover. So, if it is possible for you, let me please have the copy.

It is awfully kind of you to correct my mistakes and I really beg you to do so in future.

Have you heard anything by now about the Olympic plays in Berlin? It must be really grand. We follow events in the papers and in the wireless. The other day there was a transmission from the Olympic Stadion in Berlin and we heard the march of all the members. When Austria came in, you heard how people were roaring and shouting with pleasure.

Schwester Elvira sent me a letter the other day and told me that she will probably come and visit me here for about 2 days. That will be fine. In case she comes by car, I shall be able to show her more. To-morrow I shall make a short trip with this young priest in his motor-cycle. There is a hill here and there we will go in order that I can take some snaps from the surrounding. If they come out well you will get a copy.

We will return to Vienna about the end of this month. It is really worthwhile to stay here regarding the prices. I have never found a place so cheap. We four, father, mother, my sister and myself, cannot generally spend more for lunch than 4 or five shillings together. Isn't that cheap? There are some young men here in the tax-office, police and so on and they take their meals also in the inn where we take it. I have asked how much they pay. They pay for breakfast, lunch and dinner 2 (two) Austrian shillings and without breakfast 1.80 Austrian shillings. You get a whole pension (board and lodging), with four meals for 4.50 here.

Are you now already allowed to go out for walks? I hope so. And how is your health? I hope satisfactory. My parents and sister send you best regards. Take also from myself best wishes for your health and hearty greetings.

Yours sincerely

E. Schenkl

CENSORED AND PASSED

*c/o The Superintendent of Police*
*Darjeeling*
*The 12th August, 1936*

Dear Frl. Schenkl,

Many thanks for your letter of the 3rd inst. which was to hand this morning. It has been very cloudy and wet these days and I am therefore confined indoors. The sun, of which we have too much in the plains, has become as scarce as in Europe.

If you could send me the names and numbers, etc. of some gramophone records, I shall be thankful. No, I don't want the too classical and heavy music, whether vocal or instrumental. I would prefer the lighter music which you can get in records. Classical music is difficult to appreciate unless you are trained in it. It is the same with our music. Frankly, I could not appreciate our classical music *at all.* Now I can to some extent. The music that we generally like is ridiculed by the experts as 'no music'. I have with me a couple of Viennese Waltz music which are rather good.

If you are interested in philosophy—or rather Indian Philosophy, you may read a German translation of Bhagavad-Gita—our Bible. It may be difficult at first, but you will understand certain parts at least. There are several places which I don't understand even now—though I am an Indian and a student of philosophy also. The most important is the second chapter which deals with Karma Yoga—or 'worship through work' (or Union through work).

I have not been feeling quite well for some days. I have probably got an infection in the throat which makes me feel 'out of sorts'. As the ordinary medicines failed to cure me, I had an autovaccine prepared and am taking injections of it. This is how they do it. They take a swat from the throat, then culture it in the laboratory and find out what germs there are. From these germs (bacilli) the antovaccine is prepared. The doctors say that this is the only radical cure for throat infections, I shall let you know what results I shall get from this treatment.

I am arranging to send you the Modern Review for July. I hope you will get it in time. Please let me know if there is any other Indian magazine which you would like to have and I shall try to have it sent to you.

I shall probably be able to send you some snaps by ordinary post next week. We had a little sunshine the other day and I took some snaps which are now being developed. If they turn out to be good I shall send them, otherwise not.

My handwriting is rather bad today and I hope you will be able to read it somehow.

Yes, we are getting some reports of the olympic games. India has done rather badly in other items, but we hope that she will be able to retain the championship in Hockey at least. You see there is hardly any scientific training in India for this—and lack of funds is an important factor.

Please give my kind regards to Sister Elvira when you meet her.

My health is fairly well in spite of some minor troubles. I am allowed to walk within a radius of one mile from this house— but now-a-days weather does not permit it.

There is hardly anything else I can write about today. Hope you are well. Kind regards to your parents and yourself and greetings for your sister. Please remember me to all friends there.

Yours sincerely

Subhas C. Bose

CENSORED AND PASSED

*Supdt. of Police*
*Darjeeling*
*17th August, 1936*

Dear Mr Bose,

Your letter of . . . [illegible] reached me on the 12th inst. in a somewhat torn condition. Many thanks for it. I am glad that my letter interested you somehow. It is so difficult to write interesting things when one does not have interesting experiences. As you know from my former letters, the stay here was not at all interesting. Only since a fortnight conditions have changed tremendously. We have found a very nice party, mostly young people. We meet every week twice or thrice in an inn where we have our 'Olympic Sessions.' Out of mere stupidity, we have founded an Olympic Committee of our own. We have already made two nice excursions. One week ago we climbed a mountain. For that purpose we started at 5.30 in the morning. Of course, we had to wait for three of our boys and so could only actually start at 6 am. We reached the summit of that mountain at 8.15 am. The climb was wonderful. When we came up higher and higher and more and more of the beauty of the surroundings was unfolded to us, it was a marvelous sight. It is only difficult for me to describe this to you in English, because in my own language I could describe it much better and more vividly. On top we stayed for some hours and had a very nice time, made a lot of nonsense and got sunburnt like anything. At four in the afternoon we went home again but were forced to make a short stop on the way and came home at 7.30 pm. I came home black—burnt by the sun and am awfully proud of my wonderful colour.

The second climb was done just the day when your letter reached me. Then we were only 4 persons, my sister, a girl of our party, the clergyman and myself. We went this time to the other side and had a very nice climb too. On the way we found plenty of mushrooms, of which we are all so fond here. On top we had to stay indoors for some hours, as a heavy rain began to pour down.

But this could not make us sad. We took the guitar, began to play and sing and had a jolly good time.

Your map does not show Pøllau you say. Oh, this place is not so big and I think only on a special map of Austria you could find it. It is about 60 km to the north of Graz. Pøllau is indeed very pretty regarding scenery. The weather is not excellently good, but it is also not quite bad. We have a thunderstorm nearly every day. Just now it is pouring like anything and the thunder is grumbling continuously.

I am glad to hear that you are now allowed to go out for walks. It is of course not much to be allowed only one mile radius, but better than nothing.

It would be nice if you could send me from time to time Indian papers or magazines. I am of course still reading English, because that is now the only possibility to improve my English or at least to prevent to forget what little I know. Mrs Hargrove is now back from Ommen. She wrote me a charming letter from Tyrol where she is staying at present. She also sent me photo of Krishnaji. She wrote at great length as usual, but mostly spiritually.

Yes, you are right. 'Die Uhr' is feminine and means watch, clock and in a transferred sense also time. But it is quite correct to say 'vor ein Uhr.' Why it is so, I cannot tell you, because I never knew anything of German grammar.

I shall enquire about tea and how much duty one has to pay on it. But I can only do so when back in Vienna. I am, however, afraid, that one has to pay a tremendous duty on tea. If it was not for the duty, I would have asked you long ago to send me a parcel of Indian tea. The tea you get here is not drinkable at all. It is mere water with a light yellowish colour. Anyway, I do not take tea here, generally only coffee or milk. The German expression for 'sample post' is: 'Muster ohne Wert'.

I shall send you the German text of that poem about Shakuntala. But here I can do nothing, as I have no copies of Goethe here and I do not know of anyone here who possesses one. I will ask my friend the clergyman, maybe he has one, but I doubt it rather.

Today we had a great loss. One of our 'Olympic' girls has left us. Poor thing, she cried when she drove away and we waved the handkerchiefs.

The other day I got two interesting books from a German publisher. One is a quite modern one, which came only out this year and is about the Zeppelin. The second is a little older and is a legend about Buddha's life. This one interests me specially. I have to review these books and therefore get them free (except the usual duty which one has to pay in Austria on books and this was only 85 Groschen). Could you please advise me to which paper in India I could also send a review of these books? Perhaps to a Calcutta paper or to 'Bombay Chronicle'?

I hope your throat infection is now much better. We are feeling very well on the whole. My cousin has arrived last week here but she is not so well. Yesterday she fainted after lunch and I had the trouble with her. I had to carry her with a servant into bed, undress her and try to bring her into life again. This is an awful business.

Either this or next week I will go for a motor-drive with the clergyman. He has a fine motorcycle and we intend a longer drive and then some excursion on foot up somewhere into the mountains. We want to start early in the morning and will not return until night. I only hope that the weather keeps clear and we have not too much rain, as it is absolutely a bad business to walk in the rain.

Mrs Vetter wrote also a postcard to me some days ago and told me that she would again write to you by airmail. I think, when you get my letter, she should have got hers already.

Let me close for today my letter. There is nothing more to tell you this time. I shall send certainly some nice postcards of Pøllau with the next ordinary mail. I hope, you will get them all right. Enclosed please find a plant (I don't know how you call it in English.) We call it 'Klee' and as it has 4 leafs it is a 'Glücksklee'. Put it in your purse, it shall bring you luck. We say, if one presents you with such a Glücksklee, you have luck. But it must be found by the one who makes the present. I found it myself and as it would not bring luck to myself and I am obliged to give the luck to someone, I send you the luck. Hope, it will really bring luck to you.

My parents and sister send best regards to you.

Hope that this finds you in full health. I am sending you my best wishes and greetings.

Yours sincerely

E. Schenkl

PS Please forgive my many mistakes. But as I have not slept for some nights (we went so much into the inn), I am a bit giddy in my head and so my memory of English has faded away a bit. You would oblige me, if you would correct my mistakes.

CENSORED AND PASSED

*Supdt. of Police*
*Darjeeling*
*18th August, 1936*

Dear Mr Bose,

When you get this you will already have got my letter of the 17th. Fortunately I got hold of my friend, the clergyman and he really has got a copy of Goethe's works. I also found what you wanted. It is only very short. I copy it herewith:

Sakontala

Will ich die Blumen des frèhen, die Frèchte des spìteren Jahres,
    Will ich, was reizt und entzèckt, will ich was sìttigt und nìhrt,
Will ich den Himmel, die Erde mit einem Namen begreifen;
    Nen' ich, Sakontola, dich, und ist alles gesagt.

I hope you can understand with the help of the English translation this poem. Goethe calls Shakuntala 'Sakontala'.

I am also enclosing a few postcards of Pøllau. Further a snap which I took at about 6 pm. I liked this scenery so much. It is five minutes from our house. I find that it came out comparatively well. Don't you think so? You see, I have many snaps, but mostly people on it, my family or those friends from here and I don't think these will interest you. But if you like, I can send you also a collection of these, because sometimes the background is quite good.

I hope now that you will get this letter all right and that you like the cards a little.

We send you all best regards and good wishes for your health.

Yours very sincerely

E. Schenkl

PS ... [illegible] Demel has been called to India. Have you read anything about this in Indian papers?

*c/o The Superintendent of Police*
*Darjeeling*
*The 29th August, 1936*

Dear Frl. Schenkl,

Many thanks for your letter of the 17th August which reached me yesterday—along with the token of good luck. I find that Austrian people are very fond of plants, leaves, etc. as token of good luck. I remember that when Mrs Vetter used to go up the mountains on her summer holiday, she used to send me plenty of leaves from mountain-plants. She was particularly fond of the white plant, Edel weiss, as I think all Austrians are. In some parts of Europe I have come across other superstitions—like horseshoe, black cat, etc. which are supposed to bring good luck—but perhaps Austria specialises in plants and leaves as tokens of good luck. We in India have heaps and heaps of superstitions—with the result that I do not believe in any of them. In fact, I sometimes think that there are no superstitions outside India, because we have bagged the whole lot of them. However, it is interesting to find that you also have some superstitions. Pardon my being so rude if I hurt your feelings—but I simply cannot help saying what I feel.

During the last few days our papers are full of a sensational case in which judgement has been delivered by the judge, after a hearing lasting about 3 years. The facts of the case are so fantastic that one can very well say that 'truth is stranger than fiction'. Since you are in the habit of writing articles, I am sending you some cuttings from which you will get material for writing an article. I believe magazines like Das Magazin, Wiener Magazin or even Sunday editions of Neue Frei Presse or Wiener Tagblatt would welcome such an article for the entertainment of their readers about the 'exotic East'. I am sending you cuttings from (1) The Statesman (2) Advance (3) Amrita Bazar Patrika. The cuttings from the 'Statesman' and 'Advance' which I have marked in red will give you the story—while the cutting form the A.B. Patrika will give you the summary of the judgement. It is not necessary to read the judgment in order to understand the story, but I am sending it only for reference. As a matter of fact, the judgment is rather puzzling to one who does not know all the facts of the case. I am giving you the meaning of a few words which you will constantly find in these accounts: (1) Bhowal is the name of a place in 'Dacca' District in Bengal. (2) Kumar is the son of a Raja (3) Rani is the wife of a Raja or of a kumar. (4) Sanyasi is a monk who has given up the world. (5) Rupee is the Indian coin. R/ 3½ = 20 Austrian schillings approxiametly. (6) Plaintiff is one who brings a complaint before a court against another man. (7) Defendant is one against whom this complaint is brought and who has to defend himself or herself against the complaint. (8) Naga is a class of Sanyasi. There are different classes of Sanyasis in India who have different modes of worship ('yoga'). (9) Lac (or Lakh) = 100,000.

To understand properly, without getting confused, please read first the Statesman—then the Advance (the portion marked in red). The judgement is given in the A.B. Patrika and also on the other side of the cutting from Advance—but you need not read it at all. I am giving you a few more facts to make the matter more clear.

The plaintiff, who has won the case, says: 'he is the 2nd son, (kumar) of Raja Rajendra Narayan Roy of Bhowal. In 1909, in Darjeeling, he was poisoned and he became unconscious. He was taken to the open-air cremation-ground to be cremated at night. When a storm came, the people ran away to take shelter and they returned after some hours. In the mean-time, the Sanyasis had removed the body and brought him back to life. But the plaintiff, Ramendra Narayan Roy, the 2nd Kumar, lost his memory completely when he regained consciousness. Consequently, he had to remain with the Sanyasis. In his house, his own people got hold of another dead body during the night and next morning they had a funeral procession at the end of which the false dead body was cremated. On the other side, the 2nd kumar, having lost his memory, roamed about with the Sanyasis for nearly eleven years. In 1920, he got back his memory and returned to Dacca, still a Sanyasi—in loin cloth, long hair and his body covered with ashes. Some of his friends and relatives recognized him at once. From 1921 to 1932, he tried to get back his estate—but the authorities said that he was a cheat. Ultimately in 1933 he started a suit (case) before a court—which he has now won.

The defendant says: 'That the plaintiff is a cheat, is clear from the fact that the real kumar died in 1909. The defendant said further that the dead body was not taken to the cremation-ground at night but only the next morning and it was duly burnt and the certificate of cremation was produced before the Court'. The defendant was the plaintiff's own wife, Rani Bibhabati Debi, who denied that the Sanyasi was her husband, the second kumar of Bhowal. According to the judge, Rani Bibhabati Debi is a weak-minded woman who is entirely under the influence of her brother, Satyendra Nath Bannerji (Rai Bahadur or Hofrat). The judge further declared that after the disappearance of the 2nd kumar in 1909—this Satyendra Nath Bannerji had been enjoying the estate of his brother-in-law, through his own sister Rani Bibhabati Debi who was declared to be a widow after 1909. According to the judge, the Sanyasi-kumar could not get back his estate so long, because Satyendra Nath Bannerji was opposing him from behind. And Satyendra was the real brain behind the defendant, Rani Bibhabati Debi, Satyendra's own sister.

As Raja Rajendra Narayan Roy had three sons—the plaintiff being the second—the plaintiff will now get ⅓ of the entire annual income of the estate which is 8 lakhs (lakh= one hundred thousand). Thus the plaintiff's annual income will be more than 500,000 Austrian Schillings. He will also get all the costs of the case which dragged on for nearly 3 three years—and this will also mean a big amount.

I hope the story is now quite clear to you.

The last letter I wrote to you was on the 13th August; I do not know if you will get that letter—because the plane carrying the mails crashed near Athens—and a portion of the mails could not be saved. In case you use the airmail, please use the Imperial Airways only. The Dutch and French lines carry mails only up to Karachi—while the Imperial Airways brings the mail up to Calcutta. From Karachi to Calcutta by train takes 3 or 4 days at least for a letter.

I shall now stop as my letter is already sufficiently long. When you are back in Vienna, please ask Mrs Vecsei to open my boxes and give an airing to the clothes which may otherwise be spoilt by damp or by insects.

If you want to review German books, you may try Bombay Chronicle (of Bombay) or Modern Review or Amrita Bazar Patrika or Advance of Calcutta. These journals very often review books published in other languages, besides English. The 'Hindu' of Madras has also a weekly review of literature. In writing to these well-known papers, no address is necessary—only the town will do.

'Au revoir' or rather 'Auf wiedersehen'—as one should say in German. Kind regards.

Yours sincerely

Subhas C. Bose

CENSORED AND PASSED
Supdt. of Police
Darjeeling

*Vienna*
*8.9.36*

Dear Mr Bose,

When I reached Vienna on the 5th inst. I found your letter, dated the 12th August. Through some mistake it came late. It was posted in Darjeeling on the 13th August and reached Vienna on the 29th August. And it was not redirected to my country address, therefore the delay.

Well, now we are back and not feeling at all well. We miss the open-landscape badly and feel like prisoners in the middle of houses. When one is used, for 9 weeks, to the country, one feels unhappy in a town. Besides, you know how full of beggars Vienna is now-a-days. In the country one does not see so much poorness together as one sees in a town.We would all have liked to stay for some days more in Pøllau, but school begins on the 15th inst. and my father does not yet know what to begin with my sister so we had to return in order to get information about other schools. Up till now my sister was in a Realgymnasium (high-school). But my parents think it better to take her out and send her to some house-holding school or something like that. And this needs consideration.

I have not been able to go to town in order to find out about the gramophone records, as I had a lot of work to do when we came here. First of all I began to destroy all my old newspapers of which I had piles. Now I have emptied my drawers a little and have now space for new rubbish. I am also now arranging all my photos in order to paste them in an album because I have not done this for 2 years. This year I took about 60 snaps and some are very good.

I am so sorry to hear that your health is still not all right. Have the doctors been able to cure this throat infection? It may probably be due to the wet weather of which you write. Because I know from my own experience that during winter, when it is damp and wet I get easily an infection in the throat. But in Pøllau I got a bad cough again owing to rapid change of climate. I am still not all right, but at least somehow better.

Very kind of you that you will send me the Modern Review. I have not yet got it. No, thanks, there is no magazine I would like at present, because I do not know which is most interesting. But if you have any spare copy of any old one, of which you think it would interest me, please send it to me. I shall be thankful. Have the snaps come out well which you wrote of? I think, with a good camera one can take snaps even in bad weather. I took some snaps with another camera which I borrowed from a shop, and they came out very well. I would like to change my camera for a 'KODAK,' because they are much easier to handle and cheaper in use, because the 'roll-film' is cheaper than 'Pack film' (the one I have is Packfilm).

I have not yet seen Schwester Elvira, she has gone to Salzburg with a friend and will return only about the middle of this month. I have not yet seen any of my friends in Vienna. But I hope I shall do so next week. Mrs Hargrove is not back in Vienna, she is in Gastins, I think. I rang up Mrs Vetter but found only her husband at home. Mrs Miller seems also not to be at home, because I could not get a connection. Sen is the whole day out and I spoke only once on the phone with him.

As far as I remember, you told me once that you have written two books in Bengali. I forgot the titles. Were these not philosophical subjects which you treated? I suggest now that you should translate these books into English, that also people outside Bengal may be able to read them. I would be very interested to read these two books, but as I know only 3 words in Bengali (how are you, good day, what is your name), I think I could never read your books. Trust for you it would be some work to while away your time. What do you think about it?

I have now a very bad task before me—searching for a job. My mother is the whole day grumbling with me because she is of opinion that I am alone responsible for not having a job. As if a job were to be found on the street now-a-days! Well, my nerves are rested now, the battle with the job can begin! I have been a bit down with my nerves when we went to Pøllau but plenty of fresh air and sunshine have done me good.

You will wonder to hear that I even made some excursions into the mountain this year. But I must say this year I did not at all feel tired when climbing. I have lost in weight again and I think therefore climbing was more easy for me.

This moment Schwester Elvira rang me up, she came back this morning. She asked me to give you her kindest regards and was very sorry to hear about your throat infection.

Have you got the picture postcards and snaps which I sent under separate cover by ordinary mail from Pøllau?

I received a letter from my friend Ella and she enquired about you and also begged me to remember her to you.

From my parents and 'little' sister (who is nearly grown up now) I shall send you best regards.

Also best greetings from myself as well as best wishes for your health.

Yours sincerely

E. Schenkl

PS I shall send you in my next letter the information about the duty on tea and shall also look for the book which you asked me to send to you. If there is anything else I can do for you, please let me know and I shall gladly do what is possible.

E.S.

CENSORED AND PASSED

*c/o The Superintendent of Police*
*Darjeeling*
*The 12th September, 1936*

Dear Frl. Schenkl,

Many thanks for your letter of the 18th August, enclosing four picture postcards and two snaps. The postcards are quite good, as also your snaps. Your snaps I consider rather good for an amateur. I wish I could send you some views of this neighbourhood and of Darjeeling. My snaps have been a failure and on the top of that, I have managed to damage (if not break) the camera. Until it is repaired, there is nothing doing here. Moreover, the weather is as bad as it can be. After continuous rain for 12 days, we had brilliant sunshine for two days, followed now by wretched rain, and windy weather for three days. We are now hoping that the sky will clear up by the end of this month. Earlier than that, we can hardly hope. If I do send you some picture postcards one of these days, I must warn you before hand that they will be inferior to the ones you get over there, because the art of photography has not yet made so much progress in India.

I am grateful for the trouble you have taken in finding out what Goethe said of Shakuntala (or Sakuntala). The English translation of the German seems to be rather well done.

I have already sent you 'Modern Review' for July, as desired by you, by registered book post (Einschreiben und Drucksache) and it should reach you in due course. I do not know if you will get my letter air mail of the 12th (or 14th) August. The plane carrying the mail crashed near Greece and a part of the mail was lost. If the latter happened to be in that lost portion, then it could not have reached you. The next letter I dispatched on the 29th August by ordinary mail. I sent you some cuttings therein of a sensational case of a Rajah's son who was supposed to have been dead and cremated in 1909—but who suddenly turned up in the land of the living in 1921. He claimed his portion of the estate and the court, after a trial lasting nearly three years, decided that the claimant was the real kumar (Rajah's son) and not a pretender.

When you are back in Vienna and have time, please send me the numbers of some good records of light Viennese music. I shall then see if they could be had in Calcutta.

I have not had any reply to my letter to Mrs Vetter and on the other hand, I have not replied to two of Mrs Hargrove's letters. When you are in Vienna and have time, please enquire about the customs-duty (zoll) on tea and whether they allow a certain quantity duty-free (zoll-frei) as sample.

There is nothing else to write today—so I shall stop here. Kind regards to your parents and yourself and greetings for your sister.

Yours sincerely

Subhas C. Bose

PS Can you please ask Mrs Vecsei on my behalf to send me these two books from one of the boxes I left at her place:

(1) Statesman Year Book
(2) Visvesaraya's Planned Economy

S.C.B.

CENSORED AND PASSED

*c/o The Superintendent of Police*
*Darjeeling*
*26.9.36*

Dear Frl. Schenkl,

Your kind letter of the 8th reached me on the 22nd inst. So you got my letter of the 12th August, though somewhat late! The delay was due to the fact that the aeroplane crashed near Athens and part of the mail was lost. But the major portion of the mail was recovered and was sorted out with some difficulty. 'Better late than never', as they say in English.

Many thanks for sending me the German couplet about Shakuntala from Goethe's works. You sent it in a former letter and I do not remember if I acknowledged it in my previous letter to you.

By now you should have got my letter (ordinary post) of the 29th August and my airmail letter of the 12th September. The Modern Review for July which you asked for, was duly forwarded to you by the Superintendent of Police and will reach you in due course.

I shall be able to send you some picture postcards of Darjeeling and Kurseong within a week or two. I shall send them by ordinary post.

I am glad to know that you had a good time in the country and are feeling refreshed now.

You can let me know about the gramophone records at your convenience. There is no hurry about it.

I think I have already informed you that I have received the picture postcards (four) and the snaps (two) of Pøllau which you kindly sent me.

I am glad to have news of Miss Ella (I am sorry I have forgotten her surname, but please don't tell her). Please give her my kind regards and also to Sister Elvira. I hope the latter is better now after her 'Kur' at Franzensbad. Franzensbad is a nice little place, though not so fashionable as Marienbad or Karlsbad, with plenty of hot mineral springs.

Day before yesterday, I went to Darjeeling for a medical examination and was there for half-an-hour. Darjeeling is 1½ hours by car from Kurseong and about 2½ hours by mountain railway. I could not enjoy much of the scenery because it was rather foggy. But even the drive was good as a change. I have not been feeling so well of late—last week I had an attack of influenza—what you call 'grippe' in German.

This year has been unusually wet in India. The rainfall here has been abnormal and in the plains in two or three provinces—(Bengal, Bihar and the United Provinces) there have been floods. We are now hoping that at least from October we shall be rid of the wretched clouds and rain.

Please remember me to all friends there. Kind regards for your parents and yourself and greetings for your sister.

Yours sincerely

Subhas C. Bose

CENSORED AND PASSED

*c/o The Superintendent of Police*
*Darjeeling*
*9.11.36*

Dear Frl. Schenkl,

Please excuse me for the delay in replying to your letter of the 1st October which I received on the 16th Oct. In the meantime, I have received from Vienna the catalogues of the Gramophone records and also the Statesman Year Book. Please accept my best thanks for arranging to send them. My last letter to you (airmail) was on the 27th Sept. and on the 13th October, I sent you be ordinary mail (registered) some picture postcards of Darjeeling and some snaps.

It must be pretty cold there now. Oh, how I long for the snow! Here we cannot have any snow in winter—it is not high enough. But the mountains in the distance are gradually becoming snow-capped. It is good to see snow even at a distance.

I have not heard from Mrs Vetter—though I have written to her again. I was glad to have a few lines from Schwester Elvira in your letter. Please give her my warmest thanks and my 'herzliche Grüsse'.

I am sorry to hear of the death of Minister Paner. I am thinking of sending a message of condolence through my friend Mr Faltis.

Some of my relatives were permitted to come and stay with me for a few weeks. They have now left—except a couple of youngsters who will be leaving soon. I shall then be alone again.

How are you progressing with your French? I wonder what jokes are now going round in the Vienna cafes! Mrs. Hargrove usually writes to me about the latest joke she hears of.

My health has not been very well for some time. How are you behaving this winter? Have you had any cough again?

Please tell Mrs Hargrove, if you happen to meet her, that I have heard from her friend, Miss Greene of America. I shall reply to her letter soon. And could you please take the trouble of telephoning to my friend, Dr Sen, at 20/15 Alser Strasse to inform him that I have got his airmail letter.

Our greatest religious festival is just over—the Durga Pujah. It is customary to send 'Bijoya greetings' to relatives and friends after this festival—the idea being that after the Divine mother has been worshipped—all her children must be united in love. May I therefore send heartiest 'Bijoya greetings' to all of you? How are you all keeping.

Yours sincerely

Subhas C. Bose

CENSORED AND PASSED
Supdt. of Police
Darjeeling

*Vienna*
*4.12.36*

Dear Mr Bose,

Your letter of the 9th ult. was to hand on the 23rd ult. Many thanks. I was really already very much concerned, because I did not hear from you so long. I also got the picture postcards and the four snaps, for which please accept best thanks. They were very interesting and it is a great pleasure for me to look at them, because now I have a bit of an idea how it looks in India. The Himalayan mountains must be wonderful. But Darjeeling looks very modern and European-like. I thought there would be more of Indian buildings in Indian style. But the European influence is clearly visible.

Well, the weather in Vienna has changed all of a sudden. We had already some snow about four days ago, but unfortunately it did not last. Otherwise the weather is mostly wretched and cold, you know this type yourself. The typical 'Schnupfen-weather'. As usually I have my yearly cold and also the cough has not spared me and so I have to go through the usual winter-trouble. Otherwise I am feeling fairly well. My gall-bladder has become very quiet, it does not disturb me any more. I can eat and drink whatever I like without being afraid of getting pain. That is at least some comfort in this miserable life. I am losing in weight very much now-a-days, but this does not concern me, because it is so uncomfortable to be fat.

I do not meet any of our friends now-a-days except Dr Sen now and then, because I have plenty of work to do for X-mas. Schwester Elvira has given me some orders for X-mas presents which she wants to give to her friends and so I have still more work to do. But at least I am earning something and I like to do this kind of work. Schwester Elvira was very glad to receive your 'herzliche Grüsse' and is returning same to you. I got your letter just the moment, when I was on the point for leaving in order to visit her, so I could communicate them quite freshly.

I was glad to hear that some of your relatives had been permitted to stay with you. So you were not quite alone and had somebody to talk to. The youngsters will also occupy your time a bit. The other time you will be reading, I suppose.

I had to stop my French lessons unfortunately, because I am not earning now anything and I won't get lessons free. It is a pity, but it can't be helped. I am writing week after week heaps of offers to announcements in the press, but I never get any answer. Once I got an answer, but did not get the job. Another time I got also an answer, but I did not accept it myself, because the whole offer was useless. I should have looked after a seven-year-old boy, they would have given me board and lodging free and 25 Schillings a month. Besides that I would have had to clean my own room and help in the household. This of course I did not accept, because I am not a maid after all.

You want to know some jokes. Well, it is so difficult, because I do not often come to the Cafés now-a-days. The only joke I heard was this:

'We are getting new Schillings in Austria, made of rubber'. (Somebody asks ,'Why?') 'Well, because you can extend them (stretch them) and if the Schilling falls you do not hear it'. The joke came therefrom, that there was some possibility of the Schilling being dropping again.

I have communicated your greetings to Dr Sen. He was very glad and asked me to give you also his best regards.

Now I have to communicate a piece of news to you which will probably interest you. Sen tried to organise the Hindusthan Academical Association again. There are at present about 25 to 30 Indians in Vienna. After a lot of trouble where Gairola wanted to become the President to assure his support, he was strongly opposed by Sen. So Ali was again elected President and a compromise was arrived at by giving the Secretaryship to Gairola. At present they are meeting every Thursday in Hotel de France. Ali is taking a good interest. Although Sen is not in the Committee or anything, he is trying his best to give it a footing. At present the hopes are that it might run successfully. Trivedi has passed all his exams now and Sen has brought him into the Association as an active member. Once Professor Olbrich of the Hochschule für Bodenkultur held a very interesting lecture about his climbing the Kilimanjaro. The meeting was attended by about 100 people, though this day the weather had been as unfavourable as possible. We had sent out about 500 invitations.

I was very glad to receive your Bijoya greetings as well as my parents. Please accept heartiest thanks and same from us. (If it is possible that a non-Hindu can send Bijoya greetings.)

Our greatest religious festival will be coming soon—on the 24th inst—last year you were still in Vienna and also saw how it was celebrated. Last week I have sent you by registered sample-post a little X-mas present. Please kindly accept it with my and my parents' and sister's best wishes.

Hope your health is much better now. Please write to me soon again. With heartiest greetings from my family and myself.

Yours sincerely

E. Schenkl

PS I forgot to tell you one thing—I have arranged all your boxes and sent your clothes off. I have packed all together in the big trunk and through an Italian firm (your nephew arranged them) the box was sent.

I have given away all those things which you told me will be unnecessary for you and made a present of them to Vinzeng (the servant in Pension Cosmopolite). Further I gave him a pair of your shoes (they were already torn in the upper part) because he told me that he was in awful need of shoes. Your skiing boots I have left behind with Singh after consulting your nephew. Skating boots—with skates—I have sent to you. I also packed in the box 3 books—1) German Grammar and Dictionary, 2) The Canterville Ghost (Bilingual Series) and 3) Immersce (Bilingual Series).

There are still some clothes lying with me, which your nephew told me not to send. Most of all the dark raincoat which you never wore because it did not fit you properly. What am I to do with it?

Then some Achkan, one pair of riding breeches, and one coat European style. These three things are made of the same stuff (rough Indian stuff). Please let me know what I should do with these things.

You also did not mention whether you had got the letter in which I wrote to you about the duty on tea. For 4 pounds (half a kilo) you have to pay in Austrian about 10 shillings (Austrian 10 deka (100 grams) are duty-free.

Once more best greetings

E. Schenkl

CENSORED AND PASSED

Please reply to:
1, Woodburn Park
Elgin Road. P.O.
Calcutta

*Kurseong, the 15th Dec. 1936*

Dear Frl. Schenkl,

Many thanks for your letter dated the 4th inst. which was to hand this morning. I find that you have not received my letter dated the 26th September—at least you have not replied to it—though you have replied to my next letter dated the 9th November. In October (about the middle of the month) I sent you the picture postcards which have duly reached you. The last letter I received from you was on the 16th October and the letter was dated the 1st October. As I did not hear from you for about two months, I thought that you were possibly lying ill. But I am now glad to know that that was not the case. I am sorry I delayed replying to your last letter for about a month. I was not at all well and the weather was very disagreeable. Towards the end of the month the weather improved and I had some relatives to stay with me, which kept me busy. Now I wonder what happened to my letter of the 26th September (air mail). It must have been duly posted in Darjeeling—because I am informed officially when any of my letters is not passed by the Censor.

When replying to this letter, please write to my home address given above. I am under order of transfer and I do not know yet where I shall be going. So, if you write to my home address, they will forward the letter to me, wherever I may happen to be. About two months ago, I had asked for a transfer, because the climate of this place was not agreeing with me. I shall be leaving this place within a day or two.

About a week ago, I sent a Christmas Card for your people by ordinary post—but I am not sure if I addressed it properly according to the German etiquette. Should I have unwittingly made a mistake, I hope to excused in view of my ignorance. You will be getting this letter about Xmas time. Please accept my best wishes for a happy Xmas and an equally happy and prosperous New Year. Please convey my best wishes to the members of your family as well and also my warmest regards to your parents. Yes, I have been wondering where I was at Xmas time last year and where I shall be this year! Human life is so changing and uncertain!

I am sorry to know that you are down with your cold—though it is good to be free from the gall-bladder trouble. By the way, please do not neglect the latter. It is never cured and whenever there is irregularity of diet—the trouble pops up again. My sister in law —Asoke's mother has been suffering badly of late and whenever she neglects her diet, it appears again. That was also my experience. I have been trying to persuade her to go in for an operation—but the others are all against it.

You will perhaps be meeting Schwester Elvira during Xmas week. Please give her my warmest greetings and best wishes for Xmas and the New Year.

My brother has written to say that Mrs Fulop Miller who is now touring the East, has arrived in India. He has invited her to be his guest when she visits Calcutta.

Yes, I got your note about the duty on tea and after that, I gave up the idea of sending tea to friends there. It will certainly not be a welcome thing to pay 10 shillings duty for one pound of tea. By the way, what is the price of tea there?

I am thanking you in anticipation for the Xmas present you have sent. It was very kind of you to do so.

I am glad to know that a box of clothes which I had to leave behind in a hurry in Vienna has been forwarded to India. Please let me know how much the freight cost and who advanced the money, so that I may arrange to remit that amount. Any other clothes which may be still lying there can wait for the present. If anybody happens to pass through Vienna on his way home who happens to know me, he could be requested to bring them for me. But there is no hurry. I think I had left behind two overcoats at Pension Cosmopolite—one of a light grey colour and one of a dark (rather black) colour. Has the light grey one been sent in the box? The dark one I do not care for and it could be given away to some poor man.

My nephew was in Germany during the last few months undergoing practical training. I wonder if he was able to visit Vienna.

Kindest greetings once again.

Yours sincerely

Subhas C. Bose

CENSORED AND PASSED
[illegible]

*Vienna*
*1.1.1937*

Dear Mr Bose,

I have been very glad to receive your letter, dated the 15th December, 1936. I received it on the 28th Dec. in the afternoon. The same day in the morning we also received your Xmas-New Year card which was sent by ordinary mail. My people were extremely glad and asked me to thank you for it.

So the old year is over now and the new year begins. What will it bring? Will there be a better mend in this world situation or will we still be drawn down deeper into a worse mess? Nobody knows.

Yes, I have received your airmail letter dated the 26th September and have also replied to it. May be my letter to you was lost on the way. No, I have not been lying ill, only my usual winter cold and cough. These two are my most faithful friends. They love me so much that they visit me every year and stay the whole winter. And that you have not been well made me all very sorry. But I hope that by now your health has improved and you are feeling all right again.

During November and December I have been terribly busy with Xmas presents. I was working from morning till late in the night every day. But I could finish my task, that was good.

Have you been already transferred to another place and where? Please tell me a little about this new place, because as you know, I am a terribly curious person.

Xmas this year was quite nice. I got plenty of things, mostly necessary ones from my family and a few luxury things from friends. The other day a friend in Ireland sent me a very nice book: Basson's Flying Column, by Irwin. Do you happen to know it? Mrs Hargrove also sent me a very nice book: Die Minnesinger und ihre Matern (The Minstrels and Their Painters). There are 24 reproductions of very old German pictures. I like this book so much. It contains also some verses in middle-high German. On the 26th December Master (who is for the holidays in Wien) and Sen paid me a visit. I had invited another friend and we had a nice afternoon, we lighted the Christ Lamn and Sen was playing Indian music on the piano. By the way, Sen is going away for a few months and will probably want an extra trunk. He asked me, if I could lend him one of yours. So I will lend him this black one. I hope you do not mind. Yesterday he also told me that you wrote to him that he could have one of the Indian records. But he took two. I do not know which ones, because I cannot read the Bengali hieroglyphs.

Sylvester I passed this year in a very boring way. I went with my family to the circuna and at 11 o'clock we came home. Then we drank some tea, waited till midnight and wished one another a happy new year. After that I went to my neighbour's. She was quite alone at home with her two children. We wished each other a happy new year. Then suddenly I had the foolish idea of 'Bleigiessen'. It is done in this way. You melt on a spoon some metal (lead) and when it is melted, you pour it into cold water. At once it becomes hard and gets shaped. According to the shape, you foretell the future of the one who has poured his spoonful of metal. I had a very funny thing, looking like the map of India. At two o'clock I went to bed and was of course very sleepy in the morning when I woke up.

Schwester Elvira has left Rudolfinerhaus on the 15th of December. She went home to Upper-Austria. She will be staying there for about 3 months and then either return to Rudolfinerhaus or go for a few months to England once more. She asked me to give you her heartiest wishes and greetings when I write to you again. Also, my friend Ella wrote a very nice letter to me and asked me to give you kindest remembrances and wishes for 1937.

I knew that Mrs Fulop Miller was going to India but I only did not write to you, because she asked me to tell it to nobody. This woman must have a lot of money, when she can tour in Asia.

I do not think it is good to send tea to anyone, because duty is too high. The price of tea here is very different. You get tea from 20 Groschen per deka (10 grams) up to 70 or 80 Groschen per deka. Specially the firm MEINL, who has connections with the East through his wife, has very good tea. This duty business is dreadful. I sent for Xmas a handmade night-chemise to a friend of mine in Germany. It was very rough cotton stuff and made according to Balkan style. Poor thing's she had to pay 4.50 marks duty. That is about 9 Austrian shillings. I was so sorry when she wrote me that. Did you have to pay any duty on the Xmas present I sent you!

I did not pay the freight for the box which was sent from Vienna to India for you. Your nephew Asoke arranged the thing, I only made it ready. I told him that I have given those things, which were useless, away. The light grey coat has been sent along with the other clothes. The dark grey (rather black) is lying with me now and I shall give it to someone who is in need of it. There was one coat (European style) which I sent with a gentleman who goes to India. It will be given to your brother. Your nephew is still in Germany. I heard sometimes from him when we were corresponding about your things being transferred to India. But he has not been able to come to Vienna, though I would have been glad, because it was difficult for me to dispose about all the things. Maybe, he comes later to Vienna. I have not heard from him since a long time.

Since the 25th December, we have a bit of winter weather. On 25th we had a snow storm. But there was not too much of snow. After that we had foggy weather. And the fog settles on trees, telephone wires, etc. and begins to freeze. This gives then to trees an appearance, as if they were full of white powder—sugar. I am sorry, I cannot pluck a tree and send it with its decoration to you. It is a beautiful sight.

So, and now I have told you everything. I will go now to town and post the letter in Booreplatz in the telegraphic post office and then I will go to Café Bastes because I am meeting a friend there.

Let me once more send you my best wishes for the New Year. Also my family send best regards and wishes to you.

Oh, before I forget! Could you arrange to send me now and then a few Indian newspapers! We do not get any papers since months. Thank you in anticipation.

Heartiest greetings to you.

Yours sincerely

E. Schenkl

CENSORED AND PASSED

*Medical College Hospital*
*Calcutta*
*The 10th Jan. 1937*

Dear Frl. Schenkl,

Let me wish you and all the members of your family a happy new year (Gluckliches neues jahr—as you would say in German) and many many returns of the same!

You letter of the 1st January reached me yesterday. Since I wrote to you last from Kurseong, I have been brought down to Calcutta. I am now in Hospital—under 'internment' of course. I have been undergoing a thorough examination at the hands of the doctors since I came here ie since the 17th December last. Apart from the medical help I have been getting here, I was glad to come here for other reasons. The weather is very agreeable here now. There is plenty of sun which was lacking on the mountains—but it is pleasantly cold. Further, Government have allowed my relatives to visit me every day.

The doctors have not given out their diagnosis yet—they have only declared up till now that I am suffering from septic tonsils. For the rest of the diagnosis, I am now waiting.

I do not know how long I shall be here, nor do I know where I shall be transferred from here. But I do not expect to be here very long. So if you write to me again, please write to my home address—1 Woodburn Park, Elgin Road P.O. Calcutta. The letter will be duly forwarded to my new address.

Allow me to thank you for the Xmas present. The pictures are very interesting and they are a nice souvenir. I got it while I was still in Kurseong. They did not charge me any duty. We are not charged so much for imports as in European countries.

I do not know why they charged you 1sh 70g. for this airmail letter. Formerly they were charging only 1 sh 30 g. I wonder if they have put up the rates recently.

Mrs Hargrove has sent me a nice book, with pictures of different kinds of plants, as Xmas present. Then somebody has sent me a calendar for 1937 in book form, with beautiful pictures of Austrian scenery. The book is published by the Wiener Bank Verein.

I can only envy you the snow that you must be enjoying now. Here in the plains, we cannot even dream of snow.

Can you please tell me how you observe Xmas on the Continent? Do you light the tree and distribute the presents on the 24th or 25th December? As far as I remember, on the 25th evening. In that case, do you light the tree on any evening after the 25th—as well? Or do you pull down the tree after the 25th is over? In England, they observe Xmas on the 25th evening I think—if my memory is right.

Please convey my kind remembrances and best wishes for the new year to Sister Elvira and Miss Ella—if you have not done so already.

I am now in town after several months and at first it was a pleasant change. But it is very noisy here—both inside and outside. Outside—because of the buses and tramcars and all kinds of conveyances. Inside—because of the patients—some of whom shout when they are in pain. This Hospital is one of the biggest in India and the biggest in Calcutta. It is also the oldest in India and is in the center of the town. The rooms are not properly separated from the general ward—and that is how I get the noise whenever any patient near by is in pain. However, after a long period of isolation, the proximity (nearness) of human beings even when they are noisy, is welcome.

There is nothing more to write from here. Hope this will find your health better in spite of the cold.

The doctor hopes to cure my tonsils by treatment—otherwise I may have to get them removed by operation.

Mrs Fulop Miller of Vienna is now in Calcutta. She got permission from Government to interview me and I was glad to meet her in India. She said that she was enjoying her tour.

Best regards for your parents and greetings for yourself and your sister.

Yours sincerely

Subhas C. Bose

CENSORED AND PASSED

*Medical College Hospital*
*Calcutta*
*The 26th Jan. 1937*

Dear Frl. Schenkl

I am thankful to you for your kind letter of the 14th January which was to hand on the 25th inst. (yesterday). I trust you have by now received my letter of the 10th January. Please accept my best thanks for your good wishes and convey them to the members of your family.

The cold here in Calcutta is always mild—this year is no exception to this general rule. But in some parts of India there has been a cold wave. At Kurseong, it was of course much colder and foggy too. I had so much of foggy weather there during my stay there—that now I enjoy the sun here. But I find that people who live here do not like the sun as much as I do at present. This is but natural.

I am still in Calcutta in Hospital. On the whole, I am slightly better. At present I am undergoing treatment for my throat trouble and for congestion of the liver. I cannot know of my movements in advance and I may be transferred elsewhere any day. So you may kindly write to my home address—if and when you write (1, Woodburn Park, Calcutta). They will forward my letter to the Censoring authorities.

There is little I can write which can interest you. I have been allowed to visit my mother at home twice a week during my stay in Calcutta. I am enclosing a letter for Sister Elvira. Best regards for you parents. Cordial greetings and regards,

Yours sincerely

Subhas C. Bose

CENSORED AND PASSED
[illegible]

*Vienna*
*28.1.37*

Dear Mr Bose,

Your letter of the 10th inst. reached me on the 19th. Many thanks.

My family and myself thank you for the good wishes for the New Year. I only hope that they may be fulfilled. And we wish the same to you.

I was very sorry to learn that you are not feeling well. And I can only hope that you will soon be cured and well again. Because nothing is worse than being ill. And specially in a hospital it must be terrible I think. Have you now got further information regarding your health? Please let me know.

So you have plenty of sun in India. We have none here. Since about a week we have terribly cold weather (10 degrees below freezing point) and a comparative big lot of snow. This is of course nice, but the cold is not. I go, therefore, out as little as possible and it happens that sometimes I do not go out for three or four days at all. Because I must be very careful not to catch cold.

What do you write about pictures? I sent you as Xmas present an embroidered book-cover in blue, lined with blue silk. Did you not get that? Anyhow, I did not send you pictures. That must be a mistake.

Re: my last letter, they charged me only 1.30 shillings. Maybe the fool in the post office himself put by mistake 1.70 shillings on the cover. He must have still been drunk from Sylvester I suppose.

You want to know how we observe Xmas here. Well, first of all we buy the presents for our friends or relatives. On the 24th the Xmas tree is decorated (with sweets, candles, glass wares, etc.) On the 24th night at about 7 or 8 o'clock, the candles are lighted. Mostly the old song, 'Stille Nacht, Heilige Nacht' is sung by the members of the family. The presents are arranged below the tree. Then everybody takes his presents and thanks the other people for it, etc. Those people who are very religious go into Church at midnight into 'Mette' or 'Christmette.' (I never do so.) The 25th is a holiday. Either you get visitors or you visit somebody yourself, or you are alone at home. The Xmas tree can be lighted as often as wanted after the 24th. Mostly you light it, when some visitor is there in order to show him the tree. The tree is either pulled down on New Year's day or on the 6th of January. But there is no fixed rule even about these two days.

Sister Elvira was here a few days ago. We wrote a postcard to you and hope that you got it. But she has already left again for Upper Austria.

We have now got a radio (wireless). That is indeed a very convenient thing, because you can hear Vienna, Czechoslovakia, Germany, Italy, Poland, Switzerland, France, and even England. Only England has mostly a very tiresome programme and besides it is very difficult to get it. Father is of course furious and grumbles the whole day long that we have disturbed the peace of the family, etc. But the more he grumbles the more we play the radio.

Do you know when Mrs Fulop Miller intends to return home? It is no wonder she liked her trip in India.

Have you got already your things which I sent to you from Vienna (the big leather box with clothes, etc.)? Do you still practice some German? I am doing nothing useful the whole day long except brooding over the gloomy future. I run about like mad from one firm to the other. Introduce myself, write letters, etc. And the result is—nil. That is so discouraging, I can't tell you how. Sometimes I wonder, what for I live at all. There is rather no sense in going on living and still, one is too much of a coward to throw away life.

It seems that the Hindusthan Academical Association has stopped activity again. Because I was there once in Hotel de France to return a newspaper to Gairola. And the portier told me that they are meeting very irregular. There is no system in the whole thing. The one, who could have done something, Sen, has gone away from Vienna for a few months and the others won't do anything useful. Today I met Mr Timer. He asked me about you and wants me to convey his best wishes and greetings to you.

Are you reading anything interesting at present? I not, because I have something to do for Sister Elvira, so my whole time is occupied. And this is good, because one forgets to think about oneself.

There is nothing more to write to you. Nothing interesting happens. We are all comparatively well. I wonder, where you have been brought from Calcutta or if you are still there. Please let me know.

My family sends the best wishes and greetings to you. And also all good wishes for your birthday from myself once more and warmest greetings.

Yours sincerely

E. Schenkl

PS  Nearly I would have forgotten one thing. Mr Jenni wrote to me the other day asking me to give him your address and enquiring if I knew anything about you. He also begged to convey his and your Geneva friends' best wishes and greetings to you.

E.S.

CENSORED AND PASSED

*Medical College Hospital*
*Calcutta*
*The 10th February, 1937*

Dear Frl. Schenkl,

Many thanks for your air mail letter of the 28th January which I received on the 8th inst. You will see from my address that I am still in Hospital. My future movements are still uncertain and unknown to me.

From what you write, it appears that the Xmas present you sent me was miscarried. Did you send it registered (ein schreiben)? I have just written to the Superintendent of Police, Darjeeling, asking him to make an enquiry. But judging from my past experience, I have no hope that it will be traced. All the same, I thank you heartily for your kindness.

It is becoming quite warm here now—although in the morning it is sometimes foggy—and the sun will soon cease to be agreeable. I can only envy you the snow that you are enjoying there now. It is a pity that you are not going in for winter sports—it would have been so enjoyable for you then.

The box containing my clothes has already arrived in Calcutta and I must thank you for taking the trouble of sending it.

I have already received the joint post card which you sent me and have replied to it by air mail.

I do not remember if I wrote to you that Mrs Fulop Miller of Vienna was here in January. She was my brother's guest during her fortnight's stay in Calcutta. She was permitted to see me in Hospital. She is now travelling—and will sail from Bombay in the last week of March (next month).

When I was in Kurseong I sometimes looked into my German book. Since coming here, I have not done so. Today I am going to try a German letter to Herr Faltis. I hope he will be able to understand my faulty German, if my letter reaches him.

I think you would have done well to continue your French. Why did you stop it? It would have been useful later on.

Since coming to Calcutta, I have been feeling slightly better. Apart from that, Government have allowed me some concessions which are exceedingly welcome. I was allowed to visit my mother at home twice a week. From today I shall be able to visit her every day. In the morning, I am allowed to go out for a drive in a car in the company of a police officer. Sometimes in the afternoon I have visits from those near relatives who are allowed to meet me. The rest of the time is filled in with the help of books, newspapers and correspondence. Here in Calcutta it is not difficult to spend my time—but in Kurseong it was very boring and tiresome at times.

Kindly remember me to Mr Jenni when you write to him and to Mr Timer if you meet him. Please convey my kind remembrances to other friends as well. My address is the same as before—1 Woodburn Park. They will forward my mail to me. Please accept my sincerest regards and convey same to your parents. How are you?

Yours sincerely

Subhas C. Bose

CENSORED AND PASSED
[illegible]

*12.2.37*

Dear Mr Bose,

I have been very glad to receive your letter of the 26th Jan. which was to hand on the 3rd. inst. At once I posted the enclosure for Elvira to her and she wrote back to me immediately. She was very glad too and asked me to send you meanwhile her best thanks as well as kindest regards. She is not able now to write to you, as she is so busy. But when she has more leisure, she will answer your letter.

The other day I spoke on phone with Mrs Vetter. She told me to send you also her best and kindest regards. She would have already written to you a longer letter, but as her daughter was ill for nearly a month, she was not able to do so.

And now a piece of news about myself. Since the 2nd. inst. I have a little job. I am looking after an Indian baby in the afternoons. Is not this a joke? You know probably that I never was much for children though children hang on me like anything. And now I have to look after a baby. The child is 17 months old and very nice. Specially when his parents are not there, he is so good. Only when he sees father or mother he becomes naughty, because he knows quite well that he can do anything he likes with them. This is because he is the first child and the mother is still very inexperienced as she admitted herself. They are very nice people from Kashmir. And as I have now the opportunity of earning something, I have begun to take French lessons again. And think, though I have not taken lessons for months, I have not forgotten anything. I was surprised, myself.

Oh, so you are beginning to like the sun now! And I remember very well that you were always laughing at me when I said that I was longing for the sun in winter. We have not got much sun now-a-days. For some time we had wonderful winter- weather, but soon the snow began to melt again and the beauty vanished. Now it is very muddy and wet outside. But since a few days we have a little sunshine. Yesterday I was with baby out for a walk in Trkenschanzpark. You should have seen how people crept out of their houses. Like the worms after rain. Everybody was sitting in the sunshine and only searching for the sunny paths.

And how are you regarding your health? I hope, better. Maybe it was also due to the wet climate in Darjeeling that you were suffering from septic tonsils. I must say that this winter I am feeling exceptionally well. Since weeks I am free from cold and cough. Only sometimes, when it is very cold, I am feeling some pain in my left lung. But this is bearable. I asked a doctor about it and he told me that I should keep very warm, not go out when there is fog and try to get as much sunshine as possible.

What about your liver trouble? Is it curable? If not so in India, please come to Europe again and try Karlsbad. You know how good this is.

I was very glad to hear that you have been allowed to visit your mother while you stay in Calcutta. It will be a great comfort for you and your mother because a mother is always anxious to see her child, I think. And you will be also glad to see your mother. Has your nephew already arrived in India? He wrote to me he would embark about the beginning of February. I quite forgot to write to him, because I was so busy.

Have you heard anything from Mrs Hargrove? Though we are living in the same town I have not heard from her since Xmas last. I come out very little now. Besides there are many people gone from Vienna. Sen is in England. He wrote to me the other day that he is very busy working in hospital. Master is still in Germany. And the others I do not meet. So I am rather out of contact. Yesterday there was a lecture in the University about Ceylon. I could not attend it because it started at 6 p.m. and I am busy till 7 p.m. every day. But my parents went there. It must have been quite interesting.

And now let me congratulate you on your German letter. It was excellently written. Please allow me to send you the correction. I hope you won't mind it. And it would be very good for you if you would sometimes send me some translation or a German letter. I could easily send you the correction then.

Please accept the best wishes and greetings from my family as well as warmest greetings from myself.

Yours sincerely

E. Schenkl

Correction

Liebe Schwester Elvira

Danke vielmals fr Ihren Brief ven 14, Januar den ich gesters bekommen habe und fr Ihre freundliche Erinnerung und Glckwilnsche. Wie geht es Ihnen? Ich hoffe es geht Ihnen jetzt viel besser bach der Kur in Franzensbad. Sind Sie noch im Rudolfinerhaus? Sie haben gefragt wann ich nach Wien kommen werde. Leider, ich kann nicht getzt nach meiner Wilnschen fahren eder arbeiten—so milssen Sie selbst mach Indian kommen.

Zuerst habe ich sic bewundert, als ich Ihren englischen Brief las. Dach spter habe ich gedacht, dass Sie mit Fr. Schenkl diesen Brief geechrieben haben. Bitte sagen Sie mir die Wahrhoit ich. Ich biz jetzt in einem grossen Spital in der Hauptstadt Kalkutta. Momentan fhle ich mich etwas besser als frher. Aber ich habe nicht hier die ich im Rudolfinerhaus in wien im Jahre 1935 hatte. Jedoch kann ich mich hier mit meinen Verwanden treffen und besprechen. Ich weiss nicht bestimmt wie lange ich werde hier bleiben, aber wahrascheinlich muss ich in einigen Tagen von hier anduswe hien gehen.

Diesen deutschen Brief schreibe ich alllein, daher bitte seien Sie so freundlich meine Fehler zu entschuldigen. Herzliche Grsse.

Ihr Grgebener

CENSORED AND PASSED

*Medical College Hospital*
*Calcutta*
*The 26th February, 1937*

Dear Frl. Schenkl,

Many thanks for your airmail letter of the 12th inst. which was to hand on the 23rd. Since I wrote to you last, I have written a German letter to Kommerzialrat Faltis. I hope he will be able to understand my faulty German.

It appears from the letters I have received from Europe that the winter there has been rather mild this year. In Calcutta, of course, the winter is always mild even for India and this year has not been an exception to this rule. For the first time in my life I was glad to away from the cold and the fog of which I am generally fond.

I am still in Calcutta as you will see from the above address and my stay has been much longer than I had expected. When I first came here, I did not expect to be here for more than a fortnight. But I have been here for about 2½ months. However, it is sure now that I shall be going elsewhere soon—though I have no idea where I shall be taken. Therefore, the best course would be to write to my home address—1 Woodburn Park—if and when you write.

I am thankful to you for taking the trouble of correcting my German. Far from minding your corrections, I am grateful to you for taking all this trouble.

There is little that I can write to you which could interest you. Mrs Fulop Miller is now touring the country before she sails from Bombay in March. I read in the papers that she interviewed Mahatma Gandhi the other day. One of my nephews, who was studying in Germany, is back home after several years. Another nephew will shortly be leaving for England for higher studies.

Yes, I am allowed to go home to see my mother. The concession is welcome to both of us. I shall miss it when I am away from Calcutta.

My health is somewhat better on the whole—but certain symptoms are persisting. The attending physician thinks that it is not necessary to stay in Hospital and the treatment could be continued elsewhere.

Please accept my warmest regards and convey them to your parents.

Yours sincerely

Subhas C. Bose

*Vienna*
*26.2.37*

Dear Mr Bose,

Many thanks for your kind letter of the 10th inst. which reached me on the 19th.

Yes, of course, I sent the Xmas present for you as *registered*, sample post. Fortunately I have kept the receipt. I shall wait till I get information from you. Accordingly I shall ask them. I will then inquire from here, where the thing has gone.

My goodness, here the weather is again becoming cold, ugly, foggy, rainy. I am already quite despaired. I really envy you the sun and the warm weather. We will make a change. You come to Vienna and I go to India.

You wrote to me about Frau F. Miller's stay in Calcutta before. So she will already think now of returning home. I think she will be so sorry to come back again. Probably I shall see her, when she comes to Vienna, as I had a book belonging to her which I must return.

It is a great pity that you gave again up your German. From the letter you wrote to Elvira, I saw what a marvelous progress you have already made. If that letter, which you intend sending to Dir. Faltis, will be as well written, you have done a very good task. In my last air mail letter to you I sent a corrected copy of your letter and hope it reached you all right.

I can tell you now, that I have naturally continued my French again as I have now a little job at hand. I am glad myself. Truly, I have so little time to learn my house tasks properly.

Last Sunday I met Mrs Hargrove. She asked me to give you her kindest regards. She is herself very busy. Miss Green has gone to Italy in order to see Krishnaji who holds a meeting there. She will also write to you again.

It is very fine that you can now visit your mother daily. Specially for your mother it will be very good, as she is already old and lonely and so she will be anxious to see as much of you as possible. And how is your health? I hope, however, better. Have doctors been able to save your tonsils? And what about your liver congestion? How is the gall-bladder wound? I hope that by now you do not feel any more post-operative troubles. My gall-bladder is behaving at the present. I had the last attack in the beginning of November 1936. Since then, nothing. Today I got a letter from Frau Lowy who asked me to send her kind remembrances to you.

Please, could you send me once a copy of 'Modern Review'? Or any other paper or magazine. I am now very much out of touch with my friends except that I have this job, so I meet the family every day. That is all.

This week was a great row in Vienna. Foreign Minister V. Neuraten (Germany) arrived in Vienna on Monday. Since his arrival in the morning till in the evening, the Nazis roared and shouted in town and asked for a plebiscite. I did of course not go there, as I am always avoiding such public things. We could easily come into trouble quite innocently.

In spite of the little job, I am of course still looking for a proper job. But it is hopeless. You have no idea, how bad it is already in Austria. Everybody tries to go into other countries, as Austria is not able to give work to these 6.5 million people. And it will become worse. Owing to the crisis the number of births has become less and less. That means that within 2 or 3 years in some parts of Austria, there will be no necessity for school for some years. So the teachers will become unemployed. In Vienna, many schools had to be closed already, because there were not enough children.—

My family sends their best regards and wishes to you. Please accept also warmest greetings from myself.

Yours sincerely

E. Schenkl

CENSORED AND PASSED

*Medical College Hospital*
*Calcutta*
*The 15th March, 1937*

Dear Frl. Schenkl,

Many thanks for your air mail letter of the 26th Feb. which I received on the 11th inst.

After I wrote to you last, I was informed by the Superintendent of Police, Darjeeling, that no parcel meant for me was received in his office. As a matter of fact, when I sent out the complaint, I knew from my past experience that the parcel would not be recovered. However, I mean to take the matter up with the Postal Department if you could send me the receipt. You may also send in a complaint to the Postal authorities there—but if you do so, please do not enclose your receipt with the complaint—but mention the no., date etc. on the receipt. If you could send me the receipt, it would help the authorities here to trace the parcel.

You will see from the address at the top that I am still in Hospital in Calcutta. I have been here for 3 months, though when I came here in December, I did not expect to be here more than 2 or 3 weeks; it is warming up quickly now-a-days, the days being hot, though the nights are still pleasant. I remember that there was snow lying on the ground when I left Badgastein towards the end of March last year. Here we cannot even dream of snow—because we do not see any snow in our waking life. And seeing the Himalayan snow from a distance does not make any impression on the mind.

I am glad that you have taken up your French again. I think it is good to know other languages. For one thing—it broadens one's mind and intellect. I shall try to start my German again—when I leave this hospital and settle down somewhere else. It is difficult to do any prolonged study here—the place is too noisy. And then I am going home in the afternoons and in the mornings I am going out for a drive (accompanied by a police officer, of course, as I am not a free man).

The specialist says that the tonsils are not the cause of my trouble. The gall-bladder wound is all-right and there is no trouble due to that. The trouble is persisting either in the liver or in the lungs and on this point, medical opinion is divided. The doctor who is treating me here, Lt. Col. Vere Hodge, is, however, of opinion that the liver is causing trouble and not the lungs. I hope he is right, because that implies that the complaint is less serious than if the other diagnosis were right.

Is your family going into the country this summer? In your country, summer comes much later than it does here.

Please remember me to Mrs Lowy when you write to her next. Re. the paper you want, I am thinking what sort of paper would be interesting to you—weekly or monthly or perhaps bi-weekly. However, when I decide, I shall arrange for some paper to be sent to you. I do not know if the Modern Review would interest you, because it contains only articles—perhaps an illustrated weekly containing pictures, would be more interesting.

I hope this will find you all well. Kind regards to your parents and yourself.

Yours sincerely

Subhas Bose

*Vienna*
*18.3.37*

Dear Mr Bose,

Your letter of the 26th ult. was to hand on the 8th inst. Take my thanks for it. It is good that you wrote a German letter to Kommerzialrat Faltis. I am sure he has understood it all right. I never meet him now, as I am so busy that I do not come for weeks into town.

Yes, our winter has been comparatively mild this year though a very hard one has been foretold by the people who dare to prophesize the weather. But you can with certainty always believe the opposite of what they tell you then you will be right. Now we see slowly spring advancing. We have some times already quite fine weather and even some flowers begin to grow already. There are of course no leaves yet on the trees or bushes. This will take another month or so to come out. As I am looking after a baby now I am forced to go out every afternoon for a walk with him. This is good for the child and also for myself because when I am not forced by somebody or something I never go out for a walk.

The other day I saw in a Calcutta paper the snap of Frau Fulop Miller together with Rabindranath Tagore. Did you see it by chance also? It appeared in 'The Orient' of February 21. She looks rather haggard on this picture and I was really shocked. Because in Vienna she did not look like that.

I wonder whether you are still in Calcutta? I think now the climate must become a little disagreeable for you and it would be rather better to be somewhere up in the mountains. I was glad to hear that your health has improved. I am sure that you will improve further and send you therefore my best wishes for complete recovery.

Have you now heard anything of the book-cover that has been lost? Please let me know because if you have not I will enquire from Vienna and I am sure I will find a trace where it has gone. And if not, the postal authorities must pay a fine to me.

Schwester Elvira is now again in Vienna. The other day I went to Rudolfinerhaus to pay her a visit. She looks comparatively well, after all she has now had a long period of rest. But soon the air of hospital will bring her down again. She asked me to give you her best regards. She would have written to you and thanked you for your letter but she is dreadfully busy now in hospital because all rooms are occupied and that means very much work for the nurses.

I do not know if I have already written to you that the second part of the Vienna 'Høhenstrasse' has now been finished. You probably remember that we once saw it. We started from terminus stop of tram No. 38 and went towards Kobenzel. From there we went along the newly built road up to Kahlenberg. There the street found its end. And then we walked on an old foot-path towards Leopoldsberg once. Now they have continued the road from Kahlenberg till Leopoldsberg. I have not been there myself but I read in the papers and saw pictures. It is now the programme of our Government to build new roads and repair the old ones. That is a very good thing, because the roads in Austria are in no way to be called good roads. And specially for autos they are dreadfully bad. And as now there come so many foreigners with their cars to Austria it is rather a necessity to build new roads.

Are you continuing your German a little? It would be very good for you. I am learning French again and I am very glad to be able to do so. Unfortunately my French teacher will go away for the summer already in the beginning of May. But I hope that in autumn I will then be able to continue again, because now as I am making speedy progress I would pity it very much if I had to stop again.

When you have time and you like, please let me have a line of you again. I shall have to stop for today as I have to rush for my afternoon business again. I hope you are keeping good health now.

With my heartiest greetings and best wishes,

I am

Yours sincerely

E. Schenkl

My parents and sister send best regards and good wishes to you.

*38/2 Elgin Road*
*Calcutta*
*18.3.37*

Dear Frl. Schenkl,

This is to inform you that I was suddenly released last night. I returned home at 10 pm from the Hospital.

I am naturally very busy at the present moment and shall write to you at length next week. My freedom means that I can move about freely and that my correspondence will not be *officially* censored—though, of course, it will always be secretly censored.

Hope you are all well. Please give the above news to all friends there. Kind regards to all.

Yours sincerely

Suι  as C. Bose

*24.3.37*

Dear Mr Bose,

A few days back I read in the newspaper that you have been released. My congratulations. Sr. Elvira and myself took this as an opportunity of drinking your health today. Also hearty greetings and best wishes for Easter.

Yours sincerely

E. Schenkl

[Joint card with Sister Elvira]

*38/2 Elgin Road*
*Calcutta*
*25.3.37*

Dear Frl. Schenkl,

Last week, on the 18th, I hurriedly wrote you an air mail letter which you must have received by now. Since my release, I have been living with my mother in our old house which is a stone's throw from my brother's house. Day and night, I have a stream of visitors which keeps me busy and makes me tired. However, I am trying to leave Calcutta for change in some health resort. Today I am sending by *ordinary post* some papers giving news of my release. I am enclosing another small cutting with this. My health is not well. My release was somewhat unexpected for all of us. In future, I shall write to you by ordinary post and shall try to write a few lines every week. I am now quite free in every way, though my letters will always be secretly examined by the police censor.

How is your health please? And how is the weather there now? Here it is quite warm now. Mrs Fulop Miller has sent a telegram from Bombay saying that she is sailing from Bombay on the 25th (today). She asked me if I had any message for Viennese friends. I told her that I had no special message, but that she should give my greetings to all friends there.

You asked for some Indian paper. I am arranging to send you a weekly illustrated paper. Do you want a weekly or daily newspaper as well? I can easily arrange to send you either of them, if you want it. But I doubt if you will have time to read a daily newspaper. And the Indian news in daily papers will not be understandable to you probably. Please let me know your wishes. How is Mrs Vetter? She does not write to me regularly. Are you studying any Indian language? Why not try one? Best regards to your parents and greetings to your sister and yourself.

Yours sincerely

Subhas C. Bose

*26.3.37*

Dear Mr Bose,

Your two letters (15th inst. and 18th inst.) were to hand yesterday night at the same time. Many thanks. As a matter of fact, I knew already about your sudden release since Monday. You may imagine how glad we were all about this good piece of news. I informed as many friends as possible. But as I am very busy always, I could of course not write to every friend and will do so only in the course of the following days.

Please take my families' and my best wishes for this opportunity and may you now always remain in freedom.

Re. the lost parcel, I will, before posting this letter inquire from the post office if it is necessary to send the receipt along with the complaint, if not I enclose it for your use in India.

I can imagine that you have now a lot to do. Probably much of your time will be filled up with visits and writing of letters. Therefore I appreciate it very much that you wrote so quickly. For you it will be good to be free, because as now the warm season is approaching, you might easily be able to protect yourself against heat. Now in Vienna we have not yet had much of heat. Only twice or thrice and then only for one day. The next day was again cold and rainy. Today it is quite fine. Unfortunately I have to go downtown in the afternoon with the little boy after whom I am looking, together with his mother. As baby has a bad nose and has to go to the doctor. Very uncomfortable job, because the poor child shouts so much and that makes me quite sick. Easter we should have gone to Budapest, but owing to baby's illness, impossible.

Well, I am making good progress in French again. I am very glad because I have great interest for the subject. If I have more time and money I would learn other languages too.

Tuesday last I was out with Sr. Elvira in the evening to drink your health. We wrote a p.c. to you and hope you will receive it.

It is very nice of you that you want to send me a paper. Please select whatever you think best. I have of course now very little time to read but I will somehow manage, because without reading it is impossible for me.

When you can manage to write in detail to me it will be nice of you. But only, when you have time. I cannot write myself longer, as there is so little time and I want to post the letter with today's mail.

I also do hope that your trouble is only due to the liver. When I can do anything for you, please let me know.

My family send their best wishes and kind regards. Please take also my good wishes and warmest greetings.

Yours sincerely

E. Schenkl

I am enclosing the receipt, but if it cannot be traced, please send the receipt back to me, then I will try it from Vienna. Without receipt it is hopeless, I am informed.

Regards

E.S.

*1, Woodburn Park*
*Calcutta*
*The 5th April, 1937*

Dear Frl. Schenkl,

I am sorry I could not write to you last week—so I am writing by air mail this week. In future I shall write by ordinary mail. My health is not satisfactory—so I shall leave Calcutta soon for a change. Yes, I am now free in every way, except that all my correspondence is secretly and regularly censored by the Police. I sent you some press cuttings about my release about a fortnight ago. Tomorrow there will be a public reception for me and it will be a very big gathering. The doctors have allowed me to attend only one meeting—so after that, I shall go out for a change and I shall not accept any public engagement until I return from a change in some hill-station. Please let me know all about your health.

Many thanks for your air mail letters of the 18th March and 26th March. Please inform Mr Faltis about my release and also another friend in Berlin—Mrs Kitty Kurti, Mommsen Str. 69, Berlin-Charlottenburg. I hope you will not mind the trouble.

I have arranged to send you the weekly edition of a Calcutta paper, Amrita Bazar Patrika. Please let me know if you also receive a weekly pictorial paper from Calcutta, Orient.

Thanks for the postal receipt. I shall write to the Postal Dept. about the missing parcel. If I fail, I shall return the receipt to you.

Please remember me to all friends there and especially to Sr. Elvira.

I am glad to know that you are progressing with your French.

How do you pronounce 'Familie' in German? Familee or Familiay?

I have not yet received the p.c. which you and Sr. Elvira wrote. I hope to get it next week. Many thanks for thinking so kindly of me. Please do not bother about sending any new parcels—as they may not reach me—like the last one.

How is your health? Please send my best regards to your parents. Kind greetings for your sister and yourself.

Yours sincerely

Subhas C. Bose

*5.4.37*

Dear Mr Bose,

Many thanks for your air mail letter of the 25th ult. which was in hand on the 1st inst. According to your first letter, after your release, I have informed as many friends as possible in Vienna, but could not manage to write to anyone yet outside Vienna. I am too busy for that. But I shall do so certainly this week.

I can well imagine that the stream of visitors keeps you busy day and night. One nearly does not get time to take a breath, because people have a terrible skill to occupy one's time and energy. But I think, that when you have the opportunity to go to some health resort, you should do so, get well first and then begin the 'fight with the dragon' (called visitors) anew. By the way, what is really wrong with you now? Have the doctors found out the source of your trouble? I hope, however, it is only due to the trouble in the liver and not due to lung. Because that would be a little more persisting I think. But strong, as you are, you will certainly now be able to overcome this.. And you may also overcome it now more easily, as you know you are in freedom. Because I am sure that the constant thought that one is not free and cannot move about at his liberty, undermines the health completely.

It is very kind of you that you will arrange for some weekly paper to be sent to me. Yes, it is better I get a weekly paper, because I have now really no time to read a daily paper. I am busy from morning till evening. I am mostly very tired when I come home, but I do not mind, because the more work and responsibility I have, the quicker my energy and power grow. My health is so so but I have not the necessary time now to take special care of it and pity myself, so I do not feel the usual troubles so much. Only since a few days I have been again suffering from gall-bladder pain, which I really could not overlook. Due to that I have again lost in weight. But that does not matter so much. Otherwise I am feeling o.k. and very energetic and happy at the moment.

The weather in Vienna is dreadful. Since Easter we had rain, rain, and again rain. One could not go out which was very tiresome, because to stay indoors all the time is not an agreeable thing.

I think Mrs Miller will probably arrive in Vienna about the middle of the month. I wonder if she will phone me. She has not written one line to me the whole time she was in India though she had promised to do so. This is, how one can rely in a woman !!!

I rang up Mrs Vetter the day your letter arrived and gave her your best regards. She was very glad to hear about you. She is also always very busy and has no time to write many letters and in regular intervals. So she asked me only to give you her best and heartiest wishes. The same I should also communicate to you from Mrs Hargove who wrote to me the other day. She is also very busy because she is now meditating, as she wants to get fit for Holland in August next. I think there is again a camp of Krishnamurti this year which she wants to join. Once she told me that she would like to take me there. But I think that would not be the right environment for me at present as I do not feel the need to meditate and hear lectures on philosophy and religion. Now is the time for work. Meditating will come when I am older. Now I want work and action.

No, I am not studying any Indian language at present. It is

impossible at present. But I am continuing my French which I like very much. I must say, I am progressing rapidly. The only thing that is lacking is practice in conversation. Probably I shall now get lessons. I will have to teach German. But it is not yet quite sure. That will again take some of my free time which is now so limited. The only day that I have now free is Sunday. And then I get either a visitor or I go to visit my friend. And even then we are not lazy and both of us sit down and do some needle work or I teach her to play the guitar.

We are now thinking already of summer. We will again go to Pøllau, as this is a very lovely place and besides that we have many friends there so we will have plenty of amusements.

I think I have now told enough of myself and it is time to enquire more about you. What are you doing at present? Are you intending to write a new book? Have you got the receipt for the parcel that has been lost? Please, try to send it back to me when you are not successful because then I will enquire from this side, maybe I am successful then.

Not long ago I spoke with Direktor Faltis on the phone and he told me that he had got your German letter about which he was very much astonished. It was very well written and nearly no mistake. You should really try to continue your studies in this language because it is a pity if you give it up. You have made a very nice progress I must say. Perhaps you have once again the opportunity to come to Europe and then you will be happy to know the language. If I can help you in any way please let me know. I shall gladly do so.

My parents and my sister send you their best regards. Please take also my best wishes for your future and my heartiest greetings.

Yours sincerely

E. Schenkl

PS It is very kind that you intend to write so often to me. I shall also try to answer always as quickly as possible. So I will also write now every week by ordinary mail and only if there should be something important I will write by airmail.

*1 Woodburn Park*
*Calcutta*
*8.4.37*

Dear Frl. Schenkl,

Could you kindly forward the accompanying letter to Mr Gairola? I do not know if he is still staying at Alser Str. 20/15. If not, please find him out. Perhaps, the Hotel de France people will know his address. Please ask Gairola to do as I have requested in my letter. In case Gairola is not in Vienna, please ask Singh or some other Indian student to do the needful—as suggested in my letter to Gairola.

I am sending you today by ordinary post some press cuttings about the public meeting here on the 6th inst. Did you get the Bengali Dictionary last year?

How are you keeping now? With kindest regards,

Yours sincerely

Subhas C. Bose

*1 Woodburn Park*
*Calcutta*
*The 15th April, 1937*

Dear Frl. Schenkl,

I am glad to have your air mail letters of the 18th and 26th March and your post card of the 24th (from S. Elvira and yourself). Many thanks for all of them.

It is getting hot here now. I shall be leaving for a hill-station in the North within a week.

Please give my warmest regards to Sr. Elvira. I am not writing separately.

No, I have no time for German now. But when I am away from Calcutta, I shall try again.

My health is much the same. I am, of course, glad to be a free man—but I have not been able to improve much because of the strain caused by too many visitors. I hope to have an easy time up on the hills.

I hope you are getting on well with your French. Yes, you should keep it up in any case.

I am sorry to hear of your gall-bladder pain. Please take all possible care about your diet.

I have got the receipt of the parcel along with one of your letters but I have not been able to do anything.

I have got your air mail letter of the 5th inst. (April). When are you going in to the country (Pollau)?

My health is much the same—something is wrong with my throat, liver and lungs—but I hope I shall recover if I can take 6 months rest and change of climate. That is what the doctors say.

How are you all? Warmest regards to your parents and cordial greetings for your sister and yourself.

Yours sincerely

Subhas C. Bose

*1 Woodburn Park or*
*38/2 Elgin Road*
*Calcutta*
*The 22nd April, 1937*

Dear Frl. Schenkl,

I am writing a few lines in a hurry. I shall be leaving for the hills within a week. When you reply—please write to the following address:

c/o Dr N.R. Dharmavir
Dalhousie
Punjab
India

How are you? My health is much the same. It is quite hot here now and it makes one feel tired. When are you going to the country? Please let me know how you spend your time. Are you learning French? Did you meet Mrs Fulop Miller?

With kind regards

Yours sincerely

Subhas C. Bose

*Lahore*
*Saturday, 1.5.37*

Dear Frl. Schenkl,

Many thanks for your letter of the 14th inst by air mail which I received in Calcutta. I left Calcutta on the 25th and stopped at Allahabad for 4 days for a meeting of the Congress Party. I arrived here this morning. I shall be soon leaving for a hill station. My address henceforth will be: c/o Dr N.R. Dharmavir, Dalhousie (Punjab). I intend staying at *Dalhousie* (which is about 2000 meters high) for some months.

Please let me know if you are getting the illustrated 'Orient' and the weekly Amrita Bazar Patrika.

I did not have any talk with Mrs Fulop Miller about you at all. I think she wanted me to talk about friends there, but I simply asked her to convey my greetings to all.

This week I could not write to you by ordinary mail—so I am writing to you by airmail.

I am sorry to know that Pension Cosmopolite has been sold. Please let me know the address of Mrs Vecsei. What has happened to my boxes?

Who told you that I had made progress with my German? Please be careful with your diet. I am sorry to know that you have again the pain. It is certainly due to wrong diet.

Where is Sen now? And where is Mathur?

As I have already written before, it is not possible for me to go to Europe again. I am hoping that the change at Dalhousie will gradually put me right. I am glad that you also agree with me.

I gave up the idea of going to Puri (which is a sea-side place)—because a hill-station would be much better now.

I shall try to send you a few snaps within a week or two.

I must thank you for your long letter, though I do not usually write long letters. You know that I never forget my friends and always like to hear from them. Please let me know *in brief* when you have time—how you have spent the last year. I do not know if I shall be able to send you the bangles from here— but why don't you get them in Europe? What kind do you want? The glass bangles are all imported from Czechoslovakia or Japan.

Yours sincerely

Subhas C. Bose

*Vienna*
*4.5.37*

Dear Mr Bose,

Your two letters (ordinary mail of 15th April and airmail of 22nd April) were to hand duly, many thanks for same.

I am glad to hear that you are now going out to Punjab for a change and hope that you will soon recover completely. Probably in Dalhousie you won't have to suffer so much from the heat! We had very bad weather during the whole of April. Daily rain and very cold. Since 1st inst. it has changed and is now very nice. Everything is green in the garden and the trees in full blossom. A wonderful sight indeed.

Yes, I am getting on fairly well with French, but only have too little time to practise at home. In the morning I am busy with household and the whole afternoon I am with the baby after whom I am looking. In the evening I have to do so many other things. Reading has become a luxury for me now. So I have to look for my garderobe, you may well imagine how much of free time I have—practically none. But at least I earn a few groschen, just that I can pay my lessons, buy some of my clothes and have money for my correspondence. But nothing is left. I tried to save some money but that is rather impossible.

My health is so so. I am now often getting the pain in gall bladder. I am as careful as possible with my diet, but always I can't be, because my people eat so often meat, Kalbsfleisch, which I could take, they do not want and Rindfleisch and Schweinfleisch is bad for me. Besides I cannot ask mother to cook separately for me as this is too expensive and besides takes so much time. And mother gets tired so easily. She becomes old and cannot, of course, work as much, as a young person any more.

We will leave for the country (Pøllau) on or about the 5th of July I think. This is, when school has finished. As my sister is still in school, we have to wait for her.

Since two weeks I am getting now the weekly edition of the Patrika, but have not got 'Orient.'

Yes, I met Mrs Fulop-Miller already a few times. She is still quite charmed about India and feeling quite unhappy in Vienna. Not long ago I have brought the boxes away from Pension Cosmopolite, as Mrs Vecsei has sold the Pension. I wrote to you about it in a previous letter.

When you are in Dalhousie, please try to make a few snaps. I shall do so again in Pøllau, if only the films were not so expensive.

Mrs Hargrove I have not seen for a long time. She is now carefully meditating, as she wrote to me. Later on she will give me more typing work to do.

Otherwise, everything is unchanged in Vienna. The friends are well and send you best regards. Mrs Kurti wrote to me the other day a nice letter. She was glad to hear about your release.

Excuse me, when I stop here, but I am so busy this morning. I am quite alone at home, parents have gone to their garden and sister is in school. I will have now to prepare my meal, probably it will comprise of a cup of coffee, as I am too lazy to cook for myself. I must try to decrease the pile of correspondence. It is awful how it has accumulated.

My family sends best regards to you. Take also from me, best wishes as well as warmest greetings.

Yours sincerely

E. Schenkl

*Lahore*
*6.5.37 Thursday*

Dear Frl. Schenkl,

On Saturday last I wrote to you by airmail from here. I arrived here on the 1st inst. from Allahabad, where I stayed for 4 days. Can you follow these places in the map? We shall be moving to a place called 'Dalhousie' on the mountains, after 4 or 5 days. Please write to me

c/o Dr N.R. Dharmavir
Dalhousie (Punjab)

I have not much to write today. It was pleasant here when I first came—but now it is growing hot.

I was sorry to learn from your last air mail letter that you had been eating paprika etc. which brought on further attacks of pain. Why don't you take care of your diet, when you know that wrong diet is the main cause of your trouble? I am also afraid that you are overworking yourself—are you not? In your next letter, please let me have news that you are looking after yourself properly. I am arranging to send you some money by this mail.

I intend staying at Dalhousie for some months. When do you go into the country?

Please convey my best regards to your parents and accept same yourself. Greetings for Lotte.

Yours sincerely

Subhas C. Bose

*Lahore*
*11.5.37*

Dear Frl. Schenkl,

Your airmail letter of the 4th May was to hand this morning, having been redirected from Dalhousie. I have not left Lahore for Dalhousie yet and shall be leaving only tonight, reaching there tomorrow morning.

What do you mean by—'I have to look for my garderobe'?

I am very sorry to know that now-a-days you get the pain very often.

What is you sister studying now? I thought she had already passed her matriculation examination.

Please do not drink much coffee. If at all you take it, take plenty of milk with it and never take it in empty stomach. Black coffee in empty stomach is the best thing for bringing on pain in the gall-bladder.

I have nothing more to write today. Please take plenty of care of your health. Did you get the Indian papers I sent you, about my release (18th March) and about the meeting in Calcutta (7th April)? Any news of Mathur and of Sen?

With cordial greetings—regards for your parents. My address for some months will be: c/o Dr N.R. Dharmavir, Dalhousie, Punjab.

Yours sincerely

Subhas C. Bose

*Vienna*
*20.5.37*

Dear Mr Bose,

Your letter of the 1st inst. was to hand last week and I must apologise for not answering sooner.

You will, by now, be in Dalhousie, I suppose. How do you find it there? Have you already improved your health? I do hope so.

About your stay in Allahabad I read in the Patrika which came this week. I found that you met Mahatmaji. Must be interesting. The Patrika I get now regularly, but Illustrated 'Orient' *not.* I am, however, thankful that I get one paper as it is very interesting to be a little informed about what goes on in another part of the world.

I do not yet know about Frau Vecsei's new address. But she promised to inform me about it when she has settle down definitely. Now she will be travelling a bit. Your boxes have been transferred to another place. I have arranged all about it. Whenever you want anything, please let me know and I shall arrange for sending the things (books). You must have got by now the complete list of all books which I sent to your nephew while he was still in Europe.

I am as careful as possible about my diet but still I get sometimes a little pain, of course not such bad attacks as I got once when you were present.

Sen is now in Edinburgh and Mathur somewhere in Germany, but where, I have no idea. I do not hear from any of them. Only Katyar is a faithful friend and writes rather often though I keep him always waiting very long for my answer. He will be going home within a few weeks and wrote in his last letters that he is already counting the days and hours till he is reaching his motherland.

You want to know *in brief* how I spent the last year. Well, as you know I have no job so I was compelled to stay at home. Doing housework in the morning, afternoon French lessons, reading, writing. French was stopped in June, because (1) we went to country and (2) money was finished. And with 5 shillings per month, as pocket money I could do nothing. Sometimes I went to a café and met friends, and sometimes I went to a cinema. (One ticket for 90 groschen.) In late autumn I began making needlework for Xmas not only for my people but also something for Sr. Elvira who paid me. So I could at least give a present to my family and a few friends. Since 1st of February I am looking after an Indian baby in the afternoon. But by the end of the month the family goes and I have again nothing. Besides all this I have been writing piles of offers during the last year but without success. At present I am busy in my few free hours making dresses, bags, belts, etc. This is all.—

I have already inquired about the bangles but could not get them here. Please do not worry, if you can't send them, does not matter. I wanted simple glass-bangles of different colouring.

I spoke to Mrs Vetter today and she complained to me you do not write to her at all. Mrs F.-M. I have not met for about 3 weeks. I had to give up my French lessons again as my teacher has already gone out for summer holidays. But I am translating and studying her two translations and French letters. And she will send me the corrections. Last week I got from a friend a very interesting book: 'Labour in Irish History' by James Connolly. I am glad to have it and will begin it within a few days.—

Please let me know how you are getting on. And when you have snaps, please send them to me. My parents and sister send best regards. Also my friend Ella asked me in a letter to give you best regards. From myself hearty greetings and best wishes,

Yours sincerely

E. Schenkl

Is Dr Dharmavir a personal friend of yours or does he run a sort of sanatorium?

*Vienna*
*26.5.37*

Dear Mr Bose,

Many thanks for your kind letter of the 6th inst. which was to hand on the 26th inst. The same day American Express rang me up informing me about the money. Please let me thank you heartily for sending it. I shall put it in the bank and keep it in case you want me something to buy or arrange for you. In case I am in trouble myself I may also take some money. Anyway, I will save it. I got a very good rate, S 26.20 per £. If you remember, last year or rather two years ago, it was already down once to 25 S.

By now you will be in Dalhousie and probably have already rested from the strain you must have had in Lahore. Of course, I can spot out every place on the map. But a map can never give you an idea about the place itself. How is Dalhousie? What sort of plants do grow there? Probably the climate will be bearable for you there. Here in Vienna it is now very hot. But just that is what I like. I am simply happy when it is very hot and also feeling well.

Yes, I promise herewith that I shall be very careful about eating and will keep as strict a diet as possible. Re: overwork, there will soon be no possibility for overworking myself as the Indian family is leaving Vienna within a week. I am most sorry for that because I shall miss the child so much.

We will go into the country about the 8th of July. My address will be:

E. Schenkl,
Mrzgasse 112
Pøllau b/Hartberg
(Ost Steiermark) (Austria)

And you can just as well send your letters to my Vienna address because all our mail will be redirected. We will probably stay at Pøllau for about 6 or 8 weeks. I hope we will have a nice and hot summer. Then I shall lie the whole time somewhere in the grass and get roasted and fried by the sun. I shall also take some books and read. In all I shall lead a very lazy life and only look after myself.

Yesterday I met Mrs Fulop-Miller. She told me that she is so nervous! This always the same with people who have not much to do. If such a woman had two or three children she would have no time to be nervous. Probably I shall also get 'nervous' when I am out of a job again. At least I am then fit for society, as I find all these people are nervous.

Mrs Vetter inquired about you the other day. She said she did not hear from you since a very long time. I gave her your Dalhousie address as she will probably write to you, she said.

French lessons I had to stop, as my teacher has already gone into the country. But I shall write to her during summer and send her some work and she will correct me.

There is nothing to write this time anymore. My parents and Lotte (who is taller and stouter than myself by now) send you their best regards.

Take hearty greetings from me as well as best wishes and many thanks.

Yours sincerely

E. Schenkl

PS I have now read 'The Money Changers' by Upton Sinclair. Do you know this book? Though the book is full of banking expressions and I did not understand every word, it was very interesting.

*c/o Dr N.R. Dharmavir*
*Dalhousie*
*Punjab*
*27.5.37*

Dear Frl. Schenkl,

Many thanks for you airmail letter of the 20th inst. which reached me yesterday. I did not hear from you for nearly 2 weeks and I was feeling anxious. You perhaps know by now that I came here on the 12th May. Dr and Mrs Dharmavir are my friends and I am therefore staying as their guest—not as in a Pension. This, of course, is a common thing in India, though not in Europe.

Prof. Demel wrote to me in a letter dated the 13th April that he read in a paper the same day about my release. Did you not inform him on the 22nd March when you first heard about my release?

I shall be very happy if you will do me the favour of writing a few lines every week by ordinary mail. If you are busy, you need not write a long letter, but only a few lines.

I am feeling slightly better now—but have not improved much.

This is a quiet place on the hills 2000 meters high. On one side you see the snow covered Himalayan range and on the other side in the far-off distance you see the plains and the rivers. The air is fresh and health-giving.

I have now arranged for 'Orient' for you. At first I was told that I need not pay any subscription—but they wanted it really. So I have paid it now, you will get the paper regularly.

Yes, I duly got the list of books which you sent me.

If you like, I may give you some advice as to how you should spend your time from next month. I do not, of course, know if that advice is of any value. Haben Sie mich vergessen? Warum schreiben Sie so selten? Ich warte fur Ihren Brief—wissen Sie nicht? [Translation: Have you forgotten me? Why do you write so seldom? I wait for your letter—don't you know? – eds.] In any case you should continue your French lessons. Also speak French.

Do you have news of Lowy now-a-days? Yes, I have not been regular in my correspondence with Mrs Vetter, and she is very sensitive, unfortunately.

When you have time in hand, you may read some of my books that are lying there. There would be plenty to interest you. Do you go to the Post office now-a-days?

Please remember me to Ella. And give my best regards to your parents and greetings to Lotte.

I am enclosing herewith a snap taken when I reached Dalhousie. You need not show it to anybody if you don't like. I wonder if you will recognise me in Bengali dress.

Do you have any trouble with your lungs or throat now? Please give my regards to Schwester Elvira. Do you meet your little friend now-a-days?

With cordial greetings and best wishes.

Yours sincerely

Subhas C. Bose

PS Among my old friends, Sharma came to see me in Calcutta. He came all the way from Punjab and it was very kind of him.

S.C.B.

*30.5.37*

Dear Mr Bose,

I wonderful Sunday afternoon, sunny and warm. Mrs Fulop Miller and myself are sitting on the terrace of Kobenzl-Hotel, the place you liked so much in Vienna.

Hope you are well, best greetings,

Sincerely

E. Schenkl

[joint card with Heddy Fulop Miller]

[Undated, but from the context it is clear that Subhas Chandra Bose wrote these letters in block letters after his release in March 1937, probably some time in late April or May 1937. The first letter was posted by Frau Lowy from Karlsbad on 1 June 1937]

I HAVE BEEN LONGING TO WRITE TO YOU FOR SOME TIME PAST—BUT YOU CAN EASILY UNDERSTAND HOW DIFFICULT IT WAS TO WRITE TO YOU ABOUT MY FEELINGS. I JUST WANT TO LET YOU KNOW NOW THAT I AM EXACTLY WHAT I WAS BEFORE, WHEN YOU KNEW ME. NOT A SINGLE DAY PASSES THAT I DO NOT THINK OF YOU. YOU ARE WITH ME ALL THE TIME. I CANNOT POSSIBLY THINK OF ANYBODY ELSE IN THIS WORLD. I AM ANXIOUS TO KNOW ABOUT YOUR THOUGHTS. PLEASE WRITE TO ME SOON IN YOUR OWN LANGUAGE (SIMPLE STYLE) BY AIR-MAIL—SO THAT I MAY KNOW. I DO NOT KNOW WHAT I SHOULD DO IN FUTURE. I AM NOT ABLE TO DECIDE. I CANNOT TELL YOU HOW LONELY I HAVE BEEN FEELING ALL THESE MONTHS AND HOW SORROWFUL. ONLY ONE THING COULD MAKE ME HAPPY—BUT I DO NOT KNOW IF THAT IS POSSIBLE. HOWEVER, I AM THINKING OF IT DAY AND NIGHT AND PRAYING TO GOD TO SHOW ME THE RIGHT PATH. EVERY TIME I HEAR THAT YOU ARE NOT WELL, I FEEL SO UNHAPPY. DO TAKE CARE OF YOUR HEALTH SO THAT I MAY FEEL SOMEWHAT RELIEVED. EVER YOURS WITH MY HEART AND SOUL.

LAST WEEK I WROTE TO YOU C/O LOWY. DID YOU GET THE LETTER? DID YOU GET THE LETTER I WROTE TO YOU DURING THE JOURNEY? I WROTE AFTER 'PORT SAID' AND POSTED AT MASSAWA.

AFTER I LEFT, I INSTRUCTED THE AMERICAN EXPRESS TO PAY YOU FIVE POUNDS. THAT WAS LAST YEAR, OF COURSE. DID YOU GET THE MONEY? I HOPE IT WAS OF SOME HELP TO YOU.

HOW HAVE PEOPLE TREATED YOU (AT HOME AND OUTSIDE) DURING THE LAST TWELVE MONTHS? PLEASE LET ME KNOW.

I AM SORRY THAT YOU DO NOT TAKE CARE OF YOUR HEALTH AND THAT YOU HAVE PAINS AGAIN. DO NOT YOU KNOW HOW ANXIOUS I AM FOR YOUR HEALTH AND HOW MUCH I THINK OF YOU?

HAVE YOU SPENT ALL THE MONEY THAT YOU HAD WITH YOU?

WHAT DO YOU THINK NOW-A-DAYS? DO YOU REMEMBER YOUR OLD FRIENDS?

DO YOU PRAY NOWADAYS? WHAT ARE YOUR HOPES FOR THE FUTURE?

PLEASE REPLY BY AIRMAIL IN YOUR OWN LANGUAGE BUT IN VERY SIMPLE STYLE. I SHALL BE ABLE TO UNDERSTAND. PLEASE WRITE TO MY NEW ADDRESS IN 'KURORT' AND NOT TO MY PERMANENT HOME ADDRESS. *DON'T SIGN YOUR NAME.*

YOU WANT TO KNOW ABOUT MY HEALTH. IT IS BETTER NOW THAN BEFORE. I SUFFERED FROM ECZEMA FOR A LONG TIME AND NO DOCTOR COULD CURE ME. THEN I CURED MYSELF IN THIS WAY. I SCRAPED THE ECZEMA TILL THE SKIN WAS OFF THEN I PUT IODINE (JOD) ON IT. IT BURNT AT FIRST, BUT AFTER A FEW DAYS IT WAS CURED. IF EVER YOU HAPPEN TO HAVE ECZEMA, YOU MAY TRY MY MEDICINE. DO YOU HAVE ANY COUGH NOW?

I MET YOUR FRIEND M. (IN HAUPTSTADT) IN APRIL—BUT NOT HIS WIFE. WRITE TO HIM CAREFULLY, BECAUSE HE IS VERY MUCH AFRAID. WHEN YOU WRITE TO ME, DON'T FORGET THAT MY FRIENDS READ MY LETTERS *ALWAYS.* WHAT DOES FRAU F.M. SAY?

1. Badgastein, March 1936.

2. Badgastein, December 1937,
A.C.N. Nambiar, Heddy Fulop-Miller, Netaji, Emilie, Amiya Nath Bose.

3. Badgastein, December 1937.

4. Emilie and Anita, Vienna, November 1948.

5. Family group Vienna, November 1948.
Sitting : Bivabati, Sisir Kumar, Anita, Sarat Chandra
Standing: Roma, Emilie, Chitra

38/2 Elgin Road or
Woodburn Park
Calcutta
7. 12. 34

CENSORED AN[illegible]

Dear Fl. Schenkl,

I arrived here on the 4th December wit any trouble on the way. But I was too late. My fath left this mortal world on the 2nd December — that is about 40 hours before I reached Calcutta. My mother is utterly disconsolate, though we, brothers a sisters, are trying our best to console her. For a Westerner, it is difficult to understand our mentalit A Hindu wife's life is so bound up with that of he husband that life is unbearable to her in his abse Nevertheless, we are hoping that she will be able to stand the bereavement. Recently, there have been many other ~~calamities~~ bereavements (S.B.) in our family and all these have had a cumulative effect on my parents.

I do not know if I shall be able to write to you in future. But in case I cannot please do not misunderstand me. At present I am living like a prisoner in our house. This order of "home-internment" was served on me as soon as I landed in Calcutta. For the present, Government have allowed me to stay with my mothe

6. From Subhas to Emilie 7.12.34

LLOYD TRIESTINO

PIROSCAFO "Conte Verde"

29. 3. 36

P.S. If there is anything else to write, I shall write another letter before reaching Port Said — to another address. S.C.B.

Dear Miss Schenkl,

There are many things that I want to write to you about — but I shall write in a disconnected way — so please read this letter carefully. We are now one day's journey from Naples. The sea is fairly calm — thank God! As I am now old, I cannot stand a rough sea, which I could do, when I was a young man It is beautiful and sunny — the blue sky above — the darker blue of the ocean all around us and in front of us — an unending expanse of water.

When I crossed the Italian frontier, there was no trouble at all. They looked at me and did not even ask me to open my boxes. At Villach, I stopped at the Bahnhof Restaurant for three hours and there finished the article which I posted to you. I think there was somebody watching me there — but I did not care, as I was busy writing. If that letter did not reach you, then they must have stolen it, because I posted it myself in the Station postbox. There is not much to report about, after I crossed the frontier. I posted the pencil for you and registered it. And I spoke to Dr K. about your

7. From Subhas to Emilie 29.3.36

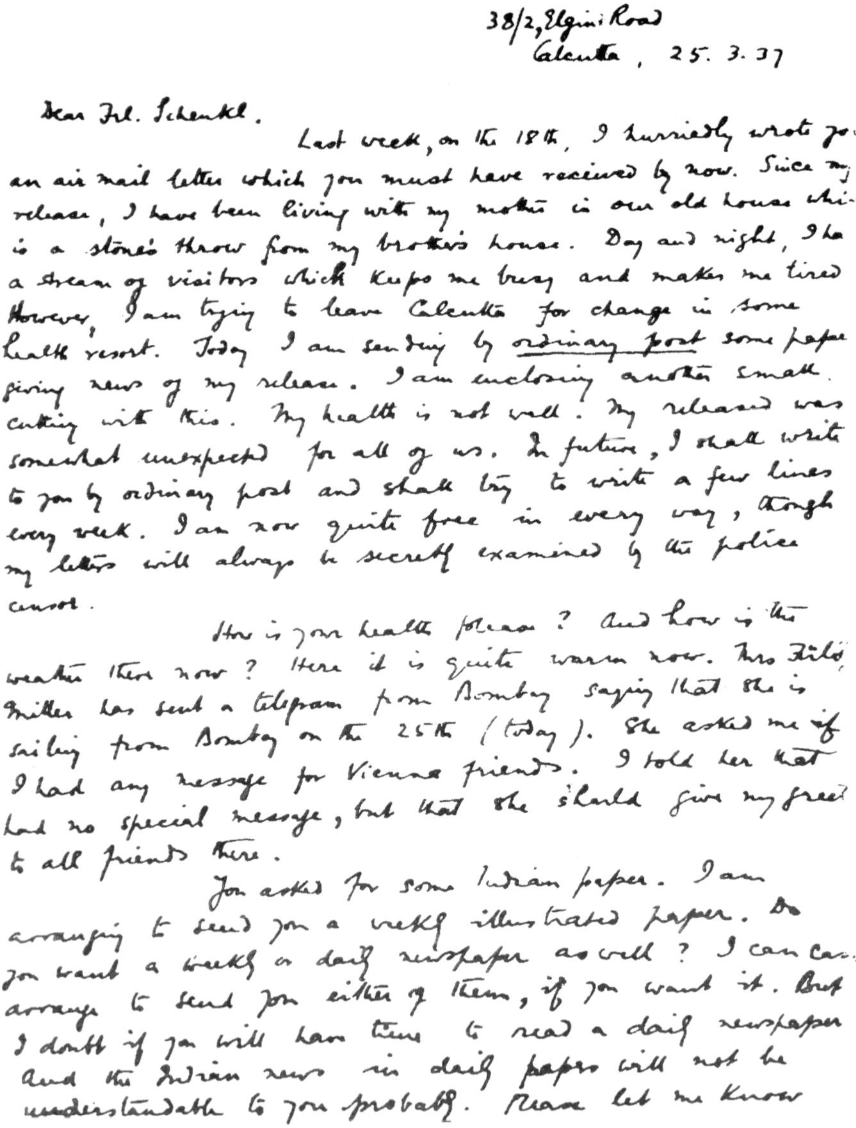

38/2, Elgin Road
Calcutta, 25. 3. 37

Dear Frl. Schenkl,

Last week, on the 18th, I hurriedly wrote you an air mail letter which you must have received by now. Since my release, I have been living with my mother in our old house which is a stone's throw from my brother's house. Day and night, I have a stream of visitors which keeps me busy and makes me tired. However, I am trying to leave Calcutta for change in some health resort. Today I am sending by ordinary post some papers giving news of my release. I am enclosing another small cutting with this. My health is not well. My release was somewhat unexpected for all of us. In future, I shall write to you by ordinary post and shall try to write a few lines every week. I am now quite free in every way, though my letters will always be secretly examined by the police censor.

How is your health please? And how is the weather there now? Here it is quite warm now. Mrs Hilde Miller has sent a telegram from Bombay saying that she is sailing from Bombay on the 25th (today). She asked me if I had any message for Vienna friends. I told her that I had no special message, but that she should give my greetings to all friends there.

You asked for some Indian paper. I am arranging to send you a weekly illustrated paper. Do you want a weekly or daily newspaper as well? I can ca[illegible] arrange to send you either of them, if you want it. But I doubt if you will have time to read a daily newspaper. And the Indian news in daily papers will not be understandable to you probably. Please let me know

8. From Subhas to Emilie 25.3.37

Vienna, 26.5.37.

Dear Mr. Bose,

Many thanks for your kind letter of the 6th inst. which was to hand on the 24th inst. The same day American Express rang me up informing me about the money. Please let me thank you heartily for sending it. I shall put it in the bank and keep it in case you want me something to buy or arrange for you. In case I am in trouble myself I may also take some money. Anyway I will save it. I got a very good rate, S 26·20 per £. If you remember, last year or rather two years ago it was already down once to 25 S.

By now you will be in Dalhousie and probably have already rested from the strain you must have had in Lahore. Of course, I can spot out every place on the map. But a map can never give you an idea about the place itself. How is Dalhousie? What sort of place is to y[illegible] there? Probably the climate will be favourable for you there. Here in Vienna it is now very hot. But just that is what I like. I am simply happy when it is very hot and also feeling well.

Yes, I promise herewith that I shall be very careful about eating and will keep as strict a diet as possible. Re. overwork, here will soon be no possibility for overworking myself as the Indian family is leaving Vienna within a week. I am most sorry for that because I shall miss the child so much.

We will go into the country about the 8th of July. My address will be:

E. SCHENKL,<br>
MÄRZGASSE 112,<br>
PÖLLAU b/HARTBERG,<br>
(Ost Steiermark) (Austria)

9. From Emilie to Subhas 26.5.37

I HAVE BEEN LONGING TO WRITE TO YOU FOR SOME TIME PAST – BUT YOU CAN EASILY UNDERSTAND HOW DIFFICULT IT WAS TO WRITE TO YOU ABOUT MY FEELINGS. I JUST WANT TO LET YOU KNOW NOW THAT I AM EXACTLY WHAT I WAS BEFORE, WHEN YOU KNEW ME. NOT A SINGLE DAY PASSES THAT I DO NOT THINK OF YOU. YOU ARE WITH ME ALL THE TIME. I CANNOT POSSIBLY THINK OF ANYBODY ELSE IN THIS WORLD. I AM ANXIOUS TO KNOW ABOUT YOUR THOUGHTS. PLEASE WRITE TO ME SOON IN YOUR OWN LANGUAGE (SIMPLE STYLE) BY AIR MAIL — SO THAT I MAY KNOW. I DO NOT KNOW WHAT I SHOULD DO IN FUTURE. I AM NOT ABLE TO DECIDE. I CANNOT TELL YOU HOW LONELY I HAVE BEEN FEELING ALL THESE MONTHS AND HOW SORROWFUL. ONLY ONE THING COULD MAKE ME HAPPY – BUT I DO NOT KNOW IF THAT IS POSSIBLE. HOWEVER, I AM THINKING OF IT DAY AND NIGHT AND PRAYING TO GOD TO SHOW ME THE RIGHT PATH. EVERY TIME I HEAR THAT YOU ARE NOT WELL, I FEEL SO UNHAPPY. DO TAKE CARE OF YOUR HEALTH SO THAT I MAY FEEL SOMEWHAT RELIEVED. EVER YOURS WITH MY HEART & SOUL.

10. From Subhas to Emilie Sep. 1937

OFFICE-BEARERS FOR 1938
President :
SUBHAS CHANDRA BOSE
Treasurer :
JAMNALAL BAJAJ
General Secretary :
J. B. KRIPALANI

अखिल भारतीय कांग्रेस कमेटी
स्वराज भवन, इलाहाबाद
آل انڈیا کانگریس کمیٹی
سوراج بھون الہ آباد
ALL INDIA CONGRESS COMMITTEE
SWARAJ BHAWAN, ALLAHABAD
TELEPHONE: 341 TELEGRAM: "CONGRESS"

President's Calcutta Address:
38-2 Elgin Road, Calcutta.
Telephone: Park 59
Telegram: "SUVASBOS"

Wardha, 27.7.38

Dear Frl. Schenkl,

My letter of the 8th inst. reached you on the 14th, while your letter of the 15th inst. reached me on the 19th. I left Calcutta on the 21st. to attend a meeting of the Working Committee. I am going back to Calcutta tomorrow morning, reaching there after 24 hours. We had a busy and anxious time here — a ministerial crisis. You will read about it in the papers. I am sorry to know that you are as careless as ever and have not been to the doctor yet. Until you write to me that you have been to the doctor and have placed yourself under his treatment, I shall not write to you again. The time you waste in writing letters, you can usefully spend at the doctor's.. Has Ami been there? I have not written to him for a long time. I shall send you the Indian Sagas with great pleasure — but only when I hear from you that you have started your treatment. I am all right now — except that I have more work than I can manage. I have written to my uncle asking him to correspond with the gentleman in Germany for stamps. Have you heard from von Hans yet? I hope you are getting both the papers regularly now. How are you spending your time now — when Lotte is away? You must be feeling lonely. Your mother must be glad and also proud of you that you are working now. What is the German for friend — isn't it Liebling? I had been to see Gandhiji at his ashrama this afternoon. There was an Englishman who has become a monk. Then there was a German lady too. His English disciple — Miss Slade or Miraben was of course there. There is nothing more to write today — so I shall end. Auf Wiedersehen mein kleines Liebling!

Yours sincerely
Subhas C Bose

11. From Subhas to Emilie 27.7.38

Berlin, 3. 4. '41

Dear Frl. Schenkl,

P.S. In case you cannot manage the expenses of one week's trip to Berlin, will you be able to borrow the money for the present and come here? Are there any restriction regarding travelling imposed by the Government owing to war conditions? S.C.B.

You will be surprised to get this letter from me and even more surprised to know that I am writing this from Berlin. I arrived in Berlin yesterday afternoon and would have written to you at once — but I was kept busy till evening. Most of the hotels are full and with difficulty a room could be found for me. I am shifting to another hotel today — "Nurnberger Hof".

My future programme is not settled — but in all probability, Berlin will be my headquarters. I do not know if I shall be able to come to Vienna. So you must come to Berlin to meet me. Can you come? You can understand how glad I would be to meet you.

It is possible that I may require a Secretary here. If so, can you come? Will your mother and sister agree to it?

My passport is not in my name but in the name of Orlando Mazzotta. So when you write, you will have to address me as Orlando Mazzotta. Please treat as

12. From Subhas to Emilie 3.4.41

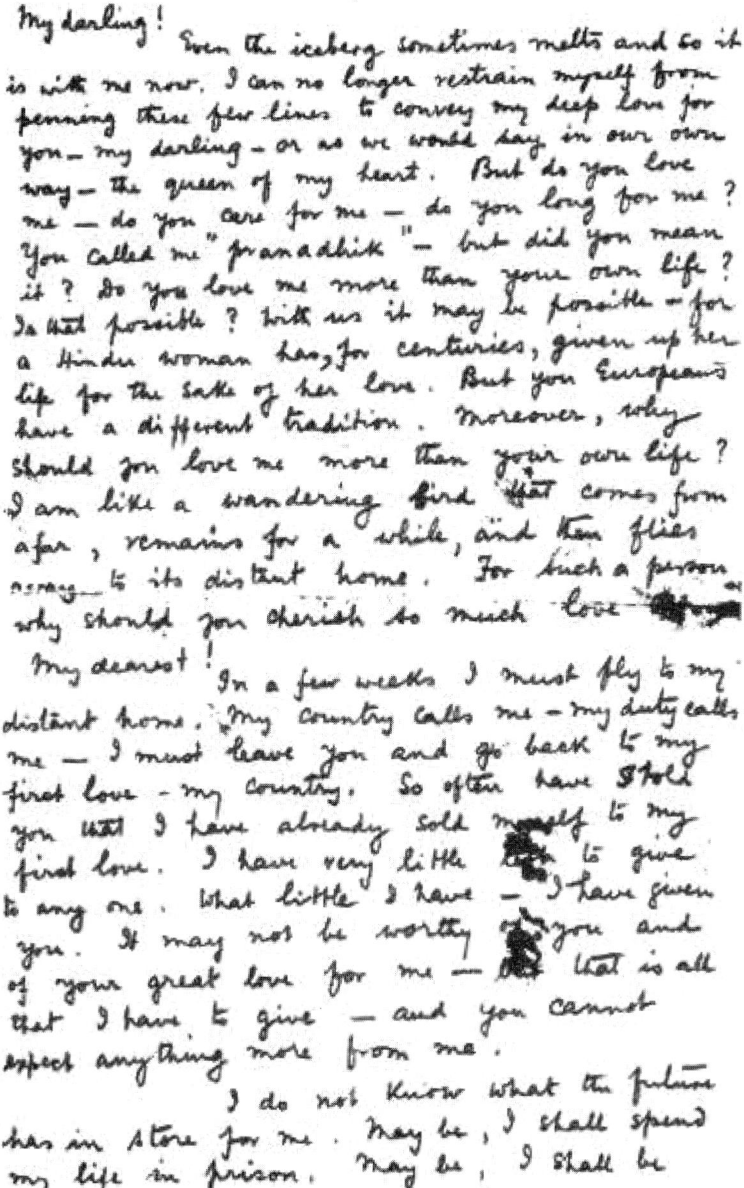

My darling!
Even the iceberg sometimes melts and so it is with me now. I can no longer restrain myself from penning these few lines to convey my deep love for you – my darling – or as we would say in our own way – the queen of my heart. But do you love me – do you care for me – do you long for me? You called me "pranadhik" – but did you mean it? Do you love me more than your own life? Is that possible? With us it may be possible – for a Hindu woman has, for centuries, given up her life for the sake of her love. But you Europeans have a different tradition. Moreover, why should you love me more than your own life? I am like a wandering bird that comes from afar, remains for a while, and then flies away – to its distant home. For such a person why should you cherish so much love

My dearest! In a few weeks I must fly to my distant home. My country calls me – my duty calls me – I must leave you and go back to my first love – my country. So often have I told you that I have already sold myself to my first love. I have very little to give to any one. What little I have – I have given you. It may not be worthy of you and of your great love for me – but that is all that I have to give – and you cannot expect anything more from me.

I do not know what the future has in store for me. May be, I shall spend my life in prison. May be, I shall be

13. First page of a 'love letter' from Subhas to Emilie, March 1936

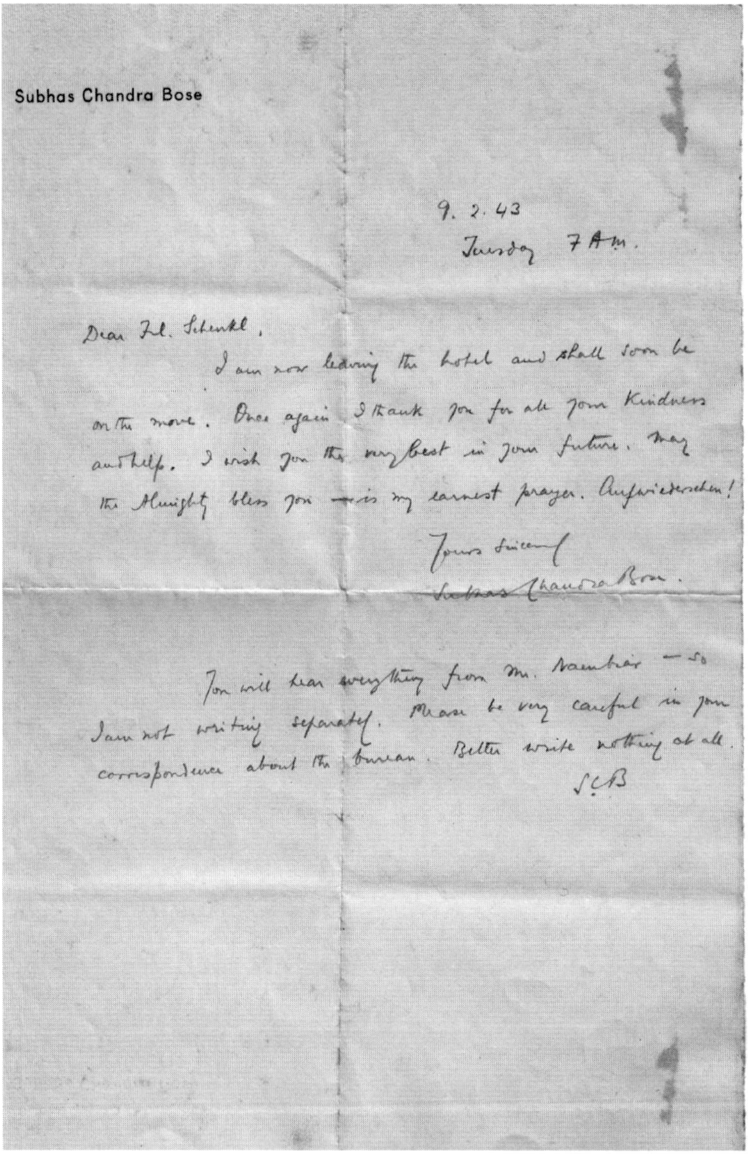

Subhas Chandra Bose

9. 2. 43
Tuesday 7 A.M.

Dear Fl. Schenkl,

I am now leaving the hotel and shall soon be on the move. Once again I thank you for all your kindness and help. I wish you the very best in your future. May the Almighty bless you — is my earnest prayer. Aufwiedersehen!

Yours sincerely
Subhas Chandra Bose.

You will hear everything from Mr. Nambiar — so I am not writing separately. Please be very careful in your correspondence about the bureau. Better write nothing at all.

S.C.B

14. From Subhas to Emilie 9.2.43

*Vienna*
*1.6.37*

Dear Mr Bose,

Your letter of the 11th May was to hand yesterday morning. Many thanks.

Sunday, the 30th May, I have been with Mrs Fulop-Miller on Kobenzl. We wrote a p.c. to you and hope you will receive it by the same mail as this letter. It was a lovely afternoon, very sunny and we had been sitting on the terrace with the magnificent view over Vienna. You also liked this place so much. Afterwards it became a little cold so we went inside the hotel and sat down in the saloon. It was quite interesting to watch all the people. The so-called 'cream of society' had gathered there. We saw the Egyptian Ambassador, some film people and plenty of foreigners. Frau Heddy told me about her journey to India and so the hours passed by very quickly.

Since today I am out of job again, as the family has left Vienna today for Italy. I am very sorry, because I am missing the child so much. I never thought that one could get so used to a child and that I would feel so sorry.

'I have to look for my garderobe'—means that I have to keep in order my dresses, sew the things and iron it, etc. I have now become very economical and do whatever it is possible, myself, so that I need not spend money on dress-making, etc.

My sister has not finished high-school. She went there only for five years (the whole high-school takes eight years). My parents came to the conclusion that it is of no value for her to pass her matriculation examination, as now-a-days you cannot get any job, even if you have your degree in this university. Besides she had trouble with Latin and mathematics, so they took her out last year and since then she had been to a house-holding school. She learns there cooking, sewing, washing, ironing,—all things which are necessary for house-holder. The course finishes in July. What they will do with her afterwards is still uncertain, probably she will have to learn typing and shorthand. The difficulty is with her that she does not want to learn any foreign language. For one year she learnt English but you cannot bring her to talk. She has an awful iron-head and has often been beaten by me for this!

My health is better now, I did not get the pain for some days. I am as careful as possible. But drinking coffee with *plenty* of milk that is a thing I cannot do. Then rather I will give up coffee altogether.

Yes, I got the Indian papers you sent me after your release. I also wrote to you about it. I am now getting every week the weekly edition of AB. Patrika. The last came yesterday. I read that you have slightly improved. I am glad to hear it and hope that now you will improve speedily. Please take a complete rest and do not, as you are in the habit, strain yourself too much by reading till 3 o'clock in the morning. When you are quite well again then you can work. And even then you must not exploit your health, because the more care you take the better work you will be able to do.

I have no news of Master or Sen. Both are lazy louts in writing.

Mrs Vetter enquired yesterday about you and told me that still she has no news about you. Please do write her a few lines at least, she will be so glad.

I wrote a letter to you last week by ordinary mail and hope you have already got it.

Did you take some snaps yet in Dalhousie? What sort of place is this? Is Dr Dharmavir perhaps the gentleman who has a German wife? I remember that you showed me once a picture of a Punjabi doctor with his wife, who was a German, she was clad in Punjabi fashion and they had a little baby. Is it the same family?

My family send best regards to you.

Warmest greetings from myself and good wishes.

Yours sincerely

E. Schenkl

Enclosed a picture of my little boy after whom I was now looking for 4 months. Isn't he sweet? I envy his parents that they can have him.

*c/o Dr N.R. Dharmavir*
*Dalhousie*
*Punjab*
*3.6.37*

Dear Frl. Schenkl,

I hope you are getting my letters regularly though I am not getting regular replies to them.

Last week I sent you a snap of myself taken when I arrived here.

I am sending along with this some stamps. Are you still collecting them? If so, I may send you more. Do you meet Schwester Elvira now? How is her health now? What is your sister doing now? Will she go up for the matriculation examination?

Please ask Singh to write to me occasionally. He was staying at Bennogasse 9/5, I think (B45-1-73 U).

When are you all going into the country? If you have any snaps of yourself—please send me some. Do you hear from Lowy now?

I think you should take lessons in French conversation. Why not join a French speaking club? Did you spend all the money you earned last year? How is your health now? I hope that with warm weather you have no trouble with the lungs? How is your eczema? Do they still trouble you? How was your health last summer (1936)—that is, in April, May and June?

I had some trouble with my throat again and was unwell for about 10 days—but it was nothing serious. I am feeling better now.

I have not been able to study German for some months but I want to do it again. Gnadiges Fraulein, was wollen Sie in Zukunft tun? [Translation: Gracious lady, what will you do in the future? – eds.] Are you continuing your French correspondence? I have nothing more to write today—so I shall close.

With kindest regards.

Yours sincerely

Subhas C. Bose

*c/o Dr N.R. Dharmavir*
*Dalhousie*
*Punjab*
*10.6.37*

Dear Frl. Schenkl,

I hope you are getting my letters regularly. I have been writing almost every week. This week I am writing by airmail.

My health is somewhat better now. A fortnight ago I had some throat trouble. This has subsided and I can go out now. If I stay here for some months—as I intend—I hope to get well and then go back to my work.

Who was this man with whom you were working? Do you know his name and address in India?

Last week I suggested that you should take lessons in French conversation. Please consider this, as it will be useful in future. If you can afford it, it is worth while. If you like, I may give you my suggestions as to how you could usefully spend your time in future. In case you have no job in hand, you can consider my suggestions.

Do you go to the Post office now-a-days?

I suddenly got a letter from Sen who is now in England (Edinburgh, I think) studying for his degree. He may go to Vienna again for further studies after he finishes his examinations in July. By the way, do you know anything about his friend Trude Weiss?

Mrs Vetter wrote to me some weeks ago that the Jews in Vienna are very much afraid of the future and are thinking of going over to America.

What are you doing about your health? Gestern habe ich Ihren Brief bekommen und alles verstanden. [Translation: Yesterday I have received your letter and have understood everything. – eds.] As I am a half-doctor, you should not mind my giving you some advice. Do you still have any pain in the lungs from your pleurisy? Does the gall-bladder give you any trouble? Do you make use of the electric heater? Ich kann nicht sagen wie glucklich ich bin, Ihren Brief zu lesen. [Translation: I cannot tell you how happy I was to read your letter. – eds.] In case you have any skin trouble like eczema, you may write to me. I have a simple but effective medicine which I have tried with good results.

Have you met Schwester Elvira recently? If so, please remember me to her and give her my best regards. Is her health all right now after her treatment at Franzenstad? Es freut mich dass Ihre Hoffnung ist noch grosser geworden. [Translation: I am glad that you have become more hopeful. – eds.] Do you hear from Ella now-a-days? Please give her my regards.

What is your sister studying now? Please give my best regards to your parents and my greetings to your sister. Take good care of your health. With my warmest regards,

I am Yours sincerely

Subhas C. Bose

PS Please let me know the address of Mrs Vecsei—if you are aware yourself. I am enclosing a letter for Mr Faltis.

*Vienna*
*15.6.37*

Dear Mr Bose,

Yesterday morning I got your kind letter of the 27th ult. together with the snap. Many thanks for both. Well, I nearly could not recognize you, not because of the dress, but because you are looking so thin. What a shame! You will have to be very careful now and please do eat plenty, so that you may increase a little, otherwise I shall be very sorry.

Yes, I will now write every week to you, at least a few lines, if not much. Last week I was so busy that I could not write to you but I hope you will forgive that.

No, I had not informed Demel personally about your release, as the boys have done it.

You know certainly that Dr B.C. Roy is now in Vienna. He

has brought his sister-in-law and his niece with him. There is an old Jewish lady, Miss Hermann, from Calcutta and a young Indian lady, Miss Huthisingh (or something like that) in his party too. Gairola has arranged that I am showing the ladies round a bit in Vienna and help Dr Roy when necessary. Yesterday I have been typing and translating the whole day for him. I must say, all of them are simply charming people. Dr Roy told me today what trouble Prof. Demel is taking to show him round the different clinics etc. I am just chewing Kardamon and Bethel, of which I got a whole tin full from Dr. Roy. You know how much I like these spices and that here you cannot get them. Renu (Miss Roy) and myself had a nice walk this morning and enjoyed it both. Afterwards we went to my place and had lunch there. She is now very anxious to learn some Viennese cooking. Unfortunately they are going away within a few days.

Thank God that you are feeling better now. I think the fresh air will do you a lot of good. Don't forget to take snaps there, because you know I am so fond of pictures.

I am now getting both the 'Orient' and the weekly edition of 'Patrika.' It is really kind of you, but please let me know the price, because why should you take all this trouble of paying.

Thank you for your advice for this month. As far as possible, I shall follow it. Only French is difficult, because I have no one to speak to and speaking to myself is no good.

Yes, I heard from Lowy. I am of course going to the Post Office. Today I saw Mrs Vetter and told her that you have written to me.

When I am out in the country I shall certainly read some of the books. But only now it is impossible. I have been sitting up till one o'clock last night translating. Then I could not read any more, as I had to get up at seven in the morning.

Well, I am not quite o.k. now with Sr. Elvira. Why, I do not know but she has suddenly adopted a very funny method of avoiding me. And I won't force myself on her, certainly not.

My little friend I saw yesterday after a couple of months again. She sends you best regards. To Ella I will probably write this month. I owe her already a letter since some weeks.

My lungs, throat and gall-bladder are at present very good, they don't behave badly.

Are you now near the place where Sharma is staying? In case you see him, please give my regards. Katyar wrote to me the other day that he will probably come here in the last week of June, but only when I am there. You see, old love is still good.

Tonight I shall go out with one of the Indian ladies and Gairola to 'Heuriger'. I shall drink your health with my heartiest greetings and best wishes,

Yours sincerely

E.Schenkl

PS My parents and Lotte (who is taller and stouter than myself) send you best regards. My mother was so fond of the picture you sent me that I will offer it to her for putting it under glass. But I have to say one thing. The sleeves of this nightgown-like shirt are a bit too long. Get them made shorter. Mrs Dharmavir will certainly be able to advise you.—I hope you don't mind this remark? But you know I always like to be frank.

*16.6.37*

Before sending off this letter, I want to tell you that yesterday we really went to 'Heuriger'. What a jolly time we had. There were some more Indians and a few Viennese ladies. We drank everybody's health there. Then we sang. Miss Huthisingh sang some Indian song, two of the ladies an Italian song and I sang Viennese songs. We came home very 'early'. Today I am completely finished as I had to go with Mrs and Miss Roy to Belvedere in the morning. How tired one gets of staying for hours in a picture gallery! We came home at 1.30 pm and there I just had quickly lunch and afterwards at once began to type something for Dr Roy. I rushed again to Cottage Sanatorium and now I am finishing this letter.

After dinner I shall go to sleep at once as I can't really keep my eyes open any more.

Best greetings.

Yours sincerely

E. Schenkl

*17.6.37*

Dear Frl. Schenkl,

I was glad to receive your kind letter of the 26th May on the 13th June. You must have already got my letters from Dalhousie. This is 2000 meters high—or rather more. From here we see the snow-covered mountains at a distance. On the other side, we can see the plains and the rivers still far away. It is a quiet hill-station—just what I like, so that there are not many visitors to worry me. I am glad to be away from the heat.

I hope you will have a nice time in the country. It seems that only a hot country will suit you—you are so fond of the sun! In any case, I hope you will read plenty of French there and spend your time usefully. Our life is so short that we should not waste our time but always learn something useful.

Re. Mrs F.M., when people say that they are nervous—do not believe that they are really so. With some people it is a pose. They want to show that they are nervous—like wearing a nice dress. Of course there is more nervousness among European women, because they smoke and drink too much and do not sleep regularly at night. Then a time comes when they cannot sleep, even when they want to. When this takes place, it is really nervousness. By the way, when will you give up smoking as you promised? How many cigarettes do you smoke a day?

It will be good if you practise a little music when you are at Pøllau. It will help you to spend the time, because you will not have much company there. If you can make time to write to me every week, then you need not write by airmail.

I shall enquire if any picture postcards of this place are available. If I can find some, I shall send you; also a group taken with my host and hostess at Lahore. If I can get them, I shall send by next mail.

My advice to you for the future would be as follows: (1) To keep your body fit, do excercise regularly. In Vienna you can join a gymnastic school, like the one I used to join. (2) To make yourself useful in later life—take lessons in domestic hygiene, domestic economy (household management) etc. (3) Also take training to be a competent secretary. For this, it is necessary to know book-keeping, a bit of accountancy and how to handle and arrange files (4) Learn some music—including playing some instrument—so that you can entertain yourself and also your family at times. (5) Learn as many languages as possible. It is more necessary to speak. (6) You should also know something of needlework, knitting, embroidery etc. (7) Regarding the subjects you should study—you may choose a subject which will fit in with your future work. Over and above this, you should study a little of Philosophy.

Excuse me for giving you this useless advice. You probably know much of what I have suggested. The fact is that this morning I was just in a mood to offer advice unasked-for. Now-a-days we have to post air mail letters on Thursday and Monday from here. When have you to post there? Ordinary letters we have to post on Thursday.

I am glad that you got a good rate for the exchange. You can spend the money just as you like.

Do you intend travelling as you did last year. Last year you were travelling with Schwester Elvira, I think. Are you still friendly with her and with your namesake (same name as yours) in Czechoslovakia? Do you spend much now-a-days? Have you spent what you earned last year or have you saved much out of it? I hope you will have fine weather at Pøllau. Sometimes I feel like writing in German, but I am afraid of mistakes. Shall I . . . [illegible]

*Dalhousie*
*24.6.37*

Dear Frl. Schenkl,

Many thanks for you letter of 1.6.37 and the enclosed snap. I also got your postcard from Cobenzl-Hotel. I wrote to Mrs Vetter by air mail towards the end of April and am also writing today. She feels angry when I write to other people but don't write to her—that is the whole thing!

I am sending by Drucksach-Einschreiben some picture post cards of this place—under a separate cover. They should reach you at the same time.

When you have time, please read the Bhagavad-Gita (German) and also Garner's Book in English. This will greatly help your intellectual development. Last week (airmail) I gave you a lot of advice gratis—please do not be annoyed with me for that. I had nothing better to do when I wrote.

From the snap it does not look as if you have lost any weight. What is your present weight?

No, Dr Dharvavir is not the person whose picture you once saw. He has an English wife—a very fine lady. I know them for a very long time.

Hope you are well. I am fairly well. Cordial greetings. Best regards for your parents.

Yours sincerely

Subhas C. Bose

*Dalhousie*
*Punjab*
*1.7.37*

Dear Frl. Schenkl,

I hope you have been getting my letters regularly. Last week I sent you by 'Drucksache' some picture post cards of this place. I hope you will get them in due time. Please send one or two photos of yourself and the places you visit.

There is nothing much to write this week, I am doing fairly well now—somewhat better than when I came here. But the progress is slow.

How are you keeping now? Please tender my regards to your parents. Cordial greetings for your sister and yourself,

Yours sincerely

Subhas C. Bose

*c/o Dr N.R. Dharmavir*
*Dalhousie*
*Punjab*
*8.7.37*

Dear Frl. Schenkl,

I received your letter of the 15th June on the 4th July. Many thanks. You are probably in Pøllau now.

I am going to slim now. I do not want to get fat any more. But I must get well, of course. What is your weight now please?

Why don't you do the French correspondence? When you did not have the addresses, you were so anxious. Now that you have some French addresses you do not correspond!

Mrs Vetter becomes very angry if she hears that I write to other people, but do not write to her. Please remember this.

When did you first notice the change in Schwester's attitude towards you? Can you guess the reason. Perhaps it is simply a woman's changeableness or whimsicality.

No, Sharma is far away from here—but he has written that he will pay me a visit. He visited me in Calcutta when I returned home. Katyar does not want to return home, I think.

The sleeves of my shirt cannot be made shorter—because that is the Indian style. It is not a shirt to be worn under a coat. It is a 'Kurta' or coat.

What work did you have to do for Dr Roy? Did you take any payment from him for the work?

Who was staying at Cottage Sanatorium? Somebody in Dr Roy's party?

So long—Hope you are well. I am fairly well. Regards to your parents and yourself.

Herewith some stamps.

Yours sincerely

Subhas C. Bose

*c/o Dr N.R. Dharmavir*
*Dalhousie*
*Punjab,*
*India*
*The 15th July, 1937*

Dear Frl. Schenkl,

Your letter of the 23rd June reached me on the 11th July. Many thanks. I find that you have given up typing your letters. Is it because your typewriter is out of order?

I got the snap you sent me some time ago together with the baby. But I was not satisfied with it. I can understand that you are sorry that the parents of the baby are now gone.

Please let me have news of Mr Faltis. Do you know how his Gesellschaft is getting on?

I can send you some more stamps, if you want. Last week I sent some. Do you know where and how Selig is?

I hope you have by now got the picture post cards I sent you (Dalhousie scenery).

Does Dr Roy know any German at all? Or is he quite ignorant?

I am glad to know that you are well now. I am better than before. Please convey my regards to your parents and greetings to your sister.

After I wrote the above, I got a long letter from Mr Faltis.

With kind regards

Yours sincerely

Subhaṣ C. Bose

*c/o Dr N.R. Dharmavir*
*Dalhousie*
*Punjab*
*22.7.37*

Dear Frl. Schenkl,

I was glad to get your postcard from Venice and your letter from Genoa. I shall not be able to write to you at length today, because I am late and I am just scribbling a few lines to catch the mail. I am fairly well. How are you? You must be in the country now. Whom did you meet at Genoa? Please write more about your journey—if you have not done so already.

Best regards for your parents. With kind regards

Yours sincerely

Subhas C. Bose

*Dalhousie*
*Punjab,*
*India*
*29.7.37*

Dear Frl. Schenkl,

Your letter of the 6th July reached me on the 25th inst. When you receive any letters late, please send me the covers. I am surprised that my airmail letters reached you by ordinary mail. I am complaining to the Postal authorities.

I am glad to know that your health is all right. I daresay Katyar was anxious to examine your lungs. I am glad that there is nothing wrong there. Please do not neglect the gall-bladder. You will be all right only when you are careful about diet.

I am better than before—but occasionally I have stomach trouble. I hope it will go with time. I wish I could take a month's cure at Badgastein—but it is not possible. I am glad that you have reduced your smoking slightly—but you may reduce it still further. Don't do it at once—but slowly. Then you will succeed.

I think you should try to learn as many things as possible. The more qualifications a man or woman has, the better in one's after life.

I wonder how Gairola passed his examinations. He really knows nothing about medicine.

I shall try to write to you next week in German.

I may send you some more picture postcards. But I want to be sure that the ones I sent have already reached you.

Yes, I got the snap you sent me some weeks ago. How do you weigh now?

With kind regards

Yours sincerely

Subhas C. Bose

*Dalhousie*
*Punjab*
*5.8.37*

Liebes Fraulein!

Es hat mich gefreut Ihre Briefe ans Venedig, Genua und Pollau (vom 6 und 13 Juli) zu erhalten. Ich mochte wissen wer Ihre Reise nach Genua arrangiert hat. Wer was der Herr der Sie nach Genua gerufen hat? Ich glaube dass war ein Inder—nicht wahr? Waren Sie nochmal in Venedig auf Ihrer Reise nach Wien zuruck? Was haben Sie in Venedig gekauft? Wer was der Herr fur denselben Sie einige Monate in Wien gearbeitet haben? Was sagte Herr Katyar? Ist er glucklich dass er nach Indien zuruck kommt oder ist er traurig? Was hat er so lange in Rom gemacht?

Ich freue mich dass Sie sich jetzt so gut fuhlen. Sie mussen sich immer errinern dass Sie Gallen Krank-heit haben und darum mussen Sie immer vorsichtig sein.

Von dem Postant in Bengal habe ich endlich gehort dass Ihr Packet—so wie alle andere Briefe—von letzem Dezember wurde in dem zug auf dem Weg gebrannt.

Ich war erstaunt zu lernen dass zwei Flugpost Briefe von mir waren mit der gewohnlichen Post Angekommen. Wenn mein Brief zu spat nach Wien ankommt bitte schicken Sie mir den Umschlag weil ich hier klagen mochte—oder bitte klagen Sie selbst in Wien.

. . . [illegible] die Judische Leute? Sind sie nicht von Gott auch geboren, wie die andere Leute? Studiet Franzi Weiss in Wien oder in London? Sen hat mir geschreiben dass er nach Wien fahren wird. Vielleicht er ist schon in Wien. Er wird einige Monate in Wien studien und arbeiten. Lebt Frau Vecsei noch in Pension Cosmopolite? Ihre Pension ist vielleicht jetzt geschlossen.

Es ist nicht gut dass Sie Cigaretten rauchen. 'Die deutsche Frau raucht nicht'. Ich weiss genau dass Sie ohne Cigaretten leben Konnen wenn Sie wollen. Sie mussen sich nicht zausen—scien Sie geduldig and ruhig und Sie worden Cigaretten nich branchen. Was machen Sie jetzt? Es ist besser wenn Sie fur Ihr kunftiges Leben alles vorbereiten. Man muss immer arbeiten.

Wollen Sie nich deutsche Bhagavad Gita studien? Das is nich so schwer fur Sie.

Ich weiss nich wie Gairola alle seine Prufungen abgelegt had. Wissen Sie?

Garner oder Gettel (ich weiss nicht genau) Sie haben bei Ihren in Wien. Das ist ein Buch uber Politik. Ich hatte dieses Buch fur Sie gebracht von Indien als ich in Wien war. Vielleicht Sie haben sohou vergessen.

54.5 kilos sind fur Sie zu wenig. Sie haben zu viel abgenommen. Sie mussen sich ungefahr 57 kilo wiegen. (1 kilo = 2.2 pfund)

Wenn Sie sind in Jahre 1910 ge boren—Sie sind sehr jung. Ich bin zu alt, weil ich im vorigen Jahrhundert geboren bin.

Ich fuhle mich yetzt viel besser als fruher aber ich bin noch nicht ganz gesund. Das Wetter hier ist gut obgleich es regnet oft. Die Temperatur is ungefahr 20 oder 21 C. Bei Tag und Nact ich esse, trinke, schlaffe, studie und manchmal gehe spazieren—aber selten lerne ich Deutsch.

Ich hoffe das Wetter in Pøllau ist jetzt besser und Sie Konnen Ausflug machen. Wie weit Kounen Sie yetzt zu Fuss gehen?

Bitte grussen Sie Ihre Eltern herzlich von mir. Wie ist Lotte—bitte geben Sie ihr meine besten Wunschen.

Mit herzlichen Grussen

verbleibe ich.

Ihr stets ergebener

Subhas C. Bose

PS Bitte entschuldiegen Sie meine Fehler.

Translation

Dear Fraulein,

I was glad to receive your letters from Venice, Genoa and Pøllau (dated 6th and 13th July). I would like to know who arranged your trip to Genoa. Who was the gentleman who called you to Genoa? I think it was an Indian—isn't that so? Were you once again in Venice on your way back to Vienna? What did you buy in Venice? Who was the gentleman for whom you worked for a few months in Vienna? What did Mr Katyar say? Is he happy that he is returning to India, or is he sad? What did he do in Rome for so long?

I am glad that you are feeling so good now. You must keep reminding yourself that you have a gall-bladder ailment and therefore you must always be very careful.

I have finally got to know from the post office in Bengal that your parcel—as well as all the other letters—of last December got burnt in the train on the way.

I was astonished to learn that two of my airmail letters had reached by ordinary post. If my letter reaches Vienna too late, please send me back the envelope as I would like to complain here – or you please complain yourself in Vienna.

. . . [illegible] the Jewish people? Are they also not created by God, just like other people? Is Franzi Weiss studying in Vienna or in London? Sen wrote to me that he would be going to Vienna. Perhaps he is already in Vienna. He will study for a few months in Vienna and also work there. Is Mrs Vecsei still living in Pension Cosmopolite? Her Pension is perhaps closed now.

It is not good that you smoke cigarettes. 'The German woman does not smoke'. I know for certain that you can survive without cigarettes if you want to. You should not get ruffled—be calm and patient and you would not require any cigarettes. What are you doing now? It is better if you prepare everything for your future life. One must always work.

Wouldn't you like to study the Bhagavad Gita in German? It wouldn't be too difficult for you.

I do not know how Gairola has fared in all his exams. Do you know?

Garner or Gettel (I do not know exactly), you have it at your place in Vienna. It is a book on politics. I had brought this book for you from India when I came to Vienna. Perhaps you have already forgotten.

54.5 kilos are too little for you. You have lost a lot of weight. You should weigh approx. 57 kilos (1 kilo = 2.2 pounds).

If you were born in the year 1910, then you are very young. I am too old, as I was born in the previous century.

Now I am feeling much better than before, but I have not yet fully recovered. The weather here is good, although it rains often. The temperature is approx. 20 or 21 C°. Day and night I eat, drink, sleep, study and sometimes go for a walk—but I seldom study German.

I hope that the weather is better now in Pøllau and you can go on an excursion. How far can you now go by foot?

Please give my hearty greetings to your parents. How is Lotte—please give her my best wishes.

With hearty greetings,

I always remain

Yours sincerely

Subhas C. Bose

PS Please excuse me for my mistakes.

*Dalhousie*
*12.8.37*

Dear Frl. Schenkl,

Your letter of the 20th July reached me on the 8th inst. You say that you did not get my letter that week—but I have been writing regularly every week. In case you get any letters late or in case the airmail letters go by ordinary mail—please preserve the covers and send them to me so that I may lodge a complaint here. I have already made a complaint about the airmail letters being sent by ordinary mail. They wanted the covers but I could not produce them. Mrs Vetter also complains about late delivery of my letters. Kindly write to her and ask her to send me all such covers, so that I may make a complaint here. Please tell her that I shall write to her next week. In English you should not say 'boil tea' or 'cook tea'—but simply 'make tea' or 'prepare tea'. You boil rice but not tea—because you put the tea in after you take the water down from the stove.

There is not much to write about here. It is the rainy season and we cannot always go out now-a-days. But by the end of this month, the rains will be over.

Last week, I wrote you a German letter. I hope there will be no delay in your getting it.

Miraben is Miss Slade—Mahatma Gandhi's English disciple

who has come here for a change. She had malarial fever and was run down in health when she came. She is better now and will soon be returning to Mahatma Gandhi. I shall see if I can send you a group photograph taken here.

My throat is better now—but liver and digestion (Verdauung) are not in order yet. After all, I am getting old now.

You have asked for some books about India—but I do not know if it is any use sending them. You do not read the books you already have with you. Unless you can get into a more serious frame of mind you will never like reading. You have plenty of books at your disposal in Vienna, on so many subjects—but I do not think you ever look at them.

I hope you are having a nice time and are keeping good health. I am fairly well.

Best regards to your parents and yourself and greetings to Lotte.

Yours sincerely

Subhas C. Bose

*Dalhousie*
*19.8.37*

Dear Frl. Schenkl,

I was glad to receive your letter of the 27th July on the 15th inst. I do not know why one of my letters (of the 1st July) missed the mail. Please send all the covers of my letters which show late delivery or carriage of airmail letters by ordinary mail. I have already complained at the local post office and they now want the covers. If you kindly send me the covers in future whenever there is some irregularity, I shall complain at once. I have been getting your letters regularly now.

By the end of this month the rains will probably go and then we shall have good weather. On the whole it is not so wet as it is in Darjeeling side. My weight is about 154 lbs. (1 kilo = 2.2 lbs) So I am less by about 20 lbs. compared to what I was when I left

Europe last year. But I am not anxious about weight if only I can get strong again.

There is nothing much to write about this place. I do not meet many people. My host is very strict and does not not allow visitors without any special business. Here in India when one is known, many people turn up just 'to pay their respects'. But this means wasting my time to no purpose. On the whole such visitors are less here, because it is an out of the way place. Dr Sharma came to see me last week and Dr Katyar will probably come next week.

Last mail brought in the Irish paper which you sent.

It is good to do gymnastics regularly—In that case you don't have any pain in the muscles. What kind of needlework are you doing now? Do you play the piano or the violin? By the way, why don't you learn to play the violin?

I am sorry to know that you are having trouble again owing to irregular diet.

I can write to you in German, but it takes too much of my time. But you may write in simple German. I wrote to Prof. Demel recently in German and got a reply in German too.

With regards to your parents and yourself and greetings for your sister,

I am yours sincerely

Subhas C. Bose

*Dalhousie*
*Punjab*
*27.8.37*

Dear Frl. Schenkl,

I am glad to have your letter of the 13th August which reached me on the 22nd inst. Many thanks for the snaps. They have come out quite well. I am sending you today by Einschreiben a group taken here when Miss Slade (Miraben) was here. She is Gandhi's disciple (English). After spending two months here, she has returned to her Ashram where Gandhi lives. She always wears Indian dress and has taken an Indian name. In the picture she is wearing provincial dress of the Punjab—which consists of loose trousers, loose shirt and a veil.

I am glad to know that you have again taken up French. Please write to me in German—easy style: I shall understand. But it takes me too much time to write in German.

How are you getting on with your gymnastics? You should do it regularly—otherwise you may get stiffness or pain in the muscles.

If you write to Mr Jenni, please tell him that I got his letter some time ago and shall write to him soon. Did you meet Mme. Horup when she was in Vienna or do you know her only by correspondence.

I have been writing to you regularly. Please let me know always on what date you receive my letter and also the date of my letters. Ordinary letters should take 18 days and airmail letters 7 days. If there is any delay in receiving, please preserve the covers (umschlag) and send them to me so that I may make complaints.

I do not want to send you any books until you are quite earnest about studying.

The first snap you sent me was not so good. The child came out quite good—aber Ihr Gesicht war nicht so schon in Foto. [Translation: but your likeness was not so good in the photo – eds.]

Has Dr Selig become a nun? Otherwise why should she go to a nunnery?

If the milk does not suit you, why don't you take yoghurt. It is much lighter and you can easily make it at home. By the way, do you know how to make yoghurt—otherwise I may tell you. Take a pinch (a very small quantity) of yoghurt or cream cheese or lemon-juice (citroen) and mix it with slightly warm milk and let it stand over night. In the morning you will have yoghurt. If it is too cold, leave the milk overnight in the kitchen.

I am getting on fairly well. I shall probably stay here till the end of September. If you like, always write to me in German. But I shall reply as I like according to the time it takes. Best regards to your parents and yourself and greetings for Lotte.

Yours sincerely

Subhas C. Bose

*2 September 1937*

Gnadiges Fraulein,

Ihren Brief vom 10 August (und den Artikel auch) habe ich dankend erhalten. Diese Woche schreibe ich mit der Luftpost. Sie Konnen mir allezeit deutsch schreiben wenn Sie wollen. Ich schicke hiermit einen Brief fur Herrn Sen der wieder in Wien ist. Ich weiss nicht genau wo er wohnt, aber ich glaube dass er in Alser Strasse wohnt—vielleicht in Nummer 18/15 oder in Nummer 20/15. Er hat mich geschrieben dass in Nummer 18/15 wohnen wird—aber ich meine dort wohnen die Familie Weiss. Fruher wohnte er in Nummer 20/15, wie Sie wissen. Bitte luerst versichern Sie sich wo er ist und dann schicken Sie ihm diesen Brief. Ich freue mich dass Sie haben nach Graz einen Ausflug gemacht. Ich habe gehort Graz eine sehr schone Stadt ist, aber ich bin leider niemal dort gewesen. Die Bilder von Graz (die Sie gescickt haben) habe ich noch nicht erhalten.

Wann kommen Sie nach Wien zuruck?

Wie is das Wetter jetzt in Pøllau—und wie viele Floh haben Sie schon ermordert? Konnen Sie bei nach ruhig schlafen?

Ich habe immer viele Briefe zu antworten and viele Artikel zu schreiben. Auch lese ich einige Bucher. Hier auf dem Berg habe ich keine Sekratarin bei mir. Die Wirthin, die sehr freudlich ist, tippt manchmal fur mich.

. . . [illegible] darum mussen Sir eine Nonne werden.

Ich weiss nicht was ich mit diesen Artikel tun soll. Vielleicht ich werde zu dem Redakteur (vom Interessante Blatt) klagen. Wissen Sie wer der Schreiber, Manzooruddin Ahmed, ist? Von welcher Nummer und welchem Datum ist dieser Artikel? Sie mussen immer die Nummer und das Datum schreiben.

Ich glaube Sie schon in Wien sind. Was wollen Sie dort jetzt machen? Bitte, treffen Sie Herrn Faltis und Prof Demel und grussen Sie die beiden Herren von mir. Ich habe so lange von Frau Hargrove nich gehort. Bitte fragen Sie sie, wie es Ihr geht. Von Wien bitte schicken sie ein gutes Bild von Ihnen. In Alser strasse 23, wohnt ein guter Photograph (sein Name habe ich vergessen), zu demselben ich einmal ging. Dort konnen Sie gehen wenn Sie wollen. Haben Sie gehort dass Prof. Demel am 30 August nach Indien fahren wird?

Ich habe letzte Woche einen Ausflug gemacht. Wir gingen ungefahr achtzehn kilometer spazieren. Jetzt fuhle ich mich viel besser, aber die Leber und die Verdauung sind noch nicht ganz gut. Bitte schreiben Sie was Sie in Wien machen. Wollen Sie nicht unsere Sprache vom Herrn Sen lernen? Grussen Sie Ihre Eltern von mir. Ich grusse Sie herzlich.

Ihr stets Ergebener

Subhas C. Bose

Translation

Gracious Lady,

I thank you for your letter of 10 August (along with the article). This week I am writing by airmail. You can always write to me in German, if you want to. I am sending herewith a letter for Mr Sen who is again in Vienna. I do not know exactly where he is staying, but I think he is staying in Alserstrasse—perhaps in number 18/15 or 20/15. He wrote to me that he would be staying in number 18/15—but I think that the Weiss family is staying there. As you know, he stayed earlier in number 20/15. Please make sure first where he is and then send him this letter. I am glad that you had an outing in Graz. I have heard that Graz is a very beautiful city. But unfortunately I have never been there. I have not yet got the pictures of Graz (which you have sent).

When are you getting back to Vienna?

How is the weather now in Pøllau—and how many fleas have you already killed? Can you sleep peacefully at night?

I always have a lot of letters to reply to and many articles to write. I am also reading a few books. Here, on the mountain, I do not have any secretary with me. The hostess, who is very friendly, sometimes types for me.

. . . [illegible] Therefore, you should become a nun. I do not know what to do with this article. Perhaps I shall complain to the editor (of Interessante Blatt). Do you know who the writer Manzooruddin Ahmed, is? In which number and on which date is this article? You must always write the issue no. and date.

I think you are already in Vienna. What do you want to do there now? Please meet Mr Faltis and Prof. Demel and give both gentlemen my regards. I have not heard from Mrs Hargrove for such a long time. Please enquire how she is. Please send a good photo of yours from Vienna. In Alserstasse 23 lives a good photographer (I have forgotten his name), whom I had been to once. You can go there if you wish. Have you heard that Prof. Demel will be travelling to India on the 30th August.

Last week I had been on an excursion. We walked for nearly eighteen kilometres. Now I am feeling much better, but the liver and digestion are not fully alright. Please write about what you are doing in Vienna. Don't you want to learn our language from Mr Sen? Give your parents my greetings. My heartfelt greetings to you.

Always yours sincerely

Subhas C. Bose

*Dalhousie*
*Punjab*
*9.9.37*

Dear Frl. Schenkl,

Your postcard of the 17th August reached me on the 5th inst. I do not understand why you did not get my letter when you wrote. I find from my diary that I did write to you. As a matter of fact, I do not miss any mail. If I do so, I inform you by the next mail. Whenever, any letter is delayed, please send me the cover, so that I may lodge a complaint here. And when you open a letter please see that the postmarks are not destroyed, because they will be necessary for making an effective complaint at the post office.

Perhaps you are now back in Wien. How do you feel after the change in the country? Ich werde noch zwei Monate hier bleiben. [Translation: I shall stay here for another two months. – eds.] The weather here is expected to be sunny and dry in October—and also in September, though this year it has still been raining. Wie viel wiegen Sie sich? [Translation: How much do you weigh? – eds.] On the 26th, I sent you Drucksache Einschreiben [Translation: Registered Bookpost – eds.]. Up till now I have written two letters in German. I am expecting to hear from you as to what you think of my German. The difficulty is that it takes me a lot of time to think out the German words and make them grammatically correct—whereas in English I can write straight away. Ar you still collecting stamps? I am sending you some herewith—because I do not collect any and just throw them away.

You did not write to me from Graz—but from Pøllau the day after you went to Graz, that is, on the 10th August. I have received the picture postcards you sent from Graz. Many, many thanks—they are very nice. The pictures were wrapt (sic) up in a paper on which you wrote—'20 photos and 1 envelope'. I found the 20 pictures all right—but there was no envelope. Was there any letter inside that? If so, it must have been stolen. Please let me know at once so that I may complain. It appears that special attention is paid to your letters, though for the life of me I cannot understand why this should be so.

Bitte schreiben Sie deutsch was Sie mit den Bildern geschrieben haben. In Wien Konnen Sie nicht unsere Sprache lernen?

[Translation: Please write to me in German when you write to me enclosing pictures. In Vienna can you not learn our language? – eds.]

My health is fairly well on the whole. Wir haben einen Schonen Ausflug gemacht. [Translation: We have had a beautiful outing. – eds.] When you are in Wien, please give my greetings to friends there.

With regards to you parents and yourself.

Yours sincerely

Subhas C. Bose

*Dalhousie*
*Punjab*
*16.9.37*

Liebes Fraulein,

Vielen dank fur Ihren Brief vom 25 August den ich am 12 September erhalten habe. Es hat auch hier stark geregnet und darum der September Monat dieses Jahr ist nicht schon gewesen. Ich werde wahrscheinlich noch zwei Monate aus dem Kalkutta bleiben, weil der Arzt sagt dass ich nach nicht ganz gesund bin. Wenn Sie genug zeit in Wien haben und dass moglich ist und Sie einen Lehrer haben, bitte lernen Sie unsere Sprache. Haben Sie das Englische Buch uber Regierungs Wissenschaft von Gettel (nicht Garner) dass ich Ihnen gegeben habe? Wenn Sie es haben, dam konnen Sie jetzt studien.

Ich habe yede Woche Ihnen geschrieben. Wenn Sie nicht yede Woche meinen Brief nicht erhalten haben bitte schreiben Sie mir und wenn Sie den Brief zu spat bekommen haben bitte schicken Sie mir den Umschlag.

Ich danke fur die Bilder von Ihnen aber diese sind nicht so gut.

Was macht die Indische-Gesellschaft? Nun in Wien mussen Sie Franzosich lernen zu sprechen.

Ich freue mich dass Sie mochten zu spinnen. Haben Sie ein Spinnrad? Von wo haben Sie es bekommen? Hier spinnen yeden Tag der Herr Doktor und seine Frau. Ich habe Ihren Faden erhalten (mit Ihren Briefe). Dieser Faden ist nicht von Baumwolle, wie unserer.

Sie mussen etwas strarker sein—ungefahr 57 kilo, wie fruher, nicht wahr?

Glauben Sie dass ich schreibe Deutsch besser als in Europa? Bitte grussen Sie Ihre Eltern und auch Lotte von mir. Mit besten Wunschen fur Sie, verbleibe ich

Ihr stets Ergebener

Subhas C. Bose

PS Ich mochte meinen Freund einen Rucksack beschenken. Bitte schreiben Sie was Kostet ein sehr guter Ruchsack. Konnen Sie einen mit Prof Demel oder Sen fur mich Schicken. Demel fahrt von Wein am 30 Oktober ab. Wissen Sie wann fahrt Sen ab?

S.C.B.

Translation

Dear Fraulein,

Many thanks for your letter dated 25th August which I received on 12 September. It rained very heavily here also and therefore the month of September this year was not very nice. I shall probably be away from Calcutta for two more months as the doctor says that I am not fully fit. If you have enough time in Vienna and if it is possible, and if you find a teacher, then please do learn our language. Do you have the English book on The Art of Governance by Gettel (not Garner), which I gave you? If you have it, you could study it now.

I have been writing to you every week. If you have not been receiving my letter every week, then please write to me and if you have received it too late, then please send me the envelope.

Thank you for the photos of yourself, but these are not so good.

What is the Indian Association doing? Now in Vienna you must learn to speak French.

I am glad that you like to spin. Do you have a spinning wheel? Where did you get it from? Here the doctor and his wife spin every day. I got your thread/yarn (along with your letter). This thread is not of cotton like ours.

You should now be weighing approx. 57 kilos and feeling somewhat stronger like before, isn't that so?

Do you think that I am writing better German than in Europe? Give my greetings to your parents and also to Lotte. With best wishes to you, I remain,

Ever yours sincerely

Subhas C. Bose

PS I would like to present my friend a rucksack. Please let me know what a good rucksack would cost? Could you send me one through Prof. Demel or Sen. Demel will depart from Vienna on 30th October. Do you know when Sen is leaving?

S.C.B

*Den 22 September 1937*

Geehrtes Fraulein Schenkl!

Vielen dank fur Ihren Brief vom 31 August den ich am 19 September erhalten haben. Ihr freund Katyar war kurzlich hier und ist gestern nach Hause gefahren. Ich suche ihn helfen um eine Stellung zu bekommen.

Die Juden in Europa haben so viele Stellungen erreichen, weil sie sehr geschickt sind und die Arier sehr dumm sind—anders wie Konnen die Auslander in Europe solche Fortschritte machen?

War der Brief vom 29 Juli, den Sie am 31 August erhalten haben, deutsch oder Englisch?

Warum sind Sie so nervos? Sie sind so Jung! Was wollen Sie werden wenn Sie vierzig Jahre alt sind, wie ich?

Mit grossem Vergnugen habe ich gehort dass Sie sehr viel arbeiten und besonders sehr viel lesen. Was fur Artikel schreiben Sie uber H.A. Verein und fur wen.

Sie haben gesagt dass Sie sehr Klein sind. Warum sind Sie so niedrig? Wie hoch sind Sie genau? Ich-bin einig dass wenn man dick ist, wird man faul. Darum mochte ich mager sein.

Wenn es Ihren moglich ist, bitte antworten Sie deutch.

Es hat mich gefreut dass Sie jetzt gesund sind aber Sie mussen gut schlafen. Ich glaube dass Sie zu viel denken und sich Kummern. Nicht wahr? Sie mussen immer ganz ruhig sein obgleich Sie mussen nach einer Stellung suchen.

Das Wetter hier ist momentan schon und sonnig. Wir werden gleich einen Ausflug zu Fuss machen. Es ist falsch was Sie uber

Meinen Diet gesagt haben. Ich esse nur was mein Arzt (und Wirt) erlaubt and er ist sehr straff.

Es ist sehr gut wenn Sie spinnen Konnen. Spinnen Sie noch jetzt? Was fur Wolle haben Sie? Hier spinnt man meistens mit Baum wolle.

Treffen Sie noch andere Inder? Ungefahr wie viele Inder sind dort and wie viele kommen zum klub?

Dreimat haben Sie die Bilder mir geschickt and alle habe ich erhalten. Vielen dank fur sie.

In Indien vierzig Jahre alter Mann ist schon alt-Wissen Sie?

Ich weiss nicht genau wie lange ich hier bleiben soll—Der Arzt meint dass ich muss biss 15 November auf dem Berg wohnen—hier oder anderswo. Momentan beratschlage ich meine Verwandte und spater werde ich entscheiden.

Bitte grussen Sie Herrn Timer von mir und andere Freunde auch.

Bitte sagen Sie mir was fur Traum Sie haben. Vielleicht ich kann er Klaren, weil ich Traum-pschologie etwas—studiert habe.

Ich habe nicht die Quittung von Ihren Paket von letzlein Dezember.

Bitte ubermitteln Sie Ihren Eltern meine herzlich Grusse.

Mit den besten Empfehlungen bin ich stets

Subhas C. Bose

Translation

Dear Miss Schenkl,

Many thanks for your letter dated 31st August which I received on 19 September. Your friend Katyar was briefly here and went back home yesterday. I am trying to help him get a job.

The Jews in Europe have attained so many positions because they are very skilful and the Aryans are very stupid—otherwise, how could the foreigners in Europe make such progress?

Was the letter dated 29 July which you received on 31 August in German or in English?

Why are you so nervous? You are so young! What would you like to become when you are forty years old, like me?

I heard with great pleasure that you are working a lot and especially reading a lot. What kind of article are you writing about the H.A. Verein and for whom?

You have said that you are very small. Why do you feel so low? What is your exact height? I agree that one becomes lazy when one is fat. That is why I always like to be thin.

If possible, please reply in German.

I am glad that you are healthy now, but you must sleep well. I feel that you think and worry too much. Is it not so? You must always be very calm even though you have to look for a job.

The weather here at the moment is very fine and sunny. We shall soon go trekking.

What you have said about my diet is wrong. I eat only what my doctor (and host) allows me to and he is very strict.

It is very good if you can spin. Do you still spin? What kind of yarn do you have? Here one mostly spins with cotton.

Do you also meet other Indians. Approximately how many Indians are there and how many come to the Association?

Three times you sent me pictures and I got them all. Many thanks.

In India a forty-year old man is already old—do you know that?

I do not know exactly how long I should remain here. The doctor feels that I must live in the hills till 15 November—either here or anywhere else. At the moment I am consulting my relatives and afterwards I shall decide.

Please give my regards to Mr Timer and other friends also.

Please tell me what kind of dreams you have. I can perhaps give interpretations because I have studied a bit of dream- psychology.

I do not have the receipt of your parcel of last December.

Please convey my best regards to your parents.

With best greetings,

I remain always

Subhas C. Bose

*Dalhousie*
*den 30 September 1937*

Sehr geehrtes Fraulein!

Vielen dank fur Ihren Brief vom 8 September den ich am 27 September erhalten habe; und auch fur die Berichtigungen. Ihr Freund Katyar war Kurzlich hier; er sah sehr gut aus. Er hat noch nicht entschilden was er tun wird und ich suche ihn zu helfen um eine Stellung zu bekommen.

Vielleicht fahre ich in einer Woche nach Hause, aber weiss ich nicht genau. Sie Konnen daher zu meinem Hause schreiben. Das Wetter in Oktober hier ist schonstes, aber leider kann ich nicht langer bleiben. Der Wirt und seine Frau mussen nach Lahore fahren und ich mochte auch nach Hause zuruck kehren.

Ich hore die Leute in dem Verein immer streiten. Ich glaube dass Gairola ein selbstsuchtiger mensch is und fur das Geld Geiz hat (bitte sagen Sie ihn nicht). Dennoch ist er sehr tatig. Sen ist grossmutig aber kann nicht so viel arbeiten wie Gairola, weil er studiert. Es ist besser wenn Sie zu den versammlungen nicht gehen.

Im vorhergehenden Briefe habe ich geschrieben, 'Sie mussen sich nicht zausen.' Das Wort 'zausen' bedeutet 'worry'. Bitte ubersetzen Sie 'you must not worry'.

Wenn Sie meine Fehler berichtigen bitte schreiben Sie nur die Worter.

Haben Sie das Buch von Gettel uber Regierungs-wissenschaft schon gefunden? Wollen Sie es nicht lesen?

Wie fuhlen Sie sich? Mir geht es ziemlich gut.

Ich bitte Sie Ihren Eltern herzliche Grusse zu ubermitteln.

Mit den besten Empfehlungen bin ich

Ihr sehr ergebener

Subhas C. Bose

PS Antworten Sie immer deutsch. Wenn Sie den Umschlag zuruckschicken, bitte schicken Sie mit den Brief marken.

Ich schicke hiermit einige Brief marken

S.C.B.

Translation

My dear Fraulein,

Many thanks for your letter dated 8 September which I received on 27 September, as well as for the corrections. Your friend Katyar was recently here. He looked very good. He has not yet decided what he would like to do and I am trying to help him find a job.

I shall perhaps go home in a week, but I don't know exactly. Therefore you can write to my home address. The weather is best here in October, but unfortunately I cannot stay longer. My host and his wife must go to Lahore and I would also like to return home.

I hear that the people in the Association are always fighting. I think that Gairola is a self-centred person and has greed for money (please do not tell him). Nevertheless, he is very active. Sen is courageous and large-hearted, but he cannot work as much as Gairola because he is studying. It is better if you do not go to the meetings.

In the previous letter I wrote. 'Sie mussen sich nicht zausen'. The word 'zausen' means 'worry'. Please translate as 'You must not worry'.

When you correct my mistakes, please write only the words.

Have you already found Gettel's book on The Art of Governance? Wouldn't you like to read it?

How are you feeling? I am fine.

I request you to convey my hearty greetings to your parents.

With best wishes,

I remain yours sincerely

Subhas C. Bose

PS Always reply in German. When you send back the envelope, please send it with the stamps. I am sending herewith some stamps.

S.C.B.

*Vienna*
*30.9.1937*

Dear Mr Bose,

When I sent off my letter by ordinary mail to you on Wednesday I had forgotten to inquire about one important thing from you for the Association though I had promised to do so. Therefore I have to write this airmail letter and request you to answer it by airmail, if possible.

We want to know the Rules and Regulations of the National flag.

[Illustrations of flags]

Now, which figure is the right one? In the papers it was said that A is correct. But there exists one Indian flag here in Vienna in which the spinning wheel is done like in B. They want me now to paint for their use two *flags* and nobody knows which is the right one. They are greatly worried about that (I can't really understand what there is to worry about.) Please find out and let me know otherwise those fellows will make my life miserable. As if I had nothing else to do than sewing and painting flags!

Then there is something else. I know it is impertinent but still I venture to request you to give a small donation to the Association. Perhaps some of your friends could also donate something. You see, there are so many things to be bought and there is not much money at hand. Dr B.C. Roy has for instance paid to keep a clerk for 6 months. But I am sure the boys had also to spend some of this money on paying rent for the rooms, papers, etc. They do not dare to request you, so I undertake this very unpleasant job without their knowledge. And please try to send or give them 2 or three books for the library which they want to start.

You may imagine now, how many things there are to worry me! Awful! If you have any idea what they should do re: the pushing of the association, please write what you suggest.

I hope you will forgive me that I give you all this trouble, though I know quite well how busy you are. But they really need help.

I read in the patrika of this week your terribly long article about the prospects of the European situation for future. How can one write such long articles. It was quite interesting, however, though I do not understand anything of politics. It took me nearly 2 hours to read it. I am attempting now to read the book you gave me as birthday present in 1935. 'Welt Pølitik von Heute' by K. Hanshofer. It is very cleverly written, but he has a horrible style. I first thought, I am the fool and don't understand it. But today my father got hold of the book and he says the same. He also has to read it twice or thrice before he understands what he means.

How is your health? Is the liver still troubling you? I have got a bad cold, but it looks as if it would stop soon.—My mother went for x raying last week and the result is—gall-bladder inflammation. So I am at least not alone. Thank God, I don't have any pain now-a-days.

I would like to write a few articles about India together with a journalist and put those articles in the Austrian papers. Could you suggest where to get the necessary information? I want to write about things like: family life, wedding ceremonies, etc.

I just remember now that the Puja festival must be over by now. Allow me to send you Bijoya greetings.

Is there anything I can do for you? If so, please don't hesitate to tell me. I shall gladly do whatever is in my power.

Do you want any of your books which are lying in Vienna? Now that you are again working you might require some. I shall send them to you. But I won't send them with anybody going to India, but only by post, as you know, how little one can rely on people in this case. They simply forget about the books.

Once more I have to beg your pardon for giving you all this trouble.

With my best wishes and warmest greetings,

Yours sincerely

E. Schenkl

*7.10.37*

Dear Frl. Schenkl,

I had your kind letter last week. I am now on my way to Calcutta and am writing in the moving train. I shall reach Calcutta after a few hours. After resting for a day or two, I shall proceed to Kurseong (near Darjeeling) where I intend spending some weeks. Please write to me to my Calcutta address.

From Dalhousie, I sent you by Book-Post (Drucksache) a magazine called 'Asia' and by Registered (Einschreiben) Book Post—two books. Hope you will receive them duly. I am fairly well. Hope all well there.

With kind regards

Yours sincerely

Subhas C. Bose

*Kurseong, D.H. Ry*
*Bengal*
*13.10.37*

Dear Frl. Schenkl,

Your ordinary letter of the 21st Sept; and your airmail letter of the 30th Sept. are both to hand. I suddenly left Dalhousie on the 5th inst. and came here through Calcutta where I met my mother and other relatives. I am now staying at Kurseong with my brother. I wrote to you last week in the train and I hope you will get this letter in due course.

I am enclosing a letter for Prof. Demel which you will kindly forward to him. Please phone to him and tell him that you will translate the letter for him if necessary.

I am writing this in a hurry and will write fully by next ordinary mail. I am enclosing the correct flag and colours as desired by you. What happened to the flag we had at the Bristol Hotel?

I am sorry I cannot give any money to the Association as subscription until I know what they are doing. Up till now, I have been very much disappointed with them. I do not think there is much use in wasting your time and energy over them. I do not want to give away [last few lines of this letter are missing]

[This letter was handwritten by Subhas Chandra Bose in block letters in German. It is clear from a small notation in the bottom left hand corner and the context that it was written on 4 November, 1937 – eds.]

GNADIGES FRAULEIN,

VIELEICHT (sic) ICH FAHRE NACH EUROPA AM MITTEL NOVEMBER. YETZT (sic) BIN ICH NICHT SICHERLICH. ICH WERDE IHNEN NACHSTE WOCHE BESTIMMT SCHREIBEN. ICH MOCHTE 4 ODER 5 WOCHE IN BADGASTEIN FUR KUR BLEIBEN. DANN KOMME ICH AM MITTEL DEZEMBER NACH HAUSE ZURUCK. BITTE SCHREIBEN SIE KURHAUS HOCHLAND, BADGASTEIN, UND FRAGEN SIE OB DORT ICH (UND SIE AUCH) BLEIBEN KANN. ICH MUSS DORT IN EINEN MONAT EIN BUCH SCHREIBEN, WIE IN 1934. FRAULEIN REICHHART IST YETZT (sic) FRAU HELMIG (WIRTHIN VON KURHAUS HOCHLAND) BITTE SCHREIBEN SIE IHR UND FRAGEN SIE WAS MUSS ICH ZAHLEN. IN 1936 HABE ICH ZEHN SCHILLING BEZALHT (INCLUSIVE) MIT KURTAXE UND GEMEINDE TAXE. ICH WERDE VIELLEICHT IN AEROPLANE FAHREN. BITTE ANTWORTEN SIE MICH NICHT. WENN ICH FAHRE, WERDE ICH IHNEN TELEGRAPHIERE WANN KOMME ICH NACH NAPOLI. VON NAPOLI KOMME ICH IN EINEM TAG NACH BADGASTEIN. SIE MUSSEN NACH BADGASTEIN KOMMEN VOR MIR UND MUSSEN SIE 'RECEIVE' MICH AUF DEM BAHNHOF. ICH WERDE

IHNEN AUF DEM WEG TELEGRAPHIEREN—(CARE POSTE RESTANTE, BADGASTEIN) WANN KOTIME ICH NACH BADGASTEIN. SIE KONNEN DANN AUF DEM BAHNHOF FUR MICH ERWARTEN.

BITTE SAGEN SIE DIESE NACHRICHT NUR IHR ELTERN.

ANTWORTEN SIE MICH NICHT UND ERWARTEN SIE MEINEM NACHSTEN LUFT POST BRIEF (ODER TELEGRAMM). YETZT (sic) BIN ICH NICHT SICHERLICH UBER MEINE REISE 4 11/37.

## Translation

DEAR GRACIOUS YOUNG LADY,

I SHALL PROBABLY TRAVEL TO EUROPE IN THE MIDDLE OF NOVEMBER. I AM NOT YET CERTAIN. I SHALL BE WRITING TO YOU NEXT WEEK CONFIRMING IT. I WISH TO SPEND FOUR OR FIVE WEEKS IN BADGASTEIN FOR CHANGE. THEN I SHALL RETURN HOME IN THE MIDDLE OF DECEMBER. PLEASE WRITE TO KURHAUS HOCHLAND, BADGASTEIN, AND ENQUIRE IF I (AND YOU ALSO) CAN STAY THERE. THERE IN ONE MONTH I MUST WRITE A BOOK AS IN 1934. MISS REICHHART IS NOW MRS HELMIG (PROPRIETRESS OF KURHAUS HOCHLAND). PLEASE WRITE TO HER AND ASK HER HOW MUCH I HAVE TO PAY. IN 1936 I PAID TEN SCHILLINGS (INCLUSIVE) WITH HEALTH TAX AND ESTABLISHMENT TAXES. I SHALL PROBABLY TRAVEL BY AIR. PLEASE DO NOT REPLY TO MY LETTER. IF I COME I SHALL SEND YOU A TELEGRAM AS TO WHEN I SHALL REACH NAPLES. FROM NAPLES I SHALL COME TO BADGASTEIN IN ONE DAY. YOU MUST REACH BADGASTEIN BEFORE ME AND MUST RECEIVE ME AT THE RAILWAY STATION. I SHALL TELEGRAPH TO YOU WHILE ON THE WAY (CARE POSTE RESTANTE, BADGASTEIN) WHEN I AM ARRIVING IN BADGASTEIN.

PLEASE MENTION ABOUT THIS MESSAGE *ONLY* TO YOUR PARENTS.

PLEASE DO NOT REPLY TO ME AND WAIT FOR MY NEXT AIRMAIL LETTER (OR TELEGRAM). I AM STILL NOT CERTAIN ABOUT MY TRIP. 4/11/37

*[Telegram dated 16.11.37]*

RADIOGRAMM

GLP/KJ 1150
W10 CALCUTTA 31 15 1125 =
DLT SCHENKL FERROGASSE 24 18 VIENNA =

STARTING AEROPLANE ARRIVING BADGASTEIN TWENTY SECOND ARRANGE LODGING AND MEET ME STATION SHALL WIRE YOU POSTRESTANTE BADGASTEIN ON TWENTY FIRST FROM NAPOLI REGARDING ARRIVAL TIME BADGASTEIN = BOSE

*[Telegram from Rome dated 21.11.37]*

TELEGRAMM

SCHENKL
POSTERESTANTE

ARRIVING VILLACH MONDAY 14/26 TAKING NEXT TRAIN.

BOSE

*8.1.38*

I am now having coffee at this Munich station with some Indian friends. All well.

Warmest greetings to all—regards to your parents.

Subhas C. Bose

*Antwerp*
*10.1.38 8am*

Dear Frl. Schenkl,

Just a line to say that I am just leaving for London. I am not going by train to Ostend. My friends are taking me in their car. So I can start from here late—otherwise I would have to start very early.

The train from Munich was very crowded—a lot of English passengers. I am all right.

If you get a film called Parnell there about Ireland—please see it—it is very good. We saw it last night. Hope all well. Regards and greetings.

Yours sincerely

Subhas C. Bose

*Artillery Mansions*
*3M Flat*
*Victoria Street*
*London S.W. 1*
*Monday 11 pm*
*[11.1.38 – eds.]*

Dear Miss Schenkl,

I arrived here this afternoon at 5.20 pm and had a good reception at the station. The sea was not so róugh. This evening I had a conference with Pressmen. I shall have a very busy time here as long as I shall be here. From Salzburg to Munich I had a nice journey. From Munich to Brussels it was very crowded and I could not sleep at all. I had a nice time with Indian friends at Antwerp and they brought me in their car to Ostende. And after the crossing I am here. How are you? I don't think I can stop at Vienna—but you need not tell anybody now.

Please excuse wretched handwriting. Can you read it?

Yours sincerely

S.C. Bose

*Artillery Mansions*
*Victoria Street*
*London S.W. 1*
*16.1.38*

Dear Miss Schenkl,

I have been frightfully busy these days and so could not write. I have recd. your two letters—many thanks.

Please buy the two watches *in steel* about which you enquired—the Diplomat no. C.K.124 and the doctor's watch no. 651 Square —both Omega. The lady's watch (Longines) you cannot get there —I understand. I shall send you money by airmail tomorrow. Please draw from the money American Express and buy the watches and come to the aerodrome. I reach Vienna at 8.40 am and again take off at 10.30 or 11 am. I am not writing to anybody else. I reach Prague on the 19th and spend the night there. On the 20th inst. I leave. [last portion of letter is missing]

*[Telegram from Prague dated 19.1.38]*

TELEGRAMM

SCHENKL
FERROGASSE
24 WIEN

BUY TWO WATCHES MEET AERODROME +

*Hotel Quirinale*
*Roma*
*20.1.38*

Dear Frl. Schenkl,

I won't have time to write to you from Naples, so I am scribbling a few lines from here. I arrived safely. We did not halt at Venice but some other airport where there was no arrangement for lunch. That was the only difficulty. Here it was all right. I am now on the point of leaving for Naples. I am rather tired, otherwise I am all right.

Hope you are well. Best wishes. Regards to your parents.

Yours sincerely

Subhas C. Bose

*Hotel Grande-Bretagne*
*Le Petit Palais*
*Athenes*
*21.1.38 Night*

Dear Frl. Schenkl,

I wrote to you from Rome by air mail and you should have got the letter by now. I am now on my way as you will see from the address. The weather was bad between Naples and Athens—a strong wind blowing straight against us. We arrived here late and could not proceed to Alexandria, as we should have done according to the programme. The Captain says that this will not affect our time of arrival in India—as he will make up for the time lost. I am writing to you again today because I have a little time in hand and because I shall have no time when I reach India. I hope you will not mind if I cannot write to you regularly in future. Please do not worry about imaginary things and take good care of your health.

Kindest regards—also to your parents.

Yours sincerely

Subhas C. Bose

Tomorrow 22nd night in Basra (Iraq)—23rd night Jodhpur—24th morning (noon) Calcutta.

Convey my message to Mr Faltis and Bad . . . [illegible] Bureau. Hope you have informed Herr Holme by now.

S.C.B.

You need not always tell people there that you have heard from me.

S.C.B.

*[Telegram dated 24.1.38 from Calcutta]*

RADIOGRAMM

40 + CALCUTTA 6/5 24 1505 EMP MCI

LC = SCHENKL FRANCEHOTEL VIENNA =
SAFE +

*[Telegram dated 24.1.38 from Calcutta]*

RADIOGRAMM

117 CALCUTTA 8/7 24 1740 EMP =
LC = SCHENKL FRANCEHOTEL WIEN =
HEARTFELT CONDOLENCE = BOSE +

*38/2 Elgin Road*
*Calcutta*
*or 1 Woodburn Park*
*Calcutta*
*25.1.38*

Dear Frl. Schenkl,

I arrived here safe yesterday and at once got into a crowded life. I have sent you a wire yesterday as follows—'Safe'. This was followed by another wire—'Heartfelt Condolence'.

I am terribly grieved to have the sad new of your father's death. Please let me know at once how this happened. It is so sudden! so awful! Was it some accident or some sudden illness? Please accept my sincerest and heartfelt condolence and convey same to all the members of your family.

I am sending herewith some Italian money. Please change it into Austrian money and use it. I am also sending you L 1/-

In haste and with all my sympathy in your grief.

Yours sincerely

Subhas C. Bose

*1 Woodburn Park*
*or*
*38/2 Elgin Road*
*Calcutta*
*8.2.38*

Dear Frl. Schenkl,

I reached Calcutta on the 24th January and was at once thrown into a whirlpool of activity. I cannot tell you how grieved I was to hear of the death of your dear father. I have been wondering how it could happen so suddenly. I thought you would write to me in details—but you have not. Please let me know at once how such a tragic event could take place so suddenly. Perhaps you have been too busy yourself to write to me.

I had to go out of Calcutta on the 28th for our Provincial Conference. I returned on the 31st and left again on the 1st February to attend the Working Committee (Party Executive) meeting at Wardha. From there I returned only yesterday. At Wardha, I met Mahatma Gandhi, Nehru and all the big leaders. I shall leave again for Haripura Congress on the 11th inst. I am now trying to make time to write my speech.

I sent you two telegrams from here on the 24th January—one about my arrival and the other about your father's death. I then wrote a registered letter on the 25th (or perhaps 27th) January. Did you receive the letter intact? Please let me know by airmail.

Please write to me also as to what you are doing now-a- days.

I hope you are getting the Patrika regularly. I shall renew its subscription in time. Do you want the Orient?

I shall be at the Congress from the 13th to the 22nd inst. From there I shall go to Bombay and I shall then return *to Calcutta by the end of this month.*

Please write to me as regularly as you can. How are you? My regards to your mother and yourself. Greetings to Lotte.

Yours sincerely

Subhas C. Bose

PS My address in Bombay will be c/o Bombay Provincial Congress Committee, Bombay. You can expect a remittance from me via London.

S.C.B.

*38/2 Elgin Road*
*Calcutta*
*Haripura Congress*
*16.2.38*

Dear Frl. Schenkl,

This is just a line to say that I am now at the Haripura Congress—very busy. Hope you are well. I have received only one air mail letter from you so far—the airmail postcard did not arrive—I do not know why.

Your article on Badgastein has appeared in the Modern Review for February. Let me know if you have not got it. I leave this place for Bombay on the 23rd inst. From there I go to Calcutta after a week. Best wishes and greetings.

Yours sincerely

Subhas C. Bose

*Wardha*
*6.3.38*

Dear Frl. Schenkl,

Many thanks for your letters of the 4/2 and 18/2. I left Haripura on the 23rd Feb. and had a very crowded time at Bombay. Bombay gave me a magnificent reception. I left Bombay yesterday and am now on my way to Calcutta. I shall be in Calcutta for 3 weeks and then begin touring. Your letter of the 18th Feb. I received in Bombay.

I have not received your airmail card and your ordinary letter of the 26th January. The former is probably lost and the latter is probably lying in Calcutta. My mail from there has not been redirected.

Please let me know if your mother will get any pension or not. If she gets, will she get the same as your father was getting.

I shall write to you at greater length from Calcutta. Now I am writing in great haste. I have to go now to see M. Gandhi who lives in a village (Segaon) 7 miles from this town.

I feel very very sorry for your family. Please give my regards to your mother. Greetings for Lotte and yourself.

Yours sincerely

Subhas C. Bose

PS How is your health? Any gall-pain?

S.C.B.

*ALL INDIA CONGRESS COMMITTEE*
*38/2 Elgin Road, Calcutta*
*(or 1 Woodburn Park, Calcutta)*
*28.3.38*

Dear Frl. Schenkl,

I am sorry I have not been able to write to you ever since I came to Calcutta from Wardha, obgleich ich denke immer an sich [Translation: even though I always think of you – eds.]. I have been terribly busy since I came here—but hence forth I shall write to you regularly. Now-a-days, the airmail to Europe goes 4 times a week. I wish your mother a quick and complete recovery and I hope she will be freed from her pains once for all after the successful operation. I shall try to write to you at some length during the course of this week. Ich schicke Ihren acht Pfund mit Luft post in einigen Tagen—hoffe es wird Ihnen etwas helfen [Translation: I am sending you eight pounds within a day by airmail—hope it will be of some help to you – eds.]. I am sorry I am beginning to forget my German once again.

I hope you will take all the care of your health that is possible. I also hope that you will now consult the doctors and find your health in order. You promised to do so. Now that your mother is back home, you should find a little time to look after your own health. I am always glad to receive your letter, though I may not have time to write to you. I am sorry to know that Mrs Vetter is so angry with you. So far, I have not received the airmail letter (postcard) you wrote soon after your dear father's death. The other letters I have got. I shall give you a list of them in my next letter. Your last letter gave a short description of Vienna after the Anschluss. Please give my regards to your mother and accept greetings for Lotte and yourself.

Yours sincerely

Subhas C. Bose

*ALL INDIA CONGRESS COMMITTEE*
*38/2 Elgin Road, Calcutta*
*5.4.38 (Tuesday)*

Dear Frl. Schenkl,

I hope you got the letter I wrote on the 28th inst. Did you get the Lira and pound notes I sent you soon after I returned home in January last?

I am awfully busy now as the Working Committee meeting is going on form the 1st April. We are sitting from morning till night. I am well but overworked. Ich habe acht Pfund letzte Woche geschickt—haben Sie beKommen? [Translation: I have sent eight pounds last week—have you received it – eds.]

How are you getting on and your mother? Is she all right? Please give her my regards and accept my greetings—also for Lotte. Ich denke an Sich bei Tag und bei Nacht. [Translation: I think of you day and night – eds.] Hope you are well. With best wishes

Yours sincerely

Subhas C. Bose

*President:*
*Subhas Chandra Bose*
*ALL INDIA CONGRESS COMMITTEE*

*38/2 Elgin Road*
*(or 1 Woodburn Park)*
*Calcutta*
*9.4.38*

Liebes Fraulein!

Ich vorstelle zu Ihnen meinen Freund Herr Seal (von London) der von Indien nach England fahrt zuruck. Ich schicke Ihnen mit ihm diese vier Sachen—Elfenbein-Halsband—ein paar Schuhe—Broche und ein Kastchen (mit Elfenbein und Sandale-Holz gemacht). Herr Seal wunscht das schone Wien zu sehen. Bitte helfen Sie ihn. Mit grossen Empfelungen fur Ihre Mutter und besten Wunschen fur Sie und fur Lotte. Ihr stets ergebener

Subhas C. Bose

PS Please send 6 copies of the speech to Prague.

S.C.B.

Translation

Dear Fraulein,

I am introducing to you my friend Mr Seal (from London) who is returning to England from India. I am sending you with him these four things—a necklace of ivory—one pair of shoes—a brooch and a small box (made of ivory and sandalwood). Mr Seal wishes to see beautiful Vienna. Please help him. With kind regards to your mother and best wishes for you and for Lotte.

I remain, yours sincerely,

Subhas C. Bose

*ALL INDIA CONGRESS COMMITTEE*
*In the train to Bombay*
*9.5.38*

I am now proceding to Bombay where I shall be for ten or 15 days. Please reply by air mail to the following address: c/o N.D. Parikh, 26 Marine Drive, Backbay Reclamation, Bombay. After 15 days I shall leave Bombay. You may then write to my Calcutta address—38/2 Elgin Road, Elgin Road P.O. Calcutta—where I am staying with my mother. My telegraphic address is—SUVASBOS, Calcutta. I have some important work in Bombay—(1) to discuss with Mr Jinnah the proposal for Hindu-Muslim understanding. (2) to preside over the Conference of the Prime Ministers of seven provinces. (3) to preside over the meeting of the Congress Working Committee.

My last letter to you was dated the 9th April in which I wrote a few lines through a friend proceeding to Europe. Since then, I have not been able to write to you. Please excuse me. I have been terribly busy. But I shall try to be more regular in future. Your subscription to 'Orient' has been renewed for 6 months. Do you want the 'Patrika'? If you have time to read, I shall of course renew it with pleasure.

I hope your mother is now doing well. What does she think of the operation now—when the agony is over once and for all? My sister-in-law had the operation last year and after the removal of the gall-bladder is relieved of the daily pain. It is difficult to write in a moving train—hence the bad handwriting.

Waren die Schuhe passend für Sie? Und had der Schachtel noch schonen Geruch von den Holz? [Translation: Did the shoes fit you?

And did the box have a nice smell from the wood? – eds.] / I do not know if my German is understandable.

I regret very much to say that I have not made any progress with my book since I returned home.

Bitte Schreiben Sie mir gewohnlich; Ich freue mich Ihren Brief zu lesen, obgleich ich kann nicht gede wochen schreiben Sie mussen dafur mich entschuldigen. [Translation: Please write to me regularly; it makes me happy to read your letters, although I cannot write to you every week for which you must excuse me. – eds.] Your letter of the 28th April reached me on the 4th May.

The trouble about the Congress flag which the Vienna papers reported was in the state of the Maharajah of Mysore.

I should like to know what happens as a result of you application to the Telegraph office. Wenn Sie etwas brauchen, bitte schreiben Sie mir. [Translation: When you come to know, please write to me – eds.]

Please write to me about friends there. I am sorry I have had to stop correspondence—no time! Herr Faltis has written to say that he is enthusiastic about the new regime.

I am sorry to know that you are not keeping well. Here we are groaning under the heat and are anxiously looking for some rain to cool the dry earth. Haben Sie den Arzt besucht, wie Sie zu mir versprochen haben? Und wie geht es Ihnen? Sie mussen immer vorsichtig sein. [Translation: Have you visited the doctor, as you had promised me. And how are you now? You must always take care of yourself. – eds.]

I have done some touring during the last 2 months—but inside Bengal province. Now I am travelling form one end of the country to the other.

Many thanks for the German magazines which you have kindly sent me. I have enjoyed the pictures but have had no time to read the text. Please let me know if there are any articles which are worth reading and if so in which magazine.

I duly received the nice postcard you sent me jointly signed by your friends and yourself. I have forgotten to inform you that I got your long letter of the 24th January which described the sad death of your dear father. It was somehow mislaid, but I got it after all.

Then I also got your letter of the 29th March. Did you go to Bad Pistyar in March or April as you said you would? Why don't you go there now on a month's holiday? Or at least a fortnight?

Hat der Direktor von Bad Pistyar bezahlt Sie fur die Artikel? [Has the Director of Bad Pistyar paid you for the article?]

I saw your article in Modern Review about Pistyar but not in Orient. Do you want any copies of these journals containing your article? I shall write to Von Have soon. You must also go on writing to him. My health is on the whole fairly good—only I have more work to do than I can manage.

I got the copy of Interresantes Blatt in which there was a picture of M. Gandhi and also of myself. I also received your letter of the 15th April. I must post the letter now—so I shall stop here. How are you all?

Yours sincerely

Subhas C. Bose

*Bombay*
*20.5.38*

Dear Frl. Schenkl,

Your airmail letter of the 12th inst. reached Calcutta on the 18th and was sent forward here, reaching me today. Many thanks for the same. I am sorry I have not written to you for a long time. I wrote to you, however, in the train on the 9th inst. when I was coming to Bombay. I have had a very busy time here. I have sent you some papers by ordinary post last week and also this week. In Calcutta I arranged to send you 'Orient' again. Please let me know your daily programme. How are you now? Did you consult the doctor and follow his treatment? Has he been able to put you right? I am glad to know that your mother is feeling better now. Please give her my best regards. I am keeping fairly well, though I am overworked. Ich denke an Sie bei tag und bei Nacht. [Translation: I think of you day and night – eds.] I am going to Poona tonight and shall return to Bombay on the 23rd. I shall then leave Bombay for Calcutta on the 24th or 25th. Poona is 4 hours' journey from here. Soll ich Ihnen etwas feld schicken? [Translation: Should I send you some money? – eds.] Please reply to this letter to Calcutta. Please accept my warmest greetings.

Yours sincerely

Subhas C. Bose

*President:*
*Subhas Chandra Bose*
*ALL INDIA CONGRESS COMMITTEE*
*Telegrams: SUVASBOS, Calcutta*
*Telephone: PARK 59, Calcutta*

*26 Marine Drive, Bombay*
*24.5.38*

Dear Frl. Schenkl,

Many thanks for your kind letter of the 15th inst. and 17th which reached Bombay on the 22nd. Your previous letter of the 12th inst. reached me on the 20th inst. and I have already replied to it. After visiting Poona for a couple of days I am now back in Bombay and am leaving for Calcutta tonight. Please reply to me there. Wie viel bekommen Sie von dem Telegraphen Amt? [Translation: How much do you get from the Telegraph Office? – eds.] I shall arrange to send you the Patrika when I am back in Calcutta.

I am writing to Von Have. If you have his address, you may also write to him.

When you use Austrian stamps, I find that you use 1 Schilling 8 Groschen—but when you use German stamps you use 70 Groschen and 25 Pfennig. What is the reason? 25 Pfenning should be equal to 50 Groschen!

I think you should meet Mr Faltis once and give him my best regards.

Is unemployment better now in Vienna?

I am sorry to hear that you have been feeling unwell. I am afraid that you are not taking proper care of your health. When will you do so? I am keeping fairly well—though I am overworked. With kind regards

Yours sincerely

Subhas C. Bose

Please forward the accompanying to Von Have. I have forgotten his address.

S.C.B.

*ALL INDIA CONGRESS COMMITTEE*

*In the train*
*26.5.38*

Dear Frl. Schenkl,

I wrote to you the other day from Bombay. Perhaps I shall not be able to write to you again for some time—so I am writing to you in the train. It is 36 hours journey from Bombay to Calcutta. I was sorry to learn from your last letter that you were not keeping well. I am afraid you are not taking proper care of your health. I understand that you have had considerable strain since your father's death and too much work at home. I hope you will now visit the doctor and get thoroughly cured of all your troubles. Why don't you take a week's holiday (or two weeks') and go for rest-cure? Please correspond with Von Have on my behalf. I think I have left his address there. Will you kindly send it to me? Ich werde von Hause Ihnen etwas geld schicken—Dass ist nur fur Ihre gesundheit. Warum besuchen Sie den Arzt nicht? Wie geht es Ihnen jetzt? Wie viel bekommen Sie von dem Telegraphenamt? [Translation: I shall send you some money from home—that is only for your health. Why don't you see the doctor? How are you now? How much do you get from the Telegraph office. – eds.]

I sent you some Bombay papers when I was in Bombay. Has

Amiya's friend visited Vienna yet? Wann wollen Sie nach Ihren Hause Kommen? [Translation: When will you come back home? – eds.]

I have already subscribed to Orient for you and shall arrange to send Patrika also. Please let me know how you spend your time now-a-days. What is your sister doing now-a-days? I am afraid that the pension your mother is getting now-a-days is not sufficient for the family. Please send me news of Mrs Miller and Mrs Vetter. Some time ago you wrote to me saying that Mrs. Vetter was again very nice to you and had made up with you. But in your last letter you tell a different story. Why don't you make up with her? Please give Mr Faltis and Mrs Faltis my best regards. How are the boys getting on with the association now? If you have any spare time, please let me know. I may then make some suggestions as to how you could prepare for your future career so that you may get quick promotion. Please make a note of my telegraphic address— SUVASBOS, Calcutta. I shall have to come to Bombay again in June. Ich denke immer an Sie. [Translation: I think of you always – eds.] I am fairly well.

Yours sincerely

Subhas C. Bose

*38/2 Elgin Rd.*
*Calcutta*
*8.6.38*

Your airmail letter of the 30th May reached me on the 14th June. Many thanks. I was glad to learn that you had passed your examination. How many hours have you got to work every day at the Buro? I left Calcutta on the 8th May for Bombay and returned on the 29th May, after visiting places on the way. I am now leaving Calcutta on a tour in the districts of East Bengal. I shall return home on the 18th June and shall probably leave Calcutta again after 2 or 3 days. Please reply to this letter to my Calcutta address where I am staying with my mother—38/2 Elgin Road, Calcutta. (Telegrams SUVASBOS, Calcutta)

Yes, I am rather overworked now. I cannot find sufficient time—I have so much to do. It is not so hot here now because we are having rain occasionally. For your mother, the best thing is occasional fasting—at least once a fortnight—preferably twice.

I am now in a hurry and shall end here. Ich schicke heute Ihnen etwas fur Sie. [Translation: Today I have sent you something for yourself. – eds.]

Hope all well with you.

Yours sincerely

Subhas C. Bose

*26.6.38*

Dear Frl. Schenkl,

I have not been able to reply to your letters for some time past. I was out on tour from the 8th to the 20th June in the interior of Bengal. I had some excitement one day when stones and bricks were thrown at our procession. I had a slight injury but am all right now. I left Calcutta ( to meet Mahatma Gandhi at Segaon near Wardha) on the 22nd June and am now returning to Calcutta. I am writing this in the train. Calcutta is 24 hours journey by train from Wardha. In spite of continuous travelling, I am keeping fairly well. I have put on weight, I think, which I do not like. I shall have to return to Wardha again on the 8th July for the meeting of the Congress Working Committee.

Many thanks for your ordinary letter of the 31st May and your airmail letter of the 15 June. I am glad to know that you expect an increment in your pay soon. Today's papers in India say that in Austria the government has ordered all factories to dismiss Jewish employees. If this is done, then there will be few Jews left in Vienna.

Please let me know what reply you receive from Have. If he does not pay now, then I shall formally transfer my claim to you. Can you find the letters which Have wrote to me acknowledging the money? They may be necessary.

I am glad to know that you are taking care of your health—though this statement contradicts another statement you made in your previous letter that you were not keeping good health. The small photo you sent was a good one—one of the best I have seen so far. If you have a bust taken of this pose from a short distance, it may turn out to be a good one. You have promised to send me a good photo. A postcard size photo will do.

If you feel tired or overworked, you should take Hellsicol. It is a good tonic. I can get this in Calcutta now—so I am taking it now-a-days. Yes, you should go to the doctor and get completely cured now that you have occasionally some time to yourself. Why don't you take a 'kur' at Badgastein this autumn? It will do you good.

The moment I reach Calcutta I shall be plunged in work and shall not have time for correspondence; hence I am writing in the train. During the whole of this year I shall have to do a lot of travelling. Please write to me from time to time, even if I do not write regularly. I have now a Secretary who knows German. If you have any spare time, please let me know. I may be able to give you some advice as to how you could usefully spend that time. Have you forgotten your German and English shorthand? Please give my regards to your mother and accept same yourself. Greetings to your sister.

Yours sincerely

S.C. Bose

*27.6.38*

On reaching Calcutta I found your airmail letter of the 20th inst. (German). I am sorry that you got only 12.30 mark for the pound or 18.45 schillings. This means that you lose now—because formerly you would get 25 or 26 schillings. How are the prices now when you calculate in marks, instead of schillings? Indian students will be better off because they will be able to get registered marks. Hope you are taking care of your health. Do you remember anything of German and English shorthand?

Kind regards,

Yours sincerely

S.C. Bose

*38/2 Elgin Road*
*Calcutta*
*8.7.38*

Dear Frl. Schenkl,

I have not heard from you for some time past—of course, I have been at fault in not writing to you. I have been moving about a lot. On Monday, the 4th inst. I had an attack of influenza from which I am still suffering. Hence I have a little time in hand, though I am still bothered by visitors.

I have renewed your subscription to the A.B. Patrika. Your subscriber's number is 1805. The subscription is from 15.3.38 to 14.9.38. Have you been getting the paper after 15.3.38?

How are you? Did you visit your doctor, as you said you were going to? I believe that foreigners in Austria will now suffer because they will get less in marks than they used to get in schillings. At least, that is what I noticed in your case.

The papers here say that people in Austria are dissatisfied with the new government. This must be altogether false—because everything seems to be quiet. Any news of my hostess in Badgastein? Any news of any other friends?

I hope to hear from you when you have time. Do you remember your English and German shorthand?

Kind regards

Yours sincerely

Subhas C. Bose

*38/2 Elgin Road*
*Calcutta*
*14.7.38*

Dear Frl. Schenkl,

Many thanks for your letter of the 6th inst. which reached me on the 11th. I have been down with influenza for a week but am feeling better now. I shall be leaving for Wardha on the 21st to attend the meeting of the Congress Working Committee and shall be back after a week. My German-knowing Secretary is gone and I have not appointed another in his place yet. He was not hard-working. I am anxious to know if Von Have replies to you. By the way, do you know if Indians in Vienna can receive registered marks as they can in Germany? That will be some help to the Indian students there—otherwise they will find living very expensive in Austria now. I am enclosing the receipt from Patrika office. So you will be getting both the Orient and the Patrika for a few months. When the time for renewal comes, please let me know in time and I shall arrange for it. Ami's father tells me that he wants to go to Vienna to bring the books, but his father thinks that it is not safe to go to Austria—so he asked me to request some friends in Vienna to send Ami the books he wants. It is amusing how people think of conditions in your blessed country. I shall be grateful if you kindly do some work for me. A firm of publishers is bringing out a book containing my speeches and writings. I think I preserved all the articles I wrote when I was in Europe. Could you collect them and send them to me by registered post? It will mean a lot of trouble for you, but will be a real help to me. These articles and statements are wanted by the publishers. You wrote to me some time ago that your father had written something about me in his diary (20th January) I would like to know what he wrote. I hope this will find you quite well. My regards to your mother and yourself. Greetings for Lotte. What does the doctor say about your health?

Yours sincerely

Subhas C. Bose

Ich Sehe Sie haben einen weisse mantel gekauft. Mit dem Sie sehr gut ans sehen. Was haben Sie bezahlt? Aufwiedersehen

[Translation: I see you have bought a white coat. It suits you very well. How much have you paid for it. So long.]

*President:*
*Subhas Chandra Bose*
*ALL INDIA CONGRESS COMMITTEE*

*Wardha*
*27.7.38*

Dear Frl. Schenkl,

My letter of the 8th inst. reached you on the 14th, while your letter of the 15th inst. reached me on the 19th. I left Calcutta on the 21st. to attend a meeting of the Working Committee. I am going back to Calcutta tomorrow morning, reaching there after 24 hours. We had a busy and anxious time here—a ministerial crisis. You will read about it in the papers. I am sorry to know that you are as careless as ever and have not been to the doctor yet. Until you write to me that you have been to the doctor and have placed yourself under his treatment, I shall not write to you again. The time you waste in writing letters, you can usefully spend at the doctor's. Has Ami been there? I have not written to him for a long time. I shall send you the Indian sagas with great pleasure—but only when I hear from you that you have started your treatment. I am all right now—except that I have more work than I can manage. I have written to my uncle asking him to correspond with the gentleman in Germany for stamps. Have you heard from Von Have yet? I hope you are getting both the papers regularly now. How are you spending your time now—when Lotte is away? You must be feeling lonely. Your mother must be glad and also proud of you that you are working now. What is the German for friend—isn't it Liebling? I had been to see Gandhiji at his ashrama this afternoon. There was an Englishman who has become a monk. Then there was a German lady too. His English disciple—Miss Slade or Miraben was of course there. There is nothing more to write today—so I shall end. Aufwiedersehen mein kleines Liebling! [Translation: So long, my little darling. – eds.]

Yours sincerely

Subhas C. Bose

*In the train*
*3.9.38*

Dear Frl. Schenkl,

I think I have almost forgotten what litte German I knew—so I shall try a few lines today.

I do not have Have's home-address. He used to change his flat very often and latterly he gave me only his Postal address. What shall I do? Why don't you write to Polizeiamt in Berlin for his address? Will it be any use my sending you his old Wohnung address? He may not be there now.

Thanks very much for the cuttings and articles. They must have given you a lot of trouble.

It was not necessary to have a German-knowing Secretary, but it so happened that he knew German.

I got a letter from Lotte from Breslau in English. I wonder who wrote it. Did she?

Thanks for the extract from your father's diary. Now—

Ich habe Ihre Brief vom 25 Juli, 10 August und 25 August

dankend erhalten. Ich habe zu erst gedacht Ihnen nicht zu [ . . . one line illegible] sehr unvorsichtig sind. Heute schreibe ich nur einmal. Wenn Sie den Arzt besuchen, dann werde ich Ihnen mit grossem Vergnugen, wie immer, schreiben. Aber wenn Sie nicht wie ich sage machen, dann kann ich nicht wieder schreiben. Es tut mir leid dass Sie noch nicht gesund sind, obgleich habe ich Ihnen so oft gesagt dass Sie den Arzt besuchen und ganz gesund sein mussen.

Diese Tage habe ich zu viel Arbeit und habe keine zeit fur mein korrespondenz. Jetzt fahre ich nach Wardha und schreibe auf dem zug. Ich hoffe dass Ungefahr 6. September Komme ich nach Kalkutta zuruck und dann fahre ich nach Madras auf eine lange Reise.

Ich freue mich dass Sie jetzt R.M. 100 prs Monat verdienen Konnen. Bitte schreiben Sir mir wenn Sie etwas brauchen.

Errinern Sie noch sich die Familie M. (in Karlovyvary). Jetzt ist Herr M. von Herzkrankheit sehr gekrankt und hat daher Pension genommen. Ich habe Ihnen vielmals gesagt dass er gleich krank Sein wird. Leider ist er arm. Glauben Sie dass ich den Unterschied zwischen Freund und Liebling vergessen habe. Ich bin nicht so dumm wie ich sehe aus. Ich habe jetzt keine zeit zu rasten (rest). Ich muss mindestens bis Februar ohne unterbrechung arbeiten. Ich danke Ihnen vielmals fur den schonen Fotographie; Jeden Tag sehe ich ihn vielmals und es hat mich sehr gefreut. Bitte schicken Sie mir noch einen wenn Sie anderen haben.

Wie geht es jetzt Ihrer Mutter. Ich hoffe sie fulht sich viel besser.

Ich hoffe Sie haben schon einen Freund von den Direktorn gefunden-ja, ich habe den Artikel von Orient gelesen. Was glauben sie? Hat er richtig geschrieben? . . . [illegible] jetzt wohne ich noch mit meiner Mutter. Ich habe von Frau Hargrove nicht gehort. Ein Flugpost Brief von Indien nach Europa ist noch zu teuer, aber nach England sehr billig. Mit besten Wunschen, verbleibe ich Ihr ergebener,

## Translation

I have received your letters of July 25, August 10 and August 25 for which thanks. I first thought . . . very careless about your health. I am writing only for once today. If you see the doctor, I will be writing to you as always with great pleasure. But if you do not do as I ask you to, then I cannot write to you again. I feel sorry that you are not in good health although I have asked you so often to see the doctor and be perfectly healthy.

Nowadays I have too much work and do not have any time for my correspondence. Now I am on my way to Wardha and am writing from the train. I expect to return to Calcutta around 6 September and then I shall proceed to Madras on a long tour.

I am happy that you can now earn R.M. 100 per month. Please write to me if you need anything.

Please remember me to family M. (in Karlovy Vary). Is Mr M. now very ill with heart disease . . .

Subhas C. Bose

*Bombay*
*13.10.38*

Dear Frl. Schenkl,

I was so glad to get your letter of the 16th Sept on the 3rd October. The delay was due to the fact that I was then at Delhi. I left Calcutta by aeroplane on the 23rd for Delhi. I had to halt at Cawnpore where I fell ill. From there, after recovery, I proceeded by 'plane to Delhi on the 26th Sept. I had a very busy time there and left for Bombay on the 5th October. Here I again fell ill from Malaria. After three days the fever left me and I am now convalescing. Your letter was registered. Many thanks for the snap—though I must say that the other one is somewhat better.

I do not remember if I have replied to Lotte. Have I? Please let me know.

At Cawnpore I met your friend Katyar. He is now doing well and earning well. I also met Singh at Delhi. He is back home.

I am glad to know that your mother is better now. I believe

living is more costly in Vienna now than before. We have often news about Austria in our papers but not in favour of the present regime.

My South India tour has been postponed. Instead, I had to go to Shillong (Assam—NorthEast) and from there to Delhi. From Bombay I go to Calcutta on the 15th inst via Nagpur. From Calcutta I have again to go to Shillong and then to South India.

Please take good care of yourself when you are crossing the road. You are generally so careless!

I am sorry to know that the Major died in Vienna.

Please let me have news of Frau Vetter—if you have any. I understand that the H. Academical Association has shifted from Hotel de France to Marianeu Gasse—for the same reason that you do not go to that Hotel.

Is Vienna more lively than before or is it much the same?

Please give my best regards to your mother and greetings to your sister. Herzliche Grusse and gute Wunsche für Sie—mein Liebling! [Translation: Heartiest greetings and good wishes for you—my darling – eds.]

Yours sincerely

Subhas C. Bose

PS I am all right now—though slightly weak. This will go in a few days time. S.C.B.

*Wardha*
*17.10.38*

Dear Frl. Schenkl,

I wrote to you by airmail from Bombay. I am now on my way to Calcutta—but doing some touring and lecturing on the way. I reach Calcutta on the 20th. I am writing this in the train—hence this shaking. I fell ill twice—once at Cawnpore on the 23rd Sept. and again at Bombay on the 5th October. I was flying in a special aeroplane from Calcutta to Delhi and halted at Cawnpore on the way where I got fever. After recovery I proceeded by aeroplane again to Delhi. From Delhi I proceeded to Bombay on the 5th October—to fall ill again. Now I am all right. From Calcutta I go to Shillong the capital of Assam (North East of India). After returning from Assam I shall go on a long tour. I have not gone to South India yet—because of several reasons.

Bitte schreiben Sie mir manschmal Deutsch. Ich bin erstamt zu horen dass des major gestorben ist. [Translation: Please write to me off and on in German. I am sorry to hear that the major has died – eds.] I hope you have been able to go to Pøllau for a holiday which you need very badly. You must not overwork and must take care of your health. Haben Sie den Arzt schon besucht? [Translation: Have you already seen the doctor? – eds.]

I hope you take care while crossing the road because the traffic is now changed from left to right.

I do not know why my letters take so much time now-a-days to reach you.

I think I have already replied to your letter of the 16th Sept. This photograph is not so good as the previous one. Ich fuhle mich immer ganz allein, obgleich arbeite ich sehr viel, bei tag und bei nacht. Das leben ist schwer fur mich, aber was kann ich tun?

Was machen Sie jetzt? Und was denken Sie? Hoffentlich Sie sind jetzt ganz gesund.

Viele liebe fur mein Liebling. Bitte grussen Sie Ihre mutter und schwester von mir [Translation: I feel completely lonely all the time, even though I work hard day and night. Life is hard for me, but what can I do?

What are you doing nowadays? What are you thinking? I hope you are now fully in good health.

Much love for my darling. Please greet your mother and sister on my behalf. – eds.]

Yours sincerely

Subhas C. Bose

*En route to Lucknow*
*19.11.38*

Dear Frl. Schenkl,

I am sorry I have not written to you for a long time. Perhaps three of your letters have not been answered by me. Please excuse me.

I am glad to know from your last letter that you are taking good care of you health. Please let me know how you feel after your return from hospital. It is not good that you feel so much run down now. May I give you one advice? Please take HELLSICOL regularly—it will do you a lot of good. This tonic is now available in India and I take it regularly. Another thing—SANATOGEN. It is a German product and should be cheap in Vienna now. Please take it with milk at least once a day and you will see what a change it will make. Will you take this advice from me? I use both these things and I know what difference they have made to me.

Do you get the papers regularly? About a month ago I renewed the Patrika for another six months. What about Orient? Do you get it regularly? Is it necessary to renew it? If so, please let me know.

I am now going to Lucknow and from there to Cawnpore where I hope to meet Katyar. After that, I shall be going to Lahore. Then I return to Calcutta for a short visit. From Calcutta I go to Wardha and from there to South India. The South Indian tour has been continuously postponed. I shall be in Calcutta in the first week of December—at Wardha on the 8th December and after that in South India.

Your short letter of the 10th inst. reached me on the 11th inst. This was written before you went to hospital. Your letter of the 28th Oct. was also to hand duly. Have I written to you that I got both the snaps. The first one was better. I am sorry that you are so overworked. Do you have depend on your mother now-a-days? What is Lotte doing now-a-days? Mit besten Wunschen fur mein Liebling [Translation: With best wishes for my Darling – eds.]

Yours sincerely

S.C. Bose

*Jodhpur*
*6.12.38*

Dear Frl. Schenkl,

Your letter of the 21st Nov. reached me at Karachi this afternoon. I have been touring Upper India since the middle of last month (viz. U.P., Punjab and Sindh). I have been constantly moving from place to place. I am now flying to Calcutta (now halting at Jodhpur for the night) from where I shall go to Wardha on the 9th inst. by train. After 4 or 5 days at Wardha, I shall begin my South India tour. This will take me till the end of December.

I take this opportunity of sending you my heartiest Xmas greetings and best wishes for a happy new year. May be I shall not be able to write to you frequently when I am on tour but please excuse me. Do write to me when you have time. I pray that God may shower his choicest blessings on you and that the New Year may bring you plenty of health and happiness.

I was sorry to read your fever chart. Please have yourself examined by Prof. Wilhelm Neumann for the lungs at once. He is the best man for lungs, I think. Please do not neglect the lungs. Where did you have the operation and who operated on you? Did you have the gall-bladder removed also? Miss Bannerji who was introduced to you by Amiya called on me a month ago at Calcutta and conveyed your greetings and message to me. Family M. are now in a bad way because M. has had to retire. Please write to me all about your health. I am anxious to know how your are keeping at present. Was your mother in Vienna? When did she return from Breslau?

It is doubtful if I shall be re-elected President for the coming year. Many people are jealous of me. Herzliche grusse, mein Liebling! [Translation: Heartfelt greetings, my Darling! – eds.]

I am well-despite the strain of constant travelling and lecturing.

What about the papers? Are you getting the Orient all right? Please let me know when renewal of subscription will be necessary.

Do you have time to read the Patrika? Dr Sharma came to see me in Calcutta and I met Mathur at Lahore. He has got a good job.

Yours sincerely

Subhas C. Bose

*In the train*
*10.12.38*

Dear Frl. Schenkl,

I am now on my way to Wardha. I shall be there for 4 or 5 days and from there I shall go to Bombay. From Bombay I shall go to Madras on the 18th or 19th inst. and I shall be touring in Madras Presidency for 2 weeks, or perhaps three. You may write to me c/o Provincial Congress Committee, Madras. I shall return to Calcutta on the 8th or 9th January.

I am so glad to know that you are out of hospital and back at home. My nephew writes to say that he will be spending a month in Vienna. Perhaps he is there already.

Your last letter is dated the 1st Dec. and I got it just before I left home. The one before that was dated the 21st Nov. written from hospital and I have already replied to it. Please write me full details about your life in hospital. Where were you? Who operated on you? Did they remove the gall-bladder also? How do you feel now? I am rather anxious about your lungs. You should be examined once by a specialist. Please do not neglect this.

I do not know why your letters take so much time to reach me. You must have noticed that my letters reach you much sooner.

Are you getting any temperature now? Have you joined your Buro yet? Do you feel strong enough to work? I hope you will try Sanatogen and Hellsicol. Both have done me good.

What does your doctor say about your throat? What is wrong with it?

This time I have toured in U.P., Punjab and Sindh. Sometimes I had to lecture 10 times a day and work 17 or 18 hours a day.

Nevertheless, I am well. The climate in winter is agreeable and I could therefore work so hard.

I hope that you will now take jolly good care of your health and not fall ill again.

There is some opposition to my re-election as President and I do not know what will happen. In any case, I shall have to work very hard till the end of February.

I met Miss Bannerji for a short while some time ago. She spoke about you. She also said that Vienna had changed considerably.

Please give my best regards to your mother and cordial greetings to Lotte. I wish you the best of luck and good health. I also wish you a very happy Christmas and New Year. I wonder how you will be feeling this Xmas and on New Year's Day. Lest I forget, please accept my best wishes and congratulations on your birth-day—und herzliche Liebe, mein Liebling! [Translation: and heartfelt love, my Darling]

Yours sincerely

S. C. Bose

*Bombay*
*26.12.38*

Dear Frl. Schenkl,

Many thanks for the book of pictures of Austria which you sent me the other day. It reached me on the 24th inst. Today is your birthday. I wish you all the best in the world and pray that you may have happiness and peace in the service of mankind—as well as the fulfilment of your heart's desires.

I am leaving for Wardha today and from there I start for Madras tomorrow. I left Calcutta on the 9th inst. for Wardha where we had the Working Committee meeting till the 16th inst. From Wardha I came here and was unwell all these days with throat trouble. I am now going on a South India tour. I shall be back in Bombay on the 10th inst. From here I go to Bardoli on the 11th inst. and the Working Committee will meet there. After the meeting I come to Bombay on the 15th January for a day or two and then return to Calcutta.

I am sorry I have not written to you for a long time—though I have been expecting your letter every day. I am anxious to know all about you health—please write in detail.

Best wishes for a happy New Year and many many returns of the same. I should like to know how you spend New Year's Eve this time. With best wishes.

Yours sincerely

Subhas C. Bose

(Christmas Card with picture of 'Lady hawking (perhaps Chand Bibi, queen of Bijapur')

With Best Wishes for a Happy Christmas and a Bright New Year

from Subhas Chandra Bose

Dec. 1938

*Wardha*
*4.1.39*

Dear Frl. Schenkl,

In my last letter I wrote to you that I would be going on a South-India tour. Once again difficulties have arisen. I came here (Wardha) from Bombay on the 27th December to meet Mahatma Gandhi and I should have left the same day for Madras but I fell ill. This time it has been throat and nose trouble. I had awful pains in the face and high temperature. The pains have subsided now, but a slight discomfort in the face and a low temperature is continuing. I hope to be quite well in 4 or 5 days' time. I shall then be going to a place called Bardoli—north of Bombay—where the Working Committee will meet on the 11th January. After a few days, I hope to return to Calcutta, where I shall stay for 8 or 10 days. Then if all goes well, I shall go to South India in February.

I have not got your letter for a long time. May be it is lying in Calcutta. My mail has not been forwarded to me from Calcutta for 8 or 10 days, because of the sudden change in my programme due to illness. But I have sent instructions to Calcutta and the accumulated mail will be coming here tomorrow. I am very anxious to know about your health. Please write me a long letter about you stay in hospital—how you liked the doctors, nurses, medicine, treatment, etc. In which hospital were you? Did you have the gall-bladder removed in order to relieve you of after-dinner pains?

Though there is a very general desire for my re-election as President—I do not think that I shall be again President. Some people have been telling Gandhiji that a Muslim (Mohammedan) should be made the President this time and that is also his feeling—but I have not had any talk with him up till now. In a way, it will be good not to be president again. I shall then be more free and have more time to myself. The election will take place by the end of this month.

Und wie geht es Ihnen, meine Liebste? Ich denke immer an Sie bei Tag und bei Nacht. [Translation: And how are you, my dearest? I think always of you day and night.]

I suppose you have enough work now to keep your hands full at home and in office. By the way, what is that instrument which you play at home? Is it the guitar? How long did you absent yourself from office? It will be good if you could go to Gastein or somewhere for 'Erholung' [Translation: recovery – eds.]. Please let me know how Herr and Frau Helmig are getting on. I suppose they are getting lots of guests now. Best regards for your mother and heartiest greetings for your sister and yourself und Liebe fur Sie [Translation: and love for you – eds.]

Yours sincerely

S. C. Bose

*11.2.39*

Dear Frl. Schenkl,

I am sorry I have not been able to write to you for a long time. Please excuse me, as I have been very busy these days. I have been re-elected as President for another year. Mahatma Gandhi and his lieutenants opposed me and Pandit Nehru was indifferent. The result of the election is a great victory for me. The whole country is full of excitement over the election, but a terrible responsibility has come on my shoulders. My work has increased considerably and I can hardly manage it now.

Where and when did you get the news of my re-election? I believe the news was cabled to all the papers in Europe. My nephew in England got the news the next morning—30th January. Did you rejoice over my victory?

Your letter of the 21st Dec. was to hand duly. From it, I got the news of your life in hospital. Are you feeling quite all right now?

How did you find my nephew in Vienna? Did you see any change in him? I mean either physical or mental change. He wrote to me that he liked Vienna immensely.

I was ill for a fortnight towards the end of December and beginning of January. Now I am well. I had throat and nose trouble.

Many, many thanks for the Xmas present you sent me—the book of pictures—which I liked so much. I am sorry that I cannot sent you anything because I am afraid that the zoll-amt will charge you too much. Can you find out if there is any arrangement whereby I can pay the duty (tax) here-in advance and you will not have to pay when you receive the parcel there? In that case I may send you something.

Can you please send me the date and exact time of your birth and the place of birth?

Please take Hellsicol and Sanatogen regularly. I hope you will act according to my advice which is based on experience. Ich denke immer an Sie—Warum glauben Sie nicht? [Translation: I think of you always—why don't you believe it? – eds.]

Please spell 'zero' and not 'cero'.

Your letter of the 21st was sent to Madras but I got it all right. I had to postpone my Madras tour owing to my illness.

Your letter of the 19th January was also to hand. I hope that the change at Weyer has done you a lot of good. How are you now in Vienna?

Do you want the Orient? Please let me know.

I have also got you letter of the 1st February which you wrote after getting the news of my re-election. Ich weiss nicht was ich in zukunft tun werde. Bitte sagen Sie was ich machen soll. [Translation: I don't know what I should do in the future. Please tell me what I should do.]

This letter is in reply to 3 of your letters. What about your typewriter? Viele liebe und Herzliche Grusse [Translation: Much love and heartfelt greetings – eds.]

S. C. Bose

*Jealgora*
*19.4.39*

Dear Frl. Schenkl,

It is quite an age since I wrote to you last. I wonder what you have been thinking of me for not replying to your letter all these days. I promise to write to you more regularly in future. I must complain that you too do not write as regularly as before.

I fell ill on the 15th February and have been ailing since then. Such a prolonged and acute illness I have not had for years. Only now I am getting well. I shall be leaving for Calcutta on the 21st inst.

While I was still ill, I went to Tripuri for the annual session of the Congress over which I was to preside. But this aggravated my illness. After the Tripuri Congress I came to this place in the province of Bihar to stay with a brother. But as soon as I am in Calcutta I shall have hard work again.

Do you get the Patrika now? Do you get time to read it? If so, you will be getting the important news. Please let me know when it is time to renew the paper.

Perhaps you know that I was re-elected President in spite of the opposition of the Gandhi group. They were greatly annoyed that I defeated their candidate. Gandhiji himself called my victory a defeat for himself. Ever since the election I have had great trouble with the Gandhi group and the trouble is not over yet. There is much conflict within the Congress, following my re-election, and this is the creation of the Gandhi group.

You will be interested to know that the Government of India have removed the ban on my book 'The Indian Struggle.' So the book can come to India now.

How is your health now? After the operation are you feeling quite well? Did the change do you much good? How is your daily work now-a-days? How do you spend the rest of the time? Have you any friends?

I wish I could go to Badgastein for 'nach-kur' [Translation: convalescence – eds.]. But I do not know if I can spare the time and the money. By the way have you any news of Frau Helmich of Badgastein? Is she still running her Pension? Are they getting more visitors and tourists than before?

Bitte entschuldigen Sie mich dass ich Ihnen nicht geschrieben habe. Aber ich denke an Sie jeden Tag wie fruher. Denken Sie auch an mich? Wirklich? [Translation: Please forgive me that I have not written. But I think of you every day as before. Do you think of me also? Really? – eds.] So you see I have not forgotten my German altogether—though I never have time to read or write. Bitte fragen Sie Helmich was ich bezahlen soll wenn ich dorthin fur kur komme. Wie fruher oder mehr? Und konnen Sie dorthin komme wenn ich fur kur komme? Wollen Sie Erlaubnis haben von Ihren Chef? [Translation: Please ask Helmich what I will have to pay if I come there for a cure. As before or more? And can you come there if I come for change. Will you have permission from your employer? – eds.]

My last letter to you was written about the 10th January. And you replied to it on 2.3.39. So you are also to blame! By the way, have you been taking Sanatogen and Hellsicol?

I was sorry to hear of the death of your cousin—dentist. Please accept my sincerest condolence. It must be so trying to see one relative after another leaving this world.

Do you have time to meet any of your old friends—I mean our common friends? I have not written to them for a year—but I shall begin correspondence again. Please give my best regards to your mother and greetings to Lotte. Und für Sie alle Liebe und beste Wunsche. Auf wiedersehen [Translation: And for you all my love and best wishes. Till we meet again.– eds.]

Yours sincerely

S. C. Bose

PS May I give you one advice? I think there is a lack of Iodine (JOD?) in your system. That is why your neck and throat are thicker than usual. Please consult a doctor if should take JOD/ in some form. This is important.

S.C.B.

ALL INDIA CONGRESS COMMITTEE

*Train*
*14.5.39*

My dear Frl. Schenkl,

I am sorry I have not been able to write to you earlier. I have been very busy for the last few months and I was ill from the 16th February to the 10th April. I went to the Tripuri Congress in a sick condition. However, I am well now—though the weakness is still there. Since the 21st April I have again been plunged in hard work. I am now going to a Conference in United Provinces (north India). I shall probably return to Calcutta on the 18th inst.

You may have heard by now that I have resigned the Presidentship of the Congress, because I could not come to an agreement with Mahatma Gandhi and his orthodox followers. It so happens that though I had a majority among the 3000 delegates of the

Congress—I do not have a majority among the 400 members of the All India Congress Committee. After the Congress is over, the All India Congress Committee carries on the work of the Congress for 12 months, till the next Congress.

I have not lost anything by resigning. As a matter of fact I have become more popular now.

I got your letter of 2.2.39 duly—but I am afraid that I did not reply to it so far. Jeden Tag denke ich an Sie. [Translation: Every day I think of you.– eds.]

I hope you have got my letter which I wrote from Jealgora where I was convalescing after the Tripuri Congress. I have now got your letter of the 17th April. Re. your going to Munich, the main point is as to your future prospects in the service. At present you will not get much in Munich—in fact, you may be worse off than in Vienna. In Vienna, you have the flat and you can share so many things with your family. In Munich, you will have to pay separately for everything. Now, you should find out whether you will get more in future in Munich or in Vienna. According to your future prospects you should decide whether to go to Munich or not. If the future prospects are bright in Munich, then you may go there—otherwise you may stay on in Vienna. If in future also you will get only 200 R.M. as against 140 R.M. in Vienna—you should stay with your family in Vienna.

Please pardon the delay in writing to you. Now that I am better, I shall write to you more regularly in future. Viele Liebe wie immer. [Translation: Much love as always.– eds.]

Yours sincerely

S.C. Bose

*In the train*
*15.6.39*

Dear Frl. Schenkl,

I am now in the train, proceeding to Lahore and from there to Peshawar (north west India). From there I shall go down to Bombay, reaching Bombay on the 21st June. I shall be in Bombay for some time and shall proceed to South India. I shall reach Calcutta on the 8th or 10th July. May be I shall return to Calcutta straight from Bombay—in which case I shall be home by the end of June.

From now, I shall also write to you regularly—that is once a week. I hope you will also have time to write. Many thanks for the small snaps you have taken and which you have sent along with your kind letter of the 30th May. This letter reached me on the 9th June because I was out on tour inside Bengal. (I had been to Dacca) But the letter reached Calcutta on the 5th June.

My resignation was the only right step for me to take. It has made me tremendously popular in some places (e.g. Bengal) and among all progressive people—but the Gandhiites are naturally angry with me. But that does not matter. I have, however, got more work in hand than before. I am now organising a new Bloc (or party) within the Congress, called the 'Forward Bloc', consisting of all radical and progressive elements. For this I have to work very hard and do a lot of touring.

India is a strange land where people are loved not because they have power, but because they give up power. For instance, at Lahore I had a warmer welcome this time than when I went last year as Congress President.

*21.6.39*

I am sorry I could not post this letter earlier. I have now finished my visit to Lahore and Peshawar and am in the train for Bombay. I shall be in Bombay for at least one week, if not more. After Bombay, I may visit South India.

At Lahore I was pickpocketed. A thief stole some money and letters from my pocket when I was in the midst of a big crowd. Among the missing letters was your letter and the snaps. I am sorry. If you can, please send me a postcard size photo of yours taken by Chitil. You sent me two post card size photos some months back. These two I have also lost after having them with me for some time.

I have to go through hard physical strain. I am sorry I cannot take rest now, because this is just the time to work— though from the health point of view I should go for a change now. I am thinking of working in June and July and then take rest in August. In August we have the rains and it is difficult to tour about. Bitte Warten Sie bis August—vielleich komme ich dann nach Gastein. Wenn ich dort komme, mussen Sie auch dorthin Kommen. Wollen Sie Kommen? [Translation: Please wait till August—probably I will come then to Gastein. If I come there you must also come. Will you come? – eds.] I do not have any time to read German now. Do you read the Indian papers? You should. Have you read the Bhagavad Gita? By the way, have I told you that my nephew Asoke is married? My second nephew, Amiya, is coming home from England in the last week of this month. Wann Kommen Sie nach Indien? Wie geht es Ihnen und Ihrer Mutter? Viele Liebe und gute Wunsche. [When will you come to India? How are you and your mother? Much love and good wishes. – eds.]

Yours sincerely

S. C. Bose

*Jubbulpore*
*4.7.39*

Dear Frl. Schenkl,

I was glad to receive your letter of the 23rd June at Bombay a couple of days ago. The letter was redirected to Bombay from Calcutta. I left Calcutta on the 14th June and have been travelling in Punjab and Frontier Province. From there, I went to Bombay via Delhi. Now I have come to Jubbulpore (Central Provinces). After a couple of days I shall be going either to Calcutta or to Bombay. The next few weeks I shall be touring continuously. My health is not yet O.K. and I am still weak. But there is so much of public enthusiasm that I must work, regardless of health. We are now organizing a new party within the Congress—the 'Forward Bloc'. Everywhere I am getting much support. I am now thinking that I shall work for one month more and then take rest for one month at least. For example, if I take rest from August 15th to September 15th—I shall then be able to work again till the end of the year. Henceforth, I shall write to you more regularly than before. My last letter to you was on the 21st June, which I posted in Bombay. You must have got it by now.

I am glad to know that you are doing well on the whole. I hope you have got over the effects of operation. I think you should take a cure at Gastein—it will make you feel all right again. I hope your gall-bladder trouble has not appeared again. If you go to Gastein, the best time will probably be August or September—not too hot nor too cold then.

My nephew who was studying in Cambridge has come home on leave. He will be staying for a couple of months or more and then return to Cambridge.

I got the letter which you sent me a month ago along with some snaps. Unfortunately, I was pickpocketed and I lost the snaps along with some money I had in my pocket. Perhaps you could send me one postcard size photo from Chitil. Those two postcard size photos I have also lost, after keeping them with me for several months.

Why did you have to learn French? Did you study again—or was your previous knowledge of French sufficient to enable you to pass this examination?

*6.7.39 (Train)*

I am now returning to Bombay after finishing my work at Jubbulpore. I do not know when exactly I shall return to Calcutta—because I have to tour a lot. However, please write to 38/2 Elgin Road, Calcutta and I shall get the letters all right.

I am glad that you had your examination in French and that you passed that examination. Will you have to learn any other language?

I must take a month's holiday at least—but I do not know if the holiday will begin in the middle of August or the beginning of September. It cannot be before the middle of August.

I am fairly well—in spite of travelling and hard work. Ich denke immer an Sie. Viele Liebe wie immer. [Translation: I think of you all the time. Much love as always. – eds.]

Yours sincerely

S. C. Bose

*Berlin*
*3.4.41*

Dear Frl. Schenkl,

You will be surprised to get this letter from me and even more surprised to know that I am writing this from Berlin. I arrived in Berlin yesterday afternoon and would have written to you at once—but I was kept busy till evening. Most of the hotels are full and with difficulty a room could be found for me. I am shifting to another hotel today—'Nurnberger Hof'.

My future programme is not settled—but in all probability, Berlin will be my headquarters. I do not know if I shall be able to come to Vienna. So you must come to Berlin to meet me. Can you come? You can understand how glad I would be to meet you.

It is possible that I may require a Secretary here. If so, can you come? Will your mother and sister agree to it?

My passport is not in my name but in the name of Orlando Mazzotta. So when you write, you will have to address me as Orlando Mazzotta. Please treat as *strictly confidential* the fact that I have come here. You may however tell your mother and sister, provided they do not speak to anybody else.

Kindly let me know by return of post—1) If you can work as my secretary *here*, if I do need a Secretary for my work here. 2) What salary you will require if you come to Berlin. 3) What salary you are getting at present. 4) In which Buro you are working now and what your hours of work are. 5) Whether you have kept your telephone and if so, whether you have the old number R 60-2-67. 6) Can you take a short leave from your Buro and come to Berlin so that we could meet? If you can come, will you be able to manage the travelling expenses and the expenses *here*, if you come for one week to Berlin? Do you know of any place in Berlin where you could stay, or shall I have to find a place for you in Berlin? I am asking this no.6 question, only in case we cannot otherwise meet.

Please write at once to *Orlando Mazzota*, Hotel Nurnberger Hof, near Anhalter Bahnhof, Berlin. Please give my best regards to your mother and greetings to your sister.

Yours sincerely

Subhas C. Bose

PS In case you cannot manage the expenses of one week's trip to Berlin, will you be able to borrow the money for the present and come. Are there any restrictions regarding travelling imposed by the Government owing to war conditions?

S.C.B.

*[Telegram dated 3 April 1941]*

E SCHENKEL FERROGASSE 24
WIEN 18

BOSE IST JETZT IN BERLIN UND BITTET SIE MOEGLICHST SOFORT HIERHER ZU KOMMEN DRAHTANTWORT = AUSWAERIT-GES AMT SCHLOBIES

[Translation: Bose is now in Berlin and asks you if possible to come here immediately. Confirm. Foreign Office. – eds.]

*17.6.42*

Dear Frl. Schenkl,

I hope you are well. Please take care of your health. This friend wants to meet you and have a talk with you. You can trust him. Please do the best you can in the circumstances.

Yours sincerely

O. Mazzotta

*[Telegram dated 8.7.42]*

ROMA
SCHENKL SOPHIENSTRASSE 6
BERLIN CHARLOTTENBURG 2

ANGENEHM REISE ALLES IN ORDNUNG HERZLICHE GRUSSE =
MAZZOTTA +

[Translation: Pleasant journey all in order hearty greetings = Mazzotta – eds.]

*[Telegram dated 1.9.42]*

TELEGRAMM

3697 BERLIN 26 11 1203
SCHENKL FERROGASSE 24 WIEN 18

ABMELDUNG DES GESTEAN GESCHICKT STOP ZUCKERKARTE IHNEN ZUSAMMENGEGBEN STOP HERZLICHE GRUSSE
MAZZOTTA +

[Translation: Abmeldung sent yesterday stop sugar cards for you sent together stop hearty greetings Mazzotta]

*Berlin*
*Tuesday, 15.9.42*

Dear Frl. Schenkl,

I returned from Konigsbruck last night. Our number there is about 740 now.

We had quite a good success at Hamburg.

I am well. Mr Faltis will probably come here on Friday on his way to Vienna.

Here are the food tickets for you. Hope you are well.

I may ring you up at night—if I have no guests. Please let me know when you intend leaving Vienna. I have posted your letter to Mrs Madan. With best wishes,

Yours sincerely

O. Mazzotta

*[Telegram dated 26.9.42]*

TELEGRAMM

1626 BERLIN CHARLOTTENBURG/2 20 26 1750 =
SCHENKL WIEN XVIII
FERROGASSE 24 WIEN

SPRACHEN FRAGE GEREGELT STOP BRAUCHEN NICHT IN DER ANGELEGENHEIT WEITER ZU BEMUEHEN HERZLICHE GRUESSE = MAZZOTTA +

[Translation: Language question resolved stop not to worry about this further stop hearty greetings = Mazzotta – eds.]

*Berlin*
*Thursday, 1/10*

Dear Frl. Schenkl,

I have sent on Wednesday, yesterday, your copy of 'Indian Struggle' by einschreiben. Hope it will reach you in due time.

Do you want any cigarettes? It will, of course, be good if you gradually give up smoking. But if you want any really—I shall try to send you some. I am arranging with Frau Didrick to send you regularly some reading matter which you want.

I have got your letter of 19/9 and 27/9. I am sending you some tickets herewith.

I am sending you some fruit today (Thursday) by express parcel. I hope they will reach you in good condition.

Frau B . . . [illegible]'s daughter will be married within a fortnight or ten days. She was enquiring if you would be then in Berlin. I said—not.

By the way, should I give her a present? If so, what? Can you suggest something?

The other day, I redirected a letter to you from Mrs Hafiz. Please be careful as to what you write to her.

I hope your mother and Lotte will like the fruit. Please give my regards to the former and my greetings to the latter. Where is Mr Peterhoff posted now? In Graz?

So long. With best wishes

Yours sincerely

O. Mazzotta

P.S. I shall probably go to Rome on Tuesday next for a week or less. I shall probably be at Konigsbruck on the 11th October.

O.M.

*[Telegram dated 6.10.42]*

SCHENKL FERROGASSE 24 WIEN 110

= BIN VERREIST WENN ZURUECK TELEFONIERE = MAZZOTTA +

[Translation: Been travelling will telephone on return = Mazzotta – eds.]

*Berlin*
*Friday*
*[no date – eds.]*

Dear Frl. Schenkl,

I was away at Konigsbruck on Wednesday and Thursday. I tried to ring you up on Tuesday night—but the Fernamt reported that there was no reply from you number at about 10 pm.

I believe that every month Spirka gets 20m. and Elizabeth 10m. Is it not?

The number at Königsbruck now is over *1100.*

I am sending you some food-tickets.

How is your mother? Please give her my best regards. How are you and Lotte? I am well.

Yours sincerely

O. Mazzotta

*Berlin Charlottenburg*
*Sophien Str. 6-7*
*Wednesday evening*
*[21.10.42? – eds.]*

Dear Frl. Schenkl,

I am enclosing herewith a letter from the Reichsbahn. Please do what you think best.

My journey to Rome has been postponed for a few days. I came to know this only yesterday (Tuesday) afternoon, on receipt of information from Rome. All the arrangements already made, had to be cancelled.

I have handed out the pastries and your letter to Frl. Jelito.

Frau Beduhn's (?) daughter has been married today. I let them use the rooms for the party.

Hope you are all right. All well here.

Yours sincerely

O. Mazzotta

[Enclosure]

*Berlin*
*den 20.10.1942*

GEPACKABFERTIGUNG

Berlin
Herrn E. Mazzotter
*Berlin-Charlottenburg 2*
Sophienstr. 6–7

Betrifft: Expre Bgutsendung Nr. 4029 Berlin Zoo — Wien Ostbf vom 1.10.1942

Nach Mitteilung der 'epackabfertigung Wien Ostbf' ist die fragl. Sendung trotz mehramaliger Bemachrichtigung von Empfanger nicht abgenommen worden. Das Gut muste, da es zum Teil verdorben war, am 15.10.42 verkauft werden. Der Verkaufserlos betrug 2,05 RS und wurde fur die aufgekommenen Lagergebuhren verrechnet. Weitere Nachfragen sind sustandigkeitshalber am die Gepackabfertigung Wien Ostbf zu richten.

*Friday, 23.10.42*
*Berlin Charlottenburg 2*
*Sophien Strasse 6-7*

Dear Frl. Schenkl,

I am enclosing herewith a letter. Please return it after perusal and answer the point about yourself.

Manzuruddin Ahmed sent a book to me, 'Geheimnisvolle

Indien', for my perusal. I want to return it—but I cannot find it. Do you know?

Herewith a photo of myself. Is this what you want?

Can you tell me where I can find the numbers of the photos of Bieber? I have to order for some more photos and I must have the numbers according to which I should place the order. Hope all well there.

Yours sincerely

O. Mazzotta

*Berlin*
*Saturday 26.10.42*

Dear Frl. Schenkl,

I am sending herewith the telephone bills, so that you may pick out the bills which do not belong to me.

The Berlin F . . . [illegible] took up the matter upon my complaint and they have told me that they have informed Vienna that I *can* speak in English.

I wrote to you yesterday a letter which you will get duly.

Yours sincerely

O. Mazzotta

*5.11.42*

Dear Frl. Schenkl,

I am leaving early tomorrow morning for Rome by aeroplane. I am sending herewith the photo that you wanted to be returned. The other photos are with me. I do not know if I shall be able to wire to you from Rome. No news should therefore be good news. Meanwhile I wish you the best of luck.

I have got the pocket lamp from your brother-in-law. Best regards to your mother and greetings to Lotte.

Yours sincerely

Subhas C. Bose

*[Telegram dated 7.11.42]*

RADIOGRAMM 7 NOV 1942

123 ROMA 10 7 1430 =
SCHENKL FERROGASSE 24 WIEN/XVIII

GUT ANGEKOMMEN HERZLICHE GRUSSE = MAZZOTTA +

[Translation: Arrived safe hearty greetings = Mazzotta – eds.]

*[Telegram dated 16.11.42]*

RADIOGRAMM 16 NOV 1942

58 ROMA 12 16 1800=
SCHENKL FERRO GASSE 24 WIENXVIII

AM DIENSTAG BIN ICH IN BERLIN = MAZZOTTA +

[Translation: On Tuesday I am in Berlin = Mazzotta – eds.]

*[Telegram dated 18.11.42]*

246 ROMA 14 18 2005 18 NOV 1942
SCHENKL FERRO GASSE 24 WIEN XVIII

KONNTE NICHT FRUEHER FAHREN STOP KOMME DONNERSTAG
MAZZOTTA +

[Translation: Cannot travel sooner stop coming Thursday Mazzotta – eds.]

*[Telegram dated 30.11.42]*

TELEGRAMM 30 NOVEMBER 1942

15 BERLIN CHARLOTTENBURG/7 14 30 1305
SCHENKL WIEN XVIII FERROGASSE 24

URLAUB VOM AMT VERLAENGERT BIS APRIL STOP AMT SCHON INFORMIERT +

[Translation: Leave from office extended till April stop office already informed – eds.]

*Thursday*
*[10.12.42—eds.]*

Hope you are well. Herewith a few tickets. Am rushing to Königsbruck.

O.M.
10/12

*Thursday*
*[no date, probably December 1942]*

Dear Frl. Schenkl,

I have sent you this morning 10 pages typed of the Special Appendix. I shall try to post some every day, till it is finished. If you cannot translate them before you go on 'urlaub' please send the stuff back to Berlin. I have got the letter which S . . . [illegible] brought me. Herewith some tickets. Best wishes and regards for your mother—greetings for your sister.

Yours sincerely

O. Mazzotta

PS *Is there anything I can do for you?*

O.M.

*Friday afternoon*
*[no date, probably December 1942 – eds.]*

Dear Frl. Schenkl,

After sending you the pages 1–23, I have made some more corrections in the pages 10–23.

Please note these corrections when you translate into German. Please return these pages to me after you have noted the corrections.

Yours sincerely

O. Mazzotta

PS The next pages will be posted tomorrow morning. I am *not* sending them einschreiben [Translation: registered – eds.] so that they may reach you quicker.

O.M.

Special Appendix

I From 1935 till today
(Contd)
Pages 1–10—sent on Thursday
Pages 11–23—sent on Friday

*Lichtenstein Alle 2*
*Berlin W 35*
*19.12.42*

Dear Frl. Schenkl,

I hope you are well and the translation work is going on satisfactorily. I am feeling well—but it appears that a slight touch of influenza is persisting. I have not heard from Mr Faltis since he left Vienna. I do not know if he has any plans for the meeting in Vienna of the I.Z. Gesselschaft—but I am sure that he will let me know as soon as something is decided. Herewith some food tickets.

Best regards for your mother. Greetings for your sister and yourself

Yours sincerely

O. Mazzotta

# *Appendices*

From Subhas Chandra Bose to Sarat Chandra Bose
[Translated from the original Bengali]

My dear brother,

Today once again I am embarking on the path of danger. But this time towards home. I may not see the end of the road. If I meet with any such danger, I will not be able to send you any further news in this life. That is why today I am leaving my news here—it will reach you in due time. I have married here and I have a daughter. In my absence please show my wife and daughter the love that you have given me throughout your life. May my wife and daughter complete and successfully fulfil my unfinished tasks—that is my ultimate prayer.

Please accept my *pronam* and convey the same to Mother, Mejobowdidi and other elders.

Berlin 8th February 1943, Your devoted brother,

Subhas

From Sarat Chandra Bose to Emilie Schenkl

*Val-mont*
*Clinique Medicale*
*Glion*
*Montreux-Territet*
*(Suisse)*
*29th May 1949*
*Sunday*

My dear Mimi,

Your registered cover containing your letter of the 21st and Anita's letter was delivered here yesterday.

This time I have come to Switzerland for treatment—and cure. In the early hours of the morning of the 18th May, I had suddenly a heart attack which continued for about eight hours. It was the first of its kind as far as I am concerned; fortunately, it was mild. My brother Sunil (the doctor) kept me in bed for ten days and advised me to come here for treatment. I would have come to Europe in any case about the middle of this month for a month's stay. But the attack I had on the 18th May has considerably restricted my movements. In fact, I have not been outside the grounds of this clinic since I came. My present intention is to stay here till the 17th of June and after that to go to Montiverita (near Locarno) for two or three weeks.

The heart was cardiographed in this clinic on the 24th. The condition is just the same as it was in Calcutta; there is no improvement yet. But I am feeling definitely better and stronger.

From next week the doctor will permit me to go outside the grounds of this clinic for walks.

Your Didi was not very well when she came, but is practically all right now. I believe she was physically fitter last year.

Now about your spending a few weeks with us in Switzerland. We have been thinking ever since we came of asking you to come to Switzerland with Anita. After receipt of your letter yesterday, I wrote to Mrs Sharma of the Indian Legation at Bern and requested her to expedite the granting of your passport as much as possible. I told her that in the present shape of our health we would like some company; moreover, there were certain family matters to be discussed. I shall write to you again as soon as I hear from her. I need hardly say that we shall look forward with great pleasure to your coming to Switzerland with Anita.

Please remember us to Dr Madan and give him our good wishes. Has he been able to make up his mind whether he will continue in Vienna or come to India?

Asoke went to Bern day before yesterday. From there he will go to Zurich, Konstanz (if he gets a visa) and Basel. He will be back here on the 5th June.

We hope you will meet with luck in your examination and, once it is over, your mind will be at rest.

Should you get your passport early, you might come here (I mean to this clinic) and take a little treatment. After that, we can go together to the Locarno side.

Please give our kindest regards to your mother and accept our love and good wishes yourself. Fondest kisses to Anita darling.

Yours very affly,

S.C. Bose

Madame Emilie Schenkl

To Emilie Schenkl March 1936

My darling!

Even the iceberg sometimes melts and so it is with me now. I can no longer restrain myself from penning these few lines to convey my deep love for you—my darling—or as we would say in our own way—the queen of my heart. But do you love me—do you care for me—do you long for me? You called me 'parandhik'—but did you mean it? Do you love me more than your own life? Is that possible? With us it may be possible—for a Hindu woman has, for centuries, given up her life for the sake of her love. But you Europeans have a different tradition, moreover, why should you love me more than your own life? I am like a wandering bird that comes from afar, remains for a while, and then flies away to its distant home. For such a person why should you cherish so much love?

My dearest!

In a few weeks I must fly to my distant home. My country calls me—my duty calls me—I must leave you and go back to my first love—my country. So often have I told you that I have already sold myself to my first love. I have very little left to give any one. What little I have—I have given you. It may not be worthy of you and of your great love for me—but that is all that I have to give—and you cannot expect anything more from me.

I do not know what the future has in store for me. May be, I shall spend my life in prison, may be, I shall be shot or hanged. But whatever happens, I shall think of you and convey my gratitude to you in silence for your love for me. May be I shall never see you again—may be I shall not be able to write to you again when I am back—but believe me, you will always live in my heart, in my thoughts and in my dreams. If fate should thus separate us in this life—I shall long for you in my next life. And if you believe in my religion—pray similarly.

My angel! I thank you for loving me and for teaching me to love you.

My sweetest! Be a good girl, be a pure girl—and above all, be unselfish. Care not for any sorrow or suffering that may come. Sorrow and suffering cannot make you unhappy if you are unselfish. If you are selfish, nothing can make you happy. This is the only advice I can give you—your 'guru' ( I think you once called me as such). I hate selfishness and I dislike selfish people. You have an unselfish heart—that is why I could love you. Make that heart more and more unselfish and you will increase your happiness in this life and after.

My queen! Should we not meet again after I leave Europe, think kindly of me. Do not blame me for not loving you more. I have given what I had—how can I give more? With these lines, I send you the tears that are now flowing.

I never thought before that a woman's love could ensnare me. So many did love me before, but I never looked at them. But you, naughty woman, have caught me. And why?

In this love of any earthly use? We who belong to two different lands—have we anything in common? My country, my people, my traditions, my habits and customs, my climate—in fact everything—is so different from yours. Then, why do you love? And what is it that you love? What is there in me that attracts you and compels you to love? Can you tell.

For the moment, I have forgotten all these differences that separate our countries. I have loved the woman in you—the soul in you. You are the first woman I have loved. God grant that you may also be the last. Adieu, my dearest!

From Subhas Chandra Bose to Emilie Schenkl

9.2.43
Tuesday 7 A.M.

Dear Frl. Schenkl,

I am now leaving the hotel and shall soon be on the move. Once again I thank you for all your kindness and help. I wish you the very best in your future. May the Almighty bless you is my earnest prayer. Aufwiedersehen!

Yours sincerely
Subhas Chandra Bose

You will hear everything from Mr. Nambiar—so I am not writing separately. Please be very careful in your correspondence about the bureau. Better write nothing at all.

SCB